The Happy Profession

THE Happy Profession

BY ELLERY SEDGWICK

AN ATLANTIC MONTHLY PRESS BOOK

LITTLE, BROWN AND COMPANY ⁊ BOSTON

1946

COPYRIGHT 1946, BY LITTLE, BROWN AND COMPANY

ALL RIGHTS RESERVED, INCLUDING THE RIGHT
TO REPRODUCE THIS BOOK OR PORTIONS
THEREOF IN ANY FORM

FIRST EDITION

Published September 1946

ATLANTIC—LITTLE, BROWN BOOKS
ARE PUBLISHED BY
LITTLE, BROWN AND COMPANY
IN ASSOCIATION WITH
THE ATLANTIC MONTHLY PRESS

PRINTED IN THE UNITED STATES OF AMERICA

TO
THE OLD HOUSE IN STOCKBRIDGE
IN HAPPY REMEMBRANCE OF
ASPIRATION, HOPE, AND FAMILY AFFECTION
SHELTERED BENEATH ITS ROOF
SINCE 1785

The power of writing one fine line transcends all the able-editor ability in this ably-edited universe.

— EDWARD FITZGERALD

By Way of Preface

"LET NOTHING," says the immortal Churchill, "interfere with the rancour and asperity of personal opinion." I am a mild-mannered man, but I have sought to abide by that counsel. Dislikes and irritations are behind me, my enthusiasms have a more enduring flame. There is nothing in this book but is set down frankly, without the ardor of a votary or the wry charity that cloaks a writer of obituaries. The truth as a man sees it, I hold to be the truth.

No one who has gone right on living in the face of the Psalmist's warning can fail now and then to ponder the meaning of the long effort. In understanding the Big Show, one difficulty is that too many people are crowded on the stage, for the records the actors leave behind them are wont to be so many justifications of parts they have played, so many libels on the parts of others. A truer impression can come from the audience. Thirty years spent in conducting the *Atlantic* has given me a comfortable seat on the center aisle and some experience in interpreting the merit of the performance. Mine has been an old-fashioned ambition. For me the good life has been the contented life and, were I to live mine over again, I should aim at the same goal.

Content does not mean smugness. I admire the great but have no importunate craving to join their company. My phi-

By Way of Preface

losophy tells me that while pebbles in the stream bed may twist the current this way and that, the river goes its own way in spite of them. It takes a boulder to alter its course but boulders are few and sometimes portentous.

The happiness of my life has been my friends, and if in this record I have set down little concerning them to whom I owe most, I hope in another to deal with them more generously.

I wish to express gratitude for the conveniences and unfailing assistance extended by the Atlantic office throughout the preparation of this book, and to acknowledge, in addition to a hundred other services she has rendered, the gentle admonitions of my secretary, Miss Madeline Goddard, restraining me from speaking with unforgiveness of those few persons who in the past have despitefully used me.

ELLERY SEDGWICK

14 Walnut Street
Boston

Contents

	By Way of Preface	ix
I	The Importance of Omitting Chapter I	3
II	Happy Valley	6
III	The Hill and the Plain	21
IV	The Old Familiar Faces	31
V	Old School Ties	46
VI	Omitted from the Curriculum	67
VII	The Metropolis Against Me	86
VIII	Alarms and Excursions	105
IX	Yellow	116
X	Friends and Crooks	124
XI	A Tornado or Two	136
XII	Sunny Weather	148
XIII	Manners and Customs in the Hub	166
XIV	A Hero, a Heroine, and People in Between	178
XV	Faraway Women	197
XVI	Men of the Species	216
XVII	Friends and Rascals	229
XVIII	Pure Prejudice	243

Contents

XIX	An Opalescent Chapter	252
XX	The Borderland of Genius	267
XXI	Home without the Bacon	276
XXII	Satisfactions	286
XXIII	Adventures by Proxy	306
XXIV	Pictures in the Night	321
	Index	333

The Happy Profession

CHAPTER I

The Importance of Omitting Chapter I

THERE is no question about it: autobiographies ought to begin with Chapter II. Luckily for you and me, this is not an autobiography in any accepted sense; that "terrible fluidity of self-revelation" against which Henry James warns us will be quite absent; but so basic a rule of criticism should stand in any record of one man's life. Pick up the nearest biography. Chapter I tells a thrice-told tale. It is about a race before it starts, and, maternal testimony notwithstanding, babies are like as biscuits in a pan. There is one pattern of life for every one of them. Their individual histories, if you can call them individual, should be confined to the family circle, which alone can appreciate the shade of distinction which divides any baby from our baby. However, one generalization should be made and I will pause long enough to call the attention of beginning fathers to one interesting and significant characteristic of babies, biographied and unbiographied, whether or not there is a flicker of difference between them. Hardly has the breath been spanked into the infant by nurse-ritual in the first ten minutes of existence and the child laid on its back to recover when, with its first gasp, *it* (the neuter gender habitually covers the first two years) stretches out its newborn hand and clutches at the universe, closing its fingers in a determined grip. That gesture

The Happy Profession

means but one thing: "What is mine is mine and nobody else's." It is Nature's protest against socialism, the primal affirmation that the world was made for individuals, whatever politicians and evangelists have to say to the contrary.

Of course, there may be something in the first chapter beside chronicles of universal babyhood. The biographers of Hercules are perfectly correct in recording the strangling of twin serpents in his cradle: that was an exceptional incident. And of course grandfathers are worth mentioning, and some grandmothers, too. My own family ascribes our cross-grainedness to one great-great-grandmother, our engaging qualities to direct transmission from the charming and accomplished spinster who was our great-aunt. These postulates are probably quite as accurate in one case as the other. I do not impugn this theory altogether, for scientists say inheritance comes from strains not individuals, but I do know, quite as well as biographers, that the dance of genes and chromosomes is of a very lively and intricate nature, that it has been going on for a long time, and that to trace its evolution in any given instance is merely to be wise after the event. One of the infinite complications of physical inheritance is the vast difference it makes to the child, not only what qualities are inherited but what is the just balance between those qualities. Too much molasses may spoil a pudding. One pinch of salt may not be quite enough. But I will let the geneticists take on from here.

Another preoccupation of that first chapter which ought to be omitted deals with descriptions of the place of birth. Very occasionally a birthplace is interesting; for example, the pinched little room where Calvin Coolidge was born, which still looks for all the world like a Tract on the Penurious Instinct. But in this country, where the face of nature changes overnight, birthplaces have commonly lost their consequence.

The Importance of Omitting Chapter I

Things of this sort matter more in England where they keep straw stacks on the same spot year after year and for generations the same antimacassars fall over the same chair-backs in the farmhouse parlor. There, the reader of the story can have a picture of what has been and there the growing hero or heroine of the biography is influenced insensibly and powerfully by the comforting illusion of a fixed spot on this whirling globe. They love it and call it home. But in America, getting on in the world means getting out of the world we have known before.

I was amused the other day by an instance of this. My wife and I were dining in a comfortable little restaurant carved out of a brownstone house in West Forty-eighth Street in New York City. As I looked at the menu the address at the top struck me and I exclaimed, "By Jove, one day in 1872 I was born here!" I called the waiter. "Where is number seventeen?" I asked. The waiter pointed across the street. "That is where the Music Hall of Rockefeller Center is." A Music Hall, I thought. What an appropriate memorial to me!

Reader, have no fear! I say once more it is not an autobiography you are in for. I and my contented life are simply the standing ground of the photographer snapping the pictures of a lifetime which has at least proved vastly amusing to me. These pictures have little enough to do with the writer but they carry the record of many scenes and many people not without interest, and if the prints have not faded, the album may be worth a few hours of idle time.

CHAPTER II

Happy Valley

AMERICAN born, I followed American fashion and number 17 West Forty-eighth Street was a memory before memory began. Within a year my father moved his family to Stockbridge, Massachusetts, but curiously enough in that migration he did not break with tradition but caught up with it. Even in that remote era Sedgwicks had lived in Stockbridge for a century or so, and it was in the house of my father's grandfather that we finally installed ourselves. Stockbridge is a village of little importance, but it is ours if love can make it so. It is seven decades at least since Tom Appleton, the wit who had the inspiration of tying a shorn lamb to a Beacon Street fence so that God would temper the wind there, chatting of the natural history of Stockbridge, used to maintain that "even the crickets there say nothing but Sedg'ick, Sedg'ick, Sedg'ick." The sixth generation is now growing up in the dear old house. This mansion house of happy memories replaced a wigwam; for it was built in 1785 on land purchased directly from the Indians. The last of the tribe, an ancient squaw known as Elizabeth, has given her name to an adjoining field, still, in family nomenclature, the Elizabeth Lot. Elizabeth had another name for it. In her day it was *Manwootania*, meaning "middle of the town." The

[6]

Happy Valley

town itself is six miles square. Elizabeth and the Sedgwicks too once lived in the heart of it.

Through all the country round the scant history that could be recalled had drifted into legend. The Yankee tongue is not good at a double twist and Indian names screw it into contortions. *Awestonook* became Housatonic. Grateful as we may be for that, it is interesting to remember that in Indian times the name *Awestonook*, meaning "over the mountain," was given not only to the river but to the entire valley. The little brook that goes sparkling through it bore a name more easily assimilated and remains Konkapot Brook, but when it came to the mountain which frames the valley to the north, guardian of Stockbridge simplicities against the sophistications of Lenox, the native *Takeecanuck* made too large a mouthful, and there was no transliteration. Rattlesnake Mountain it became. Now *Takeecanuck* means "the heart," and apparently stood as a kind of memorial to some friendly interchange between red men and white, but Rattlesnake has a sinister meaning. Behind such a transformation there seems to lie some story of treachery, some bloody drama forgotten these hundred years. It was also simply the impossibilities of linguistics which translated *Masswassehaich* (the euphonious name for "nest") into Monument Mountain.

Wherever I am, it is always from the windows of the old house on Main Street that I look out on the world and take a Stockbridge-eye-view of it. Ours is not a great house nor a beautiful, but it is delightful and built to endure. The ground plan follows the best of all designs for family living — an ample square, with four generous rooms, one at each corner, and a broad hall running through the center, opening on the view of Monument Mountain, which is the hallmark of the village. My great-grandfather had a family suited to his day, four sons and four daughters, but it was customary for the

The Happy Profession

sons to offer their wives the protection of the paternal rooftree and guests in unbroken succession were collectively quite as permanent residents as the family. In the absence of inns, any traveler with a letter to introduce him could find a night's lodging there, and humble wayfarers were invariably provided with a shakedown. Hospitality was endless and boundless. By what magic the four walls could have contained such a company mystifies the present generation. How could the less contain the greater? In my father's day a substantial wing was added for the accommodation of a much more moderate household, and I doubt whether my children would think it physically possible to find room for a company less by a third than my grandparents considered normal. Nowadays a guest or two alter the pattern of family life. It was different then. Guests simply enlarged the domestic circle.

From the beginning the Sedgwicks loved their house. It was part of them, almost the dearest part. My old Latin professor at Harvard taught me once for all that *domus* was a house but not a home. And I well know the distinction. But our Stockbridge house was certainly different from the other houses on the village street. Perhaps I can find what the difference was by quoting from a letter of a Sedgwick three generations back.

"I came down," wrote my Great-aunt Catherine in 1844, "to pass a few days at the old homestead — my only home — the only place on earth where forms, common and mute to others, have to me soul and speech; where voices linger in the walls of the rooms, and make their secret and by-gone cheerfulness and tenderness ring in my ears in the dead of night; where the stems of the old trees are still warm with the hands that once pressed them; where, in short, the dead are *not* dead."

Life with its joys and heartbreaks, death "with its train of infinite hopes," there they abide together.

Happy Valley

Like all beloved communities, Stockbridge wears two aspects. There is the Stockbridge of guidebooks and motorcars, of rockers on hotel piazzas, and of swarms of the music-struck conjured by Koussevitzky and siphoned into his show-place at Tanglewood. Pure Philistinism mingled with the titillated, the genuine, and the passionate. So far as the real Stockbridge is concerned, these are but trespassers and vagrants. The real Stockbridge is the subjective Stockbridge. It is made of a thousand memories, older than the arching elms of Main Street and more luxuriant than they, memories of the neighborliness of two hundred years, of odd characters twisted into odder shapes, of Yankee speech and Yankee silences, of sunsets over Housatonic meadows, of births and deaths intimately shared by every villager. When a Stockbridgian goes abroad he takes Stockbridge with him. To this day my yardstick of height is Monument Mountain. Marveling at the Andes I have wondered how many Monument Mountains it would take to top the crest of Illimani. Besides, it is convenient to have fixed standards like Stockbridge Bowl or Hatch's Pond when you are called on to appraise the loveliness of Lucerne or Lake Louise!

Neither Stockbridge is what it was. The census credits eighteen hundred souls or so against the twelve hundred of my time, but so many of them now are Irish or Italian souls. They are souls worth saving too, but then they have the Church to shepherd them through the Gates. My interest is in the souls of the Yankees of my youth which certainly needed salvation and as surely found it. All of us, Yankees, Irish, Italians, and the rest, are of immigrant stock of course, but we Yankees like to remember that we came over for different reasons and by earlier ships. It is interesting to trace the first trickle towards Stockbridge of the Irish blood. The spearhead of the invasion was one Larry Lynch, indentured servant of Brigadier General Joseph Dwight, a Berkshire warrior of the first magnitude in the French wars. Larry settled at the foot of West Stockbridge Mountain, outstripped his Yankee neighbors by raising fourteen children, and about the turn of the eighteenth century built a homestead for them: and Larrywang it is until this day. *Wang* is Indian for a cluster of houses, but the transliteration from Indian into American affords the learned men of Stockbridge some latitude in spelling. This I mention because the "Seelectmen" of this day seem to prefer the alternative of Larrywaug.

I owe a personal debt to Larry for in the strength of his youth, a century before I was born, he did me a signal service. An Indian raid was on. Tomahawks were in the air and my great-great-grandmother, Abigail Dwight, wife of the Brigadier and sister of that Ephraim Williams who founded Williams College, was hard put to it to bring her children to safety. Her little daughter Pamela (of whom I am an ultimate fruit), just three years old, was hurriedly entrusted to the care of a black manservant, but the chase grew hot and the Negro, incommoded by his burden, chucked it into a raspberry patch and looked out for number one. Then who should come that way, find the child and save it, but Larry of Larrywang.

I hope Larry was a saint, for it was he who first brought the Faith to Stockbridge, and bastioned it with his brood of fourteen. Next came Billy Brogan. That was the beginning. Up to 1830 there was but one Catholic family in Stockbridge. Thirty years later when the Roman Church was built the procession in its honor filled the village street from end to end. It is written of the faithful that they shall be as the sands of the sea, and of the visible fulfillment of that prophecy I hold this an instructive example.

That such things could happen in Stockbridge was a sore trial to the Puritan spirit which ever had other trials to cope

Happy Valley

with. It was two generations since Jonathan Edwards, most eloquent and impressive of American preachers, had thundered his damnations from his Stockbridge pulpit. Manners had softened, minds had ripened since then. But Unitarianism and Congregationalism were still in the Puritan tradition. Writing retrospectively in 1853 my great-aunt gives an account of the temper of the time. Underneath her humor there is a note of serious warning. She looks back upon the changes of twenty years.

"I think the Catholic influx did not begin before 1830 — and now there are two thronged churches in Berkshire and occasional Masses in all the villages where they swarm. What would dear old Dr. West, our sixty-year Defender of the Puritan faith, say to these multitudinous children of Anti-Christ. One of the oldest members of his Church, Mrs. Ingersoll, the deacon's wife, after the departure of her meek helpmate (he was the weaker vessel) rented the deacon's old hat-shop — he was hat manufacturer to the village — to Billy Brogan. It was a little unpainted one-story building in the same enclosure with her house. None but an Irish family would have gathered there. When the Irish became numerous enough, Mass was to be celebrated in the village and Billy Brogan's habitation was selected as the largest domicile among them and therefore fitted to the purpose. Nothing could exceed the indignation of the deacon's widow, nor the energy of her invectives, necessarily restrained within the decencies of Puritan objugation. To have Mass on her premises — a Catholic priest within her gates — Mass in the deacon's shop — the shop turned into a CATHEDRAL — no she had rather burn it."

But however disquieting the outlook, Wonder-Working Providence was still on the Puritan side. God's plan was proof against the influence of Masses, whether they were said in

The Happy Profession

hat shop or cathedral. The record runs on in a humane and confident spirit.

"As ignorance cannot compete with knowledge, nor get the mastery of it till there is an immense odds of brute force, as a despotic religion has neither sanction nor security in the midst of free institutions, I trust that the Irish, by the infusion of an element of warmth and generosity into our national character, would have done us more good than evil. I am inclined to think that they have already done this for us." And then amusingly enough the journal goes on to discuss Irish influence upon a facet of our lives only less important than our spiritual salvation: "I have so lively a recollection of the time when we were in the transmission stage, when the old well-trained slave had disappeared, when the few black servants to be hired were shiftless, lazy, and unfaithful, and our own people scarcely to be obtained, or if obtained, coming 'to accommodate you' and staying only until they could accommodate themselves better, that I feel grateful for Irish servants, with all their Celtic infirmities on their heads, their half savage ways, their imaginativeness, their indefiniteness, and *curved lines* every way. They desire employment. They are willing servants. They are sympathetic and progressive, and I have at this moment, June 1853, a girl in my service, Margaret Pollock, a pearl of great price. She is a Protestant to be sure, but she was born and bred in Ireland and I would not exchange her for all the service I could distil in Yankeedom."

One wonders whether the price of the pearl might have been just a little lower had Margaret passed by the Protestant Church on Sunday morning and gone on to the Cathedral.

Stockbridge denominationalism is a study in itself. The story of it would be one of the keys to New England history. Up to 1834 every citizen of Massachusetts was compelled by

Happy Valley

law to contribute to the support of some church or some sect. What complexity of bookkeeping that would imply nowadays! Happily it became plain to every citizen that obligations of that description ill consort with democratic principles, and that religion free from tithes means unrestricted faith.

The Stockbridge of my youth was almost as far removed in time from Larry Lynch as it is from his great-great-grandsons of today. We worried our heads over many things but who would have thought then that we were started toward the highroad of socialism? Since Cranford there has not been a more individualistic community. Even as a boy I felt myself no cog in the machine but an individual item in creation. The village street was and is a mile long. At one end of it just before the road drops down to The Indian Burial Ground, where a monolith dedicated To THE FRIENDS OF OUR FATHERS testifies to a decided change in the hearts of Red Men since Larry's day, lived Colonel Dwight. To us children there was a certain aura about his florid face and substantial figure, for had he not been a personal crony of President Arthur? Arthur, you remember, had disappointed "the boys" by becoming a good President, and I suspect that as a young man, Colonel Dwight had shared substantially in that disappointment. Anyway he gave the impression of a lost, more jovial age, the substance of which had largely disappeared. Certainly he sought solace, for on his sideboard there were always a bottle or two, and we boys used to watch him take up each in turn and hold it sadly to the light to make certain one final drink was not left at the bottom of it. Then with a melancholy shake of the head he would set the bottle down, exclaiming: —

> Not one damn drop o' rum
> Glory hallelujahrum!

The Happy Profession

Colonel Dwight had a witty tongue. I remember meeting him on the morning of the annual flower parade of boats which in our midsummer festival drifted down the Housatonic at very low water. The sky had a lowering look. "Colonel Dwight," I said, "I do hope it doesn't rain."

"Well," he drawled, "won't a little rain help to lay the dust in the river?"

A full mile beyond Colonel Dwight's, high above long reaches of the wandering river, stood Linwood. There in frosty isolation lived my Uncle Butler, ogre of my childhood. Charles E. Butler was a great man, there was no denying that. Had he not gone, a poor boy, to New York, and become the architect of the greatest law firm of the American ages, Butler, Evarts, and Southmayd? Uncle Butler was a notably handsome man, with bold classical features and a heart tender as a granite block. So impressive was his personality that on his entrance, conversation would flag and soon come to a full stop. In a child's ears at least, his humor roused no mirth. Often my family went for their Sunday roasts to the cold stone house, decorated with marble statuary, with marbleized wallpaper to set it off and chairs that looked immutable in their several stations. Uncle Butler would meet us at the forbidding walnut-paneled entrance. He loved my mother, nobody could help that, but he would turn to me as the youngest of the party with the air of a playful mastodon.

"Well, Stick-in-the-mud, brought your dinner with you? If you've left it behind, go down to the coal hole." The inevitable greeting froze the cockles of my heart.

Half a mile below the gates of Linwood on the way back to the village lived Mr. Butler's junior partner, Mr. Charles F. Southmayd. He was the only man I ever saw who dressed after the pattern of Mr. Pickwick in black broadcloth with the characteristic square flap of the trouser buttoned up in front, and a huge collar which was only the slightest modification of a stock. On Sundays he would walk to church in his gray beaver hat and never without a silver-headed cane, exclusively I imagine a Sunday ornament. His costume never altered. For nigh forty years it had been Mr. Southmayd's custom to save time and trouble by writing a brief semiannual note to his tailor ordering "two more of the same." Pinched and alert, caustic and formidable, Mr. Southmayd looked for all the world as if "Phiz" had just drawn him for a new novel by Charles Dickens. Certainly Dickens in all his rambles never picked up a more congenial subject for his artist's pencil or his own pen.

Charles Southmayd's education was remarkable. As a child he was sent to a small private school and there displayed so unusual a precocity that at the age of twelve years and six months his schoolmaster confided to his astonished father that since he had taught the boy all he knew and since the boy had perfectly assimilated the whole of that learning, he could do nothing more for him. It was the beatific quandary parents dream of before they wake to the realities. How was the boy to go on from there? Providence, responsible for the conundrum, stood ready with an answer. A lawyer of distinction, one Elisha P. Hurlbut, heard of the young prodigy through a friend of his and asked to have a look at the phenomenon. Now this Mr. Hurlbut, very wise in the ways of the law, had as an amateur practised a "science" much in vogue at the time. Phrenology he thought might give the answer, and phrenology did. Mr. Hurlbut passed his hands over the small boy's bumpy head and announced that inside of it was the very stuff lawyers are made of. And so it was that, long before his thirteenth birthday, Charles was presented with Black-

The Happy Profession

stone and a Kent's *Commentaries* and went to work as office boy for the firm of Hurlbut and Johnson, 73 Cedar Street, New York City.

Charles was not a boy to let the grass grow under his feet. During the next four years he read, marked, learned, and inwardly digested the principles of the law. He learned them from top to bottom, outside and in, and by the time he was seventeen the whole office knew him as the "Chancellor." Legends began to grow about his phrenologic head. It was said that when clients turned up they would find the two senior members of the firm in the front office discussing public questions and that one of them was sure to say, "Do you want to talk politics? If so, here we are. But if you happen to come on law business, you will find the Chancellor inside." Boys like this are very different from your sons or mine but they get on. Charles worked in the office. He lived in the office. He slept in the office. After the shutters were closed for the night, he would eat his bread and cheese and wash his supper down with water from the tap. Then out would come the *Commentaries* and he was lost in them till midnight. As the clock struck twelve, he would slip into his cot conveniently made up under the counter and squander six hours in idle sleep.

Charles was not a poor boy to begin with, and having no rent to pay nor fees for instruction he began early to grow rich. Unencumbered he shot ahead. He became the office partner in the firm of Butler, Evarts, and Choate (he was Choate's senior), living his own shrewd, ingrowing life, seldom going into court, and making himself utterly indispensable to Mr. Choate, whose forensic brilliance rested squarely on Mr. Southmayd's briefs.

Mr. Southmayd was a man of intense conviction. That was the interesting part of him. Property was a sacred thing, immutable, ordained of God. When the Elevated Railroad was built, destroying property rights without one penny of damages to the abutters, as its engines rattled every pane of glass the length of Sixth Avenue, he made the resolution never to pay tribute to that iniquity. Daily he traveled four miles by the slow streetcar, up and down from Forty-seventh Street to his office, losing one hour every day. After years of litigation, righteousness triumphed and the Elevated was compelled to pay for the evil it had wrought. But Mr. Southmayd's sense of injustice was not to be assuaged. "No," said he, "it's a fraud anyway and I will never ride in it." And he never did.

"Thou shalt not speculate" was Mr. Southmayd's first and great commandment, and he embraced speculation to mean a probable return of more than three per cent unless a prime mortgage was concerned. He was saving. Almost he was penurious. He held out to himself the decent hope of living on his income's income. But he was not mean and, as I can affirm from personal knowledge, he could be generous — provided he could be generous in secret. Mr. Gradgrind was not more a man of principle than he.

Such was Charles F. Southmayd. Dickens would have made of him an avaricious Scrooge. Not so his Maker. Beneath the reinforced concrete of his principles, utterly hidden from the world, glowed a strain of romance. Who would have suspected it! Who could have imagined it! One solitary flame of devotion kindled in his youth (assuming that he had a youth) burned to the very end.

Before Uncle Butler married my Aunt Susan, his first wife had borne him a large family. The eldest daughter, noble in mind, manners, and appearance, moved like a goddess across Mr. Southmayd's field of vision. He adored her, this weazened, narrow, intelligent man, as much as the rights of property; as much as the majestic law itself, he worshiped her. It was not in the stars she should accept him. She was kind, but she

The Happy Profession

was obdurate. He understood. He had no hope, but his affection was unchanged. And so without a glimmer of expectancy, but knowing that at least he should see her pass on her way to church, he bought a large and beautiful place, bounded by the Oxbow of the Housatonic, put up a large and ugly house just below the hill whereon she lived, and there for decades spent his summers. He retired at sixty, but it was ten years later that he volunteered to write the most brilliant brief of his life, the brief by whose aid Mr. Choate won his great income tax case and quashed an Act of Congress. I never knew Mr. Southmayd to go into another man's house, I never but once knew another to go into his, but when I was old enough to understand his story I felt the magnificence of his lonely devotion. Under his quaint American disguise he was a Cyrano. And how he would have sniffed at the comparison!

Poor Mr. Southmayd! Toward the end of his gnarled and twisted life he had a terrible adventure. One night he was undressing and had tossed those Pickwickian trousers of his across a chair, when a violent knock came at the door and a rough voice cried: "Your house is afire!" Mr. Southmayd ran to the window. Light was streaming from the parlor below. He threw open the door and there stood a gigantic Negro, a mask over his eyes and in his hand a naked axe. The burglar had lighted the lamps below. His ruse succeeded. He stripped the pitiful old gentleman of his watch and cash. The loot was small but the terror remained and the next season the house was empty.

Before I leave Mr. Southmayd I want to pay his memory a personal tribute which I have carried in my heart for sixty years. Perhaps there is no one left who holds him in affectionate remembrance, but it is his due, and I set the story down.

For some reason deep in the human heart, my father, the

Happy Valley

looting of whose comfortable fortune had left him in chronic difficulties, found it impossible to talk of his troubles to grown-up people and found relief in making a confidant of his youngest son, scarcely fourteen years old. Bills, mortgages, and notes of ninety days crept into my dreams. Of course I did not understand them, but I felt the aura of horror that surrounds such things and my sympathies could always be relied on.

There came a summer day when my father said to me: "Ell, if I am to save the Old House, I must borrow seven thousand dollars and I have decided to ask Mr. Southmayd for it." Now I did not regard Mr. Southmayd as an ogre; our greetings on Sunday mornings were too manly for that, but more than once I had heard our farmer, Jimmy MacMonigle, speak of him as "near," and I had a notion of what that meant. I knew too that Mr. Southmayd was formidable and felt certain he was a man not easily to be dispossessed; so although I fell in with my father's plan, there was fear in my heart where hope ought to be. At any rate, it was arranged that on the following day we two were to drive over behind old Conrad in the pony phaeton, and that I was to hold the horse while my father transacted business in the grim parlor.

That drive might have happened yesterday. Somehow or other Conrad walked the entire way. Papa's spirits were at an all-time low, so I held the reins while he bit his nails. The crunch of the gravel before the door is still in my ears, and I see my father with the desperate look of the debtor doomed, visible across his face. In a moment he had gone within and I was left to loop the reins about the whip and sit back shivering in the warm sun. Visions of the Old House slipping inexorably into the river were before my eyes. We were homeless; I had little doubt of it. Then suddenly the door was flung open and out came my father, his ruddy face glowing with happiness. There was no need for words, but as we trotted home, my father kept exclaiming: "What a kind man! What a good man!"

Mr. Southmayd, it seemed, had made everything easy. He had agreed to give his check for seven thousand dollars and take in exchange our meadows lying beyond the river. The Old House was safe.

The full extent of Mr. Southmayd's generosity my father never knew. Those meadows, which must have been a mere encumbrance to him, were left by his will as a bequest to my brother, Alexander, who in those days ruled as master in the Old House.

CHAPTER III

The Hill and the Plain

THE GREAT of Stockbridge lived for the most part on the Hill, overlooking a prospect far beyond the village street; the winding willows of the river, the meadows of the Happy Valley beyond, stretching far till they reached the encircling mountains framing the view and dominated by the majestic Dome which forms the southern pinnacle of the Berkshire Range. Here on the Hill was entrenched the famous Field family. I commend their careers to novelists and historians, for it is not often that so many winged arrows are found in a family quiver. The head of the house was David Dudley Field, a monument to the majesty of undisputed eminence. From the modest level of the Plain, as the village street was called in my grandfather's day, I watched him with awe: the central pillar of the temple, codifier of the laws of the State of New York, unassailable defender of the very rich, embodiment of the serenity of order and of law. It was on his arm that Abraham Lincoln walked to the rostrum of Cooper Union. And yet, and yet, there were some who said he was a colossal sham, a whitened sepulcher on a monumental scale, protecting not the small villainies but the great, shield and buckler of any scoundrel whose plunderings had passed the million mark. The buccaneers, Drew, Fisk, Gould, and the rest, were supposed habitually to consult him.

The Happy Profession

Senate and House in Albany listened deferentially to him, and had he not been senior counsel for Boss Tweed in his time of trouble, with Elihu Root for his junior? To the historian of corruption, America, land of opportunity, offers no such enticing field as New York in the '60s and '70s. Read *Chapters of Erie* by Charles Francis Adams, ponder Albert Stickney's essays on the time and place, and you will find there records not unfit to be compared with the malefactions of Borgia or Malatesta. And it was whispered that these magnificent rascals owed their wealth and their immunity to the acumen and respectability of David Dudley Field.

After this introduction to the Field family let me add, modestly and parenthetically, that when Mr. D. D. Field first practised in New York it was in the law office of my two grandfathers, Henry and Robert Sedgwick, yet two more upright men than they never trod the devious paths of the law.

The second Field, Stephen, left Stockbridge to join the rough-and-tumble of California, social and political, in the '50s. He emerged from politics as an Associate Justice of the Supreme Court of the United States and had the additional distinction of being the only Justice in the history of the High Court directly implicated in a man's death. Some there were who called it murder. Others used the happy synonym, dear to lawyers, of justifiable homicide. At any rate, although it was Stephen's guard who fired the shot, it was Stephen's quarrel.

No description of the Field temperament would be complete without some account of this remarkable incident which occurred in 1889. It had its origin in the filing of will by one Miss Sarah Althea Hill. This will was found to be a forgery, and there was drama in the making when Miss Hill's attorney, David S. Terry, formerly an associate of Judge Field's on the Supreme Bench of California, fell in love with his client and

The Hill and the Plain

married her. On account of the outrageous behavior of the pair in open court they were indicted for contempt, and Terry, who already had a notch in his revolver, one killing to his credit, openly announced the intention of shooting Mr. Justice Field on sight. In this state of affairs the Justice was reluctantly induced to accept the companionship of an armed guard and was breakfasting with him in a dining car at Lathrop, California, when Terry suddenly made his appearance. He wore a look vividly described by the guard, one Neagle, as "the most desperate expression that I ever saw on a man's face, and I have seen a good many in my time. It meant life or death to him or me."

What followed I borrow from Mr. Justice Field's own testimony.

"I supposed at the time Judge Terry was going out to meet his wife as she had not returned so I went on with my breakfast. It seems, however, that he came around back of me. I did not see him and he struck me a violent blow in the face, followed instantaneously by another blow. Coming so immediately together, the two blows seemed like one assault. I heard 'Stop, stop!' cried by Neagle. Of course I was for a moment dazed by the blows. I turned my head around and saw that great form of Terry's with his arm raised and fist clinched to strike me. I felt that a terrific blow was coming, and his arm was descending in a curved way as though to strike the side of my temple when I heard Neagle cry out: 'Stop, stop, I am an officer.' Instantly two shots followed. I could only explain the second shot from the fact that he did not fall instantly. I did not get up from my seat, although it is proper for me to say that a friend of mine thinks I did, but I did not. I looked around and saw Terry on the floor. I looked at him and saw that particular movement of the eyes that indicates the presence of death. Of course it was a great shock to me. It is impossible for anyone to see a man in the full vigor of life, with all those faculties that constitute life, instantly extinguished without being affected, and I was. I looked at him for a moment, then went around and looked at him again, and passed on. Great excitement followed. A gentleman came to me whom I did not know, but I think it was Mr. Lidgerwood, who has been examined as a witness in this case, and said: 'What is this?' I said 'I am a Justice of the Supreme Court of the United States. My name is Judge Field. Judge Terry threatened my life and attacked me, and the deputy marshal has shot him.' The deputy marshal was perfectly cool and collected, and stated: 'I am a deputy marshal and I have shot him to protect the life of Judge Field.' A few moments afterwards the deputy marshal said to me: 'Judge, I think you had better go to the car.' I said 'Very well.' Then this gentleman, Mr. Lidgerwood, said: 'I think you had better.' And with the two I went back to the car. I asked Mr. Lidgerwood to go back and get my hat and cane, which he did. The marshal went with me, remained some time, and then left his seat in the car and as I thought went back to the dining room. He returned and either he or someone else stated that there was great excitement; that Mrs. Terry was calling for some violent proceedings. I must say here that, dreadful as it is to take life, it was only a question of seconds whether my life or Judge Terry's life should be taken. I am firmly convinced that had the marshal delayed two seconds both he and myself would have been the victims of Terry!"

The next brother was Cyrus Field, who belonged to the world as well as to Stockbridge. His epitaph in the village graveyard tells a noble story: CYRUS WEST FIELD, TO WHOSE COURAGE, ENERGY, AND PERSEVERANCE THE WORLD OWES THE ATLANTIC TELEGRAPH.

The Hill and the Plain

The fourth brother, Henry, unlike his brother Stephen, was too mild to kill, but he made up for it by marrying a lady who played her own heroine's part in a murder case. Of that drama you can read a capital account if you will turn to *All This, and Heaven Too*, written by Rachel, a greatniece of the hero of the story. Henry Martyn Field was the gentlest of men and one of the kindest, an evangelistic editor and copious writer of Fireside Travel; whose blackest sin I always thought was the unction with which he would wash his hands in invisible soap and address me as "My dearr Boy."

Even this does not summarize the vigorous race of Fields. A nephew, another Stephen, owned a barn just off the village street. On the bare floor ran a toy railroad train, fascinating me with its intricate convolutions. It seemed the perfect plaything for grownups. Tiny poles lined the tracks, supporting the lightest of electric wires, and on the rails sped tiny cars with no engine to pull them, driven as I saw at a glance by pure magic. Stephen was inventing the trolley car.

At the other end of the village street, just after it turns to climb Yale Hill, lived a heroine, though you wouldn't think so, for she was a schoolma'am by profession and incidentally a sister of Mr. Justice Brewer of the Supreme Court. The telegraph octopus was attempting to embrace the village streets, its gaunt and ugly poles destroying the loveliness of the leafy elms. The company insisted upon planting one precisely in front of Miss Adele Brewer's trim little cottage. She protested but to no avail, and a pit four feet deep was dug just opposite the front door. The next morning the black skeleton of a pole was fated to be set there. But the spirit of Barbara Frietchie was in Miss Brewer. She secured an army tent and, with the help of her little maid, pitched it right over the hole. Driving tent pegs at the corners, they snugged down the guy ropes, made everything trim in accordance with the

The Happy Profession

best traditions of the Army of the Potomac. Then both women disappeared into the house, returning with a cot bed, blankets, pillows, and a coverlet. Inside the tent the bed was made neatly as a New England spinster could make it — and then and there Miss Brewer went quietly to bed. The company was euchred.

Binding together the old-fashioned Unitarians and the new-fashioned Episcopalians of the village were the church, built by Uncle Butler in memory of my Aunt Susan, and its rector, Arthur Lawrence. Unchristian as it is to lay stress upon it, the Rector was a gentleman as well as a man of God, and it was a comfort to many of us to hear the Sunday service read without too great evangelistic fervor and to listen to a sermon which did not disturb the congregation by pleading too passionately for the refashioning of satisfactory lives. Of his ministrations it could certainly be said in the words ascribed to his Maker that his yoke was easy and his burden light. In his youth, however, as an army captain, our Rector had marched with Sherman from Atlanta to the sea, and that was enough to make me realize that he had his adventures and needed none. Besides, he was my "Lordfather" as I called him at six years old, since five years before he had baptized me and had stood as my sponsor. The weight of that responsibility he occasionally felt, for I was too speculative a boy to be satisfied with the revealed outline of Truth as Sunday School presented it. It amuses me today to note in my child's Bible penciled marks against crucial verses of which I seem to have doubted the validity or suspected an interpolation, stimulated probably by a precocious reading of Gibbon.

Mr. Lawrence felt, I say, the weight of responsibility, for he occasionally questioned me, and as occasionally intensified his own misgivings. But certainly it was the Rector who first

The Hill and the Plain

led me to ponder the eternal problem — I must have been passing college age then — whether justice is really an abiding concern of the Lord or merely an aspiration of mankind apparently in direct opposition to the laws of nature. For Mr. Lawrence had suffered as I sometimes think only a good man can suffer. He had lost his wife and his beloved daughter. His son alone was left and after college the boy showed signs of weakening of the brain. The agonized father had taken Billy to see the great Dr. Dana in New York and the verdict had been pitiless. As I passed the Rectory one day, Mr. Lawrence threw open the long window of his study and beckoned me to come in. He told me his story very simply and touchingly, and then he said: "Ellery, I can't believe it. I won't believe it. I have tried to do my duty and such cruelty cannot be visited upon me."

Years afterward I witnessed the still more cruel sequel. I was on a riding trip in the South and was walking my horse up a hill in the city of Asheville, North Carolina, when just ahead of me I saw a muscular young man in the center of the road engaged in rolling up the steep grade an enormous ball of stone. He put his back into it and pushed it with his powerful arms. I checked my mare to see more. Then I stared at the Sisyphus. It was Billy Lawrence. He looked up. "Hello, Ellery," he said as casually as if we had parted that morning. "It's hard going but I shall get it up." And then he went on with his labor. Billy was living in a physician's retreat, and in default of the possibility of mental exercise, he was called on to expend every physical faculty. When the stone reached the summit, the long day's work was done and he let it roll down again so that his task might be ready for the morrow.

The incident photographed on my thoughts the most desperate problem in human life.

Our Rector was a handsome man with regular features and

a benign expression. After the fashion of an earlier day he wore whiskers of a flamboyant Burnside cut, but after Mr. Choate saluted them as "flying buttresses of the Church" they quietly disappeared. Hardly a pastoral priest, he was everybody's friend, a good and kindly man.

The Rectory was next door to us and a broad lawn separated our piazzas. The Rector often wandered over for an evening chat and amenities flowed back and forth between the houses. Many were the jests between us, but one I recall to which no Sedgwick ever alluded in the presence of a Lawrence.

A dog was always an integral part of our family. Only the other day, wandering about the old place, I counted eighteen stones in the tiny graveyard, Dog's Acre, which lay close to the Rectory line, eighteen memorials of passionate and requited affection. At the time of the incident of which I speak, Scud, an Irish terrier, was in charge of our household and of my father in particular. Whenever the rattle of Papa's cane was heard in the hall, there was Scud ready to take his daily walk. On Sundays when the paternal stroll led to church there was always a particular bustle. Just ten minutes before eleven, it was the weekly duty of Nelly Farrell, the maid, to make Scud secure. Generally he was consigned to the cellar, but it was observable that the church bell never ceased tolling before Scud had squeezed himself out of some unnoticed aperture and was racing down the street precisely in time to enter the church doors between my father's legs. So decent was his demeanor, so downcast his look, so inextricably was he confused with my father's legs, that not infrequently he was able to reach the immunity of the family pew, and it is fair to add that during the service, Scud's character was sanctified. At those moments one could always see a flicker of the Rector's

The Hill and the Plain

eyelids, for Sunday after Sunday the spectacle never lost its ludicrous novelty.

The particular incident I speak of occurred on one of those Sunday mornings. Church was over. Scud had returned from worship and was sitting reflectively on the porch steps. The Rectory windows were thrown wide to the delicious summer day, and the Rector's maid had just placed upon the table the Sunday leg of mutton and flanked it with the boat of caper sauce. For sixty seconds, the interval usually allowed in detective stories, the room was vacant. Then the Rector came to his dinner. There before him was the caper sauce, there was the big platter, but the twelve-pound leg of mutton had vanished. Not a trace remained until the Rector looked closely. Then he caught sight of a thin trail of mutton fat. Across the white cloth it led, across the carpet, across the window seat, the window ledge, the piazza — and then it utterly disappeared.

Direct evidence of the thief there was none. The Rector gave thanks for all he was not about to receive and with Miss Lena, his sister-in-law, sat down to caper sauce and mashed potato. True he remembered the Ninth Commandment and in despite of it harbored a suspicion of his neighbor's dog, but where there was no proof there should be no protest.

As for the suspected; Scud had disappeared. It was an odd thing for him to do when scraps from Sunday dinner were in the offing. Two o'clock and he was nowhere to be found, but we children, one and all, scouted the idea that he could in any possible way be implicated in crime. It was contrary to Scud's nature. From that day to this I have made no admission but there was corroborative evidence. Towards seven o'clock that evening, I had caught sight of Scud creeping across the lawn. He had left us a terrier; he returned a mastiff,

The Happy Profession

with a body so enormous that his scraggy legs gave way and he crawled on his belly to the back door.

A long and beloved procession of the companions of my youth passed before me as I stood at the foot of Scud's grave and recalled that afternoon. I remembered my boyhood sympathies for those too clever to be caught. I reflected on the injustice of circumstantial evidence. I felt the intensity of doggish temptation, and then my gaze wandered to all those other graves in Dog's Acre. I thought of all the devotion and all the derelictions of those comrades of generations of Sedgwicks. Eighteen little graves were huddled under the locust trees. One slate was graven with the name "Zozo," most petulant of French poodles, and close beside stood the white stone of "Kai," dog of dogs, friend of friends. His inscription bears true witness: —

> *Hic jacet Kai*
> *Amicus fidelis*
> *Non sine peccatis*
> *Sed supra modum canis*
> *Amans, amatusque.*

Benvenuto Cellini, too, lies there, Benny just a year my senior, causing my brothers to hold me back at dinnertime so that my elder might enter first. And there, too, lies the beloved Chou-fleur, once a ball of fluffy whiteness, who thought nothing of journeys to other homes of his master in Paris and in Athens. I leaned over to read the inscription on his white stone; the end of all adventure was there: —

> *Nous n'irons plus au bois.*

CHAPTER IV

The Old Familiar Faces

THE CHARM of the Stockbridge mind in those days was its complete lack of self-consciousness. Today it seems to me the Village never quite forgets itself. There used to be no time for the interpretation and analysis which in the post-Freudian world takes such toll of individual and community reflection and tends to make us all alien to one another. There was too much work to be worked and talk to be talked and gossip to be gossiped. Were I to do what might be called a "Middletown" upon our primitive village, I think I should begin with the churches. A church was something more than a church; it was so to speak a layer of the social cake. The frosted top, of course, was Episcopalian, with a little old-fashioned Unitarianism in the batter which gave it consistency and a flavor now forgotten and perhaps, in its memory, almost scandalous. The Episcopal Church being quite as social as it was clerical, no stress was laid upon dogma. My father, for instance, a simon-pure Unitarian of what today we call the old school, was Senior Warden of the Episcopal Church, and I recall how often in later years Bishop Lawrence used to laugh over that anomaly. Even in the '80s dogma had begun its long march toward oblivion. Phillips Brooks used to call it "Truth packed for transportation." But however tight the bag is packed, its transportation grows more difficult

The Happy Profession

year by year. At any rate, there was little *odium theologicum* then to poison village relationships.

But to get on with the cake-making. The second layer was compounded of Congregationalists. Just as the summer people were Episcopalian by social habit, so the solid all-the-year-rounders, headed by Deacon Williams, trooped to the Congregationalist Church — the red meetinghouse with the white steeple standing on its green lawn at the far end of the village — together with their Presbyterian brothers, exchanging church discipline for brotherly love.

The third layer of our cake was Methodist, and a skimpy layer it was, for by the rules of Methodism the minister was transferred to pastures new at the end of each third year, and where is the crop of Methodists — or any other Christians for that matter — which matures after three years' growth? Just underneath the Methodists in the social scale ought to have been the Baptists, but in Stockbridge the Baptists flourished not. Perhaps the drama of village life was not up to their standard, perhaps the Housatonic was too shallow for total immersion. At any rate a Baptist Church was not on hand, and the lowest layer, the undercrust (if a cake has an undercrust), was Roman Catholic. The Catholics were a society of their own, household servants almost exclusively, and laborers. In my youth there was among them but a solitary recruit from the gentry. This convert from the Unitarianism of the fathers was a portent in those days, and although the event had taken place years and years before, the wonder and dismay of it had not quite passed from Stockbridge memories. Especially had this been felt in my family, for the convert was none other than my father's sister, my dear Aunt Jane, who, setting out as a young girl on the grand tour in Europe with education and pleasure as her goal, fell under the eternal

The Old Familiar Faces

spell of Rome and afterwards devoted a lifetime to the Church. Long after Billy Brogan's translation of the deacon's hat shop she had her share in the building of the Catholic Church, and after years of prayer to her patron, Saint Joseph, succeeded in transplanting in the neighboring village of Lee a sisterhood of the Order of the Sacred Heart, who, poor women, born and bred in France, must have found it hard in Our Lady to condemn them to the slow martyrdom of Yankee living. At any rate, Aunt Jane was certainly "an influence." That was universally acknowledged, as you can see from the following episode.

One day in New York she dropped into St. Patrick's Cathedral for a quiet prayer. As she knelt, a sense of dizziness came over her and in need of some immediate restorative she felt in her reticule and took out a tiny flask of brandy, always carried there for precaution. Asking Saint Patrick to excuse her for an instant she rose and, slipping behind a pillar, put the bottle to her lips. That instant an uninstructed sacristan was upon her. The scene was embarrassing but hardly had a word been spoken, when up came a Monsignor hurrying to her assistance. He turned upon the sacristan and impatiently exclaimed, "Don't you know who *she* is? Why, next moment the Vatican will excommunicate you *by cable*."

Full thirty years after Aunt Jane's death I was first introduced to Cardinal O'Connell. A prelate never forgets. "Sedgwick, Sedgwick," he repeated to catch the name accurately, "why, what relation are you to *Madre Americana* at whose feet I passed four of my student years in Rome?"

But not the Catholics were the near friends of my youth (always excepting Aunt Jane, and Nelly and Ella in our kitchen), not the Methodists nor yet the Congregationalists. My "society" was Episcopalian, and it was in that society that

The Happy Profession

I learned a little of the quirks and oddities of human nature which know no boundaries of creed or class. I suppose you will find them in every village where the rector is a bachelor or has lost his wife, but about Dr. Lawrence was always hovering a chorus of spinster ladies devoted to good works and singing praises to the Rector's name. It was they who taught Sunday school, hung green festoons about the church at Christmas, filled the chancel with lilies for the Easter service and kept fresh flowers upon the altar. On Thursday afternoons they "sewed for the Indians." How quaint that occupation seems now! On Fridays I forget what they did — it was something as useless as it was devoted — and throughout the week they fluttered about the Rector, who would perhaps have been happier without them. Vestal virgins we called them ironically, but not without a sense of their devotion. In those days no serious civic work called to women, and their meager lives were spent as moths round the church candle.

The pride and boast of the village was Mr. Choate, and when he was made Ambassador to the Court of St. James's, we considered it Stockbridge which had honored him. His was a manly person, beautiful to look upon: a leonine head and, until his stooping days, a figure for Hermes. His humor was like a sunburst. When we children were on our way to a play in the Village Casino it was Mr. Choate who warned us, "Have a care, boys, lest you dilate with the wrong emotion." His wit never relied upon a story but kept bubbling up through his talk in unexpected phrases. In public he was never guilty, but in private I shudder to remember the puns he perpetrated for the delectation of us children. I see him now in what seemed his eternal youth, and I recall on his sixtieth birthday his saying to me as I chanced to be swimming alongside him in Stockbridge Bowl, "Ellery, they tell

The Old Familiar Faces

me I am sixty. The calendar lies. I feel just as I did when I was forty."

Mr. Choate inherited all the gods had to give. But he gave to himself the essential quality which made his career — audacity. *Toujours de l'audace* might have been his motto. He feared no cause, no audience, not even himself. True, he told me that he had never risen to speak without trepidation, and when I showed my incredulity, "Yes," he said, "when I am on my feet I am always afraid, till my knees shake under the table. When they knock together, then I know I am going to make a good speech."

His knees must have knocked together pretty sharply one evening in 1893 when he was to make the speech of the evening at a dinner of "The Friendly Sons of Saint Patrick," at Delmonico's on St. Patrick's Day. Home rule was the question of the hour. Every Irishman in New York was howling for it, though to do much about it was not on the cards. The leaders were much too busy in making Tammany Hall rule in New York. I quote from the proceedings with thanks to the *New York Sun*.

"After a few graceful compliments, Mr. Choate went on to say that he would not speak upon the subject nearest to Irish hearts, Home Rule. 'I leave that to Mr. Depew who is to come later. I leave that to Mr. Depew and to Mr. Gladstone, who understand it so much better than I. But I prefer to speak upon a kindred subject more familiar to me. That is, how Irishmen rule away from home,' and then Mr. Choate went on to speak of Irish victories in New York City. 'For what offices great and small have the Irishmen not taken? What spoils have they not carried away? From Mayor Gilroy — I am glad to hear your applause — I am the only man here tonight, I doubt not, who did not vote for Mayor Gilroy. I voted for the other man. I've forgotten who he was. But no matter who he was. No man could stand against Thomas F. Gilroy and his seventy-five thousand majority.

" 'But, gentlemen, now that you have done so much for America, now that you have made it all your own, what do you propose to do for Ireland? How long do you propose to let her be the political football of England? Poor, downtrodden, oppressed Ireland! Hereditary bondsmen, know ye not who would be free themselves must strike the blow.

" 'You have learned how to govern by making all the soil of other countries your own. Have you not learned how to govern at home; how to make Ireland a land of Home Rule?'

"There was a confused murmur in the room, a cry of 'Mr. Choate is carrying his sarcasm too far.' Mr. Choate went on with a sarcastic smile of good humor on his face: 'There *is* a cure for Irish woes and feebleness today. It is a strong measure that I advocate. I am here tonight to plead for Ireland with the retaining fee in my possession, and I propose to plead. I propose that you should all, with your wives and children, and your children's children, with the spoils you have taken from America in your hands, set your faces homeward, land there, and strike the blow.

" 'Gentlemen, the G.O.M. [Gladstone was of course the "Grand Old Man"] needs you. He is clamoring for you, and the G.O.P. to which I belong, has been so severely disciplined that it can get along without you. Think what it would mean for both countries if all the Irishmen in America, from the Atlantic to the Pacific, should shoulder their muskets and march to the relief of their native land! Then, indeed, would Ireland be for Irishmen and America for Americans!' Then, amid the rising hubbub he continued his satirical discourse and ended thus, 'It would be a terrible blow to us. It would take us a great while to recover. Feebly, imperfectly, we should

The Old Familiar Faces

look about us and learn for the first time in seventy-five years how to govern New York without you. But there would be a bond of brotherhood between the two nations. Up from the whole soil of Ireland, up from the whole soil of America, would arise one paean, Erin go bragh.'"

Many Americans perhaps have dreamed this iridescent dream but none other than Mr. Choate have had the audacity to put it into words.

To outward seeming, Mr. Choate was the most fortunate of men, the happiest, the most contented with his lot. And yet it fell to him to suffer misfortunes that would have crushed a man of lesser will or weaker faith. His eldest son, pride and joy of the family, inheritor of his father's talent, died at the threshold of manhood, and before she reached womanhood, his eldest daughter, Effie, made to be loved, was taken also. His second son had a still more tragic fate. George gave early proof that his mind was not in balance. He was a carefree, generous, likable boy, quite without mental stamina and overbold in his physical risks. I recall his father giving him the absolute injunction never to go on the river except in company with an older man. George was an obedient son. The next day he sought out his chief crony, my brother Alick. Now Alick was precisely twenty-four hours older than George, so no commandment was broken when they rollicked off together in a rickety canoe. The dereliction was reported to Mr. Choate, but Mr. Choate was just. Respecting the letter of the law, he felt he had been fairly checkmated.

Soon however it became evident that George's mind could not be trusted to guide his life. He was sent to a private sanitarium, and there for nearly thirty years lived a harmless and unthinking existence. At Christmas he would come home for the holidays. Think of his loving parents on those Christmas days.

The Happy Profession

Beneath this triple blow Mr. Choate never faltered but pressed resolutely on. It was his greatest victory.

In our village the lesser characters permitted no cramping of their individualities. They filled in the human comedy as milkmaids and yokels do in the Shakespearean scene. In a piazzaed house on Main Street Miss Nellie Gavitt kept her Dame School. I was turning six when I insisted on walking there alone, a hot potato in each pocket of my pea jacket to keep my fingers warm on a brisk day. Miss Nellie's sisters were her assistant teachers — Miss Pussie and Miss Chloe. They guided our plump, little, clumsy hands as we traced our imperfect copies of the faultless Spencerian script, printed in unattainable symmetry at the top of the page. The impeccable Mr. Spencer had furnished American youth with a purely commercial model of penmanship but legible and neat as a scrivener could make it. *Haste makes waste;* just so, I would copy on the twelve ruled lines below the example. Would I had acquired for a lifetime that legible hand, ugly and serviceable: my secretaries and correspondents wish so too! Nowadays schools do these things better, and the letter in handwritten print is the groundwork of all instruction in handwriting. Fifty years later in Japan, I watched a more imaginative method. In place of pothooks, the children, not five years old, traced the delicate likeness of a blade of grass dipping in the wind. Scores of times, hundreds, the pupils would copy the consummate natural line of that curve of perfect grace. At last they would catch it — the arrowy upward shoot, the inevitable droop of the tired grass, the bare suggestion of a stir in the air. They do these things well there, and their lovely screens with their golden backgrounds bear ultimate witness to it.

To Miss Nellie I owe my first training in English composi-

The Old Familiar Faces

tion. On the very first Prize Day, I was called upon to read to a select group of parents a composition of my very own. I seem to detect the fascinating influence of Paul du Chaillu and his gorillas, for my brothers never allowed me to forget my lisping introduction.

"The owrang owtang isth a very interestible animal."

Every successful day when I returned from school, I brought home to my mother a tiny square of paper marked "Good" in Miss Nellie's hand. The other days were heavy and sad.

Village faces crowd back upon me. There was Mr. Hofmayer, the Hungarian fishmonger, so far as I know the only Jew in the village. How common and insignificant he looked with his scaly apron, his fishlike smell, and his big nose, peddling his flounders and mackerel at the kitchen door. I should hardly have liked then to acknowledge his acquaintance on the street. But on festal days, oh the difference! It was Mr. Hofmayer who led the band. His bearskin busby, the height of a small barrel, made him a full head taller. His glittering baton with its great brass ball at the top caught the sun as he whirled it with dizzying speed. His nose dominated the procession. What a pleasure it was then to have him turn his friendly head and wink at me! Then there was "Skip" Kilfoil, the bandy-legged hostler of Pratt's livery stable. Who but Skip, on special holidays, would drive us in his carryall, twelve picnickers bound for Goose Pond or Shaker Village with four horses to pull them there. If there was a torchlight procession with Republican banners flaunting the breeze, it was Skip on horseback that would lead the procession. Who would be a Democrat when Skip was in the saddle!

The barber was Frank Rathbone. May he live forever in a Fisherman's Paradise, for never yet did Sunday trout elude him in the shadows of an earthly brook. But on weekdays he stumped his cork leg round the tight circle of his barber's chair. It was from Frank I learned the democratic doctrine of perfect equality. First come, first served. He explained to me that if Queen Victoria dropped in twelve inches behind me she would have to wait right in that chair till her turn came round. There was a legend in his shop that once a customer, impatient to be shorn and to go about his business, said to the man just ahead, "Let me have your place and I'll pay your bill." The stranger assented. When it came the latter's turn Frank asked, "What will you have?" "Well," drawled the man, "let's see. A shave with lotion, then a haircut with a rub-in of Herpicide. Then you had best give my hair a good singeing to keep it from bleeding to death, and then a shampoo won't do me any harm. Make it an oil shampoo."

The bill came to $2.75.

The drygoods store (in Yankeedom a store is never a "shop") was presided over by Mr. Dean, who had brought a stiff leg home with him from Lookout Mountain or thereabouts. He it was who showed me the miracle of tearing a yard of gingham straight across, neatly as if you had cut it with shears. But Mr. Dean was not good at conversation with small boys and I felt more at home with George Seymour, the plump and smiling grocer across the street, his shirt sleeves held in place by bright red garters.

"Well, Bubby, what can I do for you?" was Mr. Seymour's comfortable greeting. "Five cents' worth of citron if you please and five Gibraltars." Then across the street to the drugstore for a sarsaparilla, where bang went the last nickel of my fifteen weekly cents. Mr. Clarke, the proprietor, never erred, I am sorry to remember, on the side of amiability, and since the drugstore was our Boys' Club, that was a dereliction. It was whispered too that in the evening behind the

The Old Familiar Faces

rear partition, business went on not in strict conformity with the "Maine Law," and on Sunday morning the empty bottles along the village street were held to have belonged in Mr. Clarke's establishment. What a fraud that "Maine Law" was! Once when my parents took me on a trip to its natural habitat, the State of Maine, my mother expressed a wish for a cup of tea. Now afternoon tea in a country hostelry is an unknown rite, and I followed the waiter to the kitchen door to see whether I could not help to compass it. To my mystification the waiter turned on me and winked one eye. "Tea," he said with knowing emphasis and disappeared to return with a cold teapot filled with bourbon.

Right next the horse trough which bears the irrefutable sentiment UTILITY IS PREFERABLE TO GRANDEUR stands the village library, a frequent haunt. There Miss Fanny Wells, her twin curls nestling at the nape of her neck, would advise me upon my next choice of books. Biography and history were my favorites but Miss Wells's fancy seldom strayed from the realm of fiction. The library itself had been presented to the town, as the inscription on its cornerstone commemorates forever, by Mrs. J. Z. Goodrich. This ancient lady had been comfortably endowed by her husband, J. Z. Goodrich, deceased, who had been in his day the successful owner of woolen mills at Glendale and a diligent worker in the vineyard. The widow bestowed his money generously and cared not who knew it. Almost stone-deaf, she never allowed a compliment to escape her spreading ear trumpet and was famous for the reception of deserved praise. My father, at a "Sunrise Meeting" in the library held at 7.30 on January first to herald the arrival of a better year, laid it on with a trowel, much to his own amusement and to Mrs. Goodrich's delight. His theme was the Age of Woman, in the '80s just dawning above the horizon. His peroration would have done honor to

The Happy Profession

Bossuet. There were four great ages he said, ushered in by four women, famous in song and story: "From Semiramis to Cleopatra, from Cleopatra to Queen Elizabeth, and from Queen Elizabeth to Mrs. J. Z. Goodrich!"

Mrs. Goodrich had had her difficulties and had triumphed over them. During his latter years, the mind of her strictly methodical husband had begun to wander. One day, most unfortunately, he tried to remember when he had been married. The mists of half a century hung about that crucial date. He could remember nothing of the circumstances. Could it be possible that he, unfailing in attendance at church, upright in his dealings, with a life open as the day, had taken a woman whom he had not made his wife? Had the lady who had faced him across the breakfast table, the dinner table, the supper table, for fifty years and more, worn a false ring upon her finger and assumed a false name? Had they two in wanton wickedness been living for half a century in sin? It was too terrible. The horrid idea took root. Mrs. Goodrich gave her helpmeet most positive assurance, but no witnesses were available to support her testimony. The clergyman had died a score of years before. The bridesmaids had vanished with the snows of yesteryear. Then a blessed thought occurred to her. Slipping her arm through Mr. Goodrich's, she drew him to the rear door of the parsonage. Again they made their vows and even as Isaac and Rebekah his wife they were made one. The burden of sin rolled away from Mr. Goodrich. He died in the comforting assurance that his transgression had been forgiven, his iniquity had been pardoned. And besides, he had made Mrs. Goodrich an honest woman.

Never have I heard of a philosopher, political or social, who did not extol a country boyhood. Never a God-made or self-made successful man who did not congratulate himself upon having been brought up in the country. And yet the

The Old Familiar Faces

tides of human existence run all the other way. But in thinking of the country as a place to grow up in, it is not fame and fortune I have in mind, but rather happiness and understanding. The proper study of mankind is man; the rewarding study of boys is the unaccountable behavior of their elders. People are a queer lot. Watch them in a city crowd, and you will say it is human nature that makes them act so. But watch them as individuals in the country and you well know that John Smith and Billy Jones act just as Billy Jones and John Smith make them act, without response to any orthodox human orbit whatsoever. People in the mass are not a mass of individuals. Something extraneous, a sixth unhappy sense, has been added. You have arrived at quite a different product. Some Gresham's law seems to be at work, the bad driving out the good. Apparently it works progressively. A group loses something of the individuality of its components. In a crowd it rapidly diminishes. In a mob it is lost. The country recruit does not refresh the city. He is lost in it. So it was in Rome. So it is in New York and Chicago.

But before we lose ourselves in this pessimistic philosophy let us remember with thankfulness all that country living does for us in explaining men to boys, filling their minds with all sorts of entertaining and desirable information. What fun those early lessons were! Somewhere in *The Fortunes of Nigel,* a favorite with my youth, Sir Walter throws in this sagacious bit of personal philosophy. "If we have ever been able to afford amusement to the reader," he writes, "it is owing in a great degree to this cause — that we have never found ourselves in company with the stupidest of all possible companions in a post-chaise, or with the most arrant cumber-corner that ever occupied a place in a mail coach, without finding that in the course of our conversation with him we had some ideas presented to us either grave or gay, or some information communicated in the course of our journey which we should have regretted not to have learned and which we should have been sorry to have immediately forgotten."

I think of the cumber-corners of Stockbridge as well as of the up-and-doing. They were all of them schoolmasters of my youth. Bless their memories, and may the quiet mounds in the village graveyard never be disturbed by the perturbation of one restless soul!

A last word about the village. There is an imaginative influence at work for the benefit of every child who lives his own life there. Among the children of the gentry in my day, it was rather a lonely life. There were few boys for me to play with and I lived largely in adult companionship. But with my cousin Nathalie, a child of my own age who came to live with us, I never failed to find some new and amusing game. It was the spirit of the place. We could always blacken our faces on a stormy night and scowl suddenly into the kitchen window, frightening the "girls" into fits, or we could stir the Irish in them by shouting in derogation of some friend, newly arrived from Erin: —

> Paddy from Irreland,
> Paddy from Corrk,
> With a howle in his breeches
> As big as New Yorrk.

But occasionally we climbed to more imaginative heights. One evening at nightfall, I cried: "Let's have a wake." There was perfect understanding between us, and with a single thought we ran to the parlor and lifted the serene white bust of the young Augustus from its marble pedestal. By a miracle we did not drop it on the way to the library, and rested the pallid features on a pillow of the long sofa. Sheets and pillow

The Old Familiar Faces

slips came from the linen closet. We gave the couch all the pale serenity of death. Two tall candlesticks, a yard high, stood on either side of the library fireplace, each bearing a two-foot ornamental candle. These we placed at the head and foot of the bier, and when the curtains were drawn and light came only from the two tapers, we had almost convinced ourselves we were in the presence of tragedy. We raised our shrill lamentation and then it only remained for me to call in a hollow voice to the gardener. "Oh Haley. Come. Come! He is dead!" Haley dropped his rake and as he came into the doorway his jaw dropped too. "My God," he said in a sepulchral whisper, "he *is* dead." "Yes," I murmured, "dead as Caesar."

CHAPTER V

Old School Ties

It is a well-kept secret among parents that boarding schools are primarily for their convenience, but for boys too they have their importance. First and last I know a good deal about boarding schools for I was once schoolboy, master, and trustee. My feelings about them are mixed. Certainly so far as the civilizing process goes they are imperfect substitutes for home life, and it seems hardly natural that boys and girls should be brought up apart, when in the long run they are destined to be so exceedingly dependent upon each other. But here the tradition of the race runs right against me. We are still under the spell of the monastic habit. There are obvious advantages in the opportunity for a boy to devote undivided attention to study and preparation for the long struggle of competing with his fellows. The experiment of our coeducational colleges throws light on the moot question. I have not the statistics before me, but I am certain that in our state universities, so far as paper education goes, the rating of women is higher than that of men. Why is it then that professors, eight out of ten of them, would banish women if they could? In their classrooms, that everlasting Gresham's law which operates in so many unexpected places is steadily at work. As the proportion of women rises in a class, so surely does the number of men decline. And as women are very apt

Old School Ties

to plump for the humanities, I suspect that the fatal trend against civilizing studies among men is accelerated by the influx of women. But in these matters no choice is involved. The expense of a double program of education is prohibitive, and every institution supported by taxes must combine the sexes.

Considering then the advantage of boarding school, I should say it is entirely relative. If a boy has space to play in, companions enough, and if he belongs to a family of boys and girls good at educating each other, as every real family should be, boarding school offers a poor alternative to the home. But boys so favored grow rarer year by year.

How terrible is that day when boarding school is first mentioned. You have long dreaded it in secret and suddenly you hear your eldest brother declare it high time you should be packed off. Next your parents take it up; your father would "like to talk with you after supper," and pretty soon you hang your head and go.

It is a fashion now that when a writing man reaches the eminence of forty years he discusses in his autobiography the painful effect his boarding school has had upon his brilliant gifts. Commonly it seems to have curbed a generous spirit and cramped bright possibilities. Particularly is this the case with literary Grotonians. But in the instances which happen to have fallen under my notice I judge the author's youth to have offered difficult problems which the school would have been glad to escape. If a boy has individuality so has a boarding school. It would be of little worth if it had not. To be true to itself the school must decide every question by asking not so often what is best for the boy but what is best for the school. And what is best for the school is usually a group of normal boys growing up in a normal way. The exceptional boy, unless he excels as a scholar, and in particular the aesthetic

The Happy Profession

boy, the incipient artist, is a knot in the log as it goes through the mill. This is not to say that exceptional boys may not be the hope of the world, but merely that no school intent upon its job can be run in their especial interest.

It is the penalty of talent. Odd boys must be their own schoolmasters, they and the Lord who made them, and that chance friend who comes into so many lives bringing a peculiar sympathy and some eccentric but wise advice. The exceptional boy with his talent goes through the world crying, "Who will understand me? I am so worth understanding." The shadow of talent is egoism, and conscious of that, most men pass him by. But if the candle of talent shines bright enough, someone will catch sight of it and then the boy will go his glittering way, maintaining to the very end that schools are kept by Philistines and only in their teeth was he able to save his birthright.

Much as I have loved Groton, I cannot say that I enjoyed the school, not at least until I went back there as a master. I was an untalented boy, biddable, reasonably unattractive, and most content when unnoticed. And yet from the first day there I felt there was a possible heaven above me, for the truth was I had come out of the pit of hell.

My story was this. When the family conclave decided that I really must grow up and be a man I was despatched to a boarding school that shall be nameless. At the time, I merely knew that school was hateful to me, but I think of it now less as a school than as a sink of iniquity. Not that there were not a number of nice boys there, but the tone of the place was the tone of a penal institution. What could a boy of fourteen learn of manliness, when, unseen himself, he watched the headmaster creep in slippered feet to a door and satisfy his suspicions by peeping through the keyhole! It was a military school. The young lieutenant fresh from West Point, who looked like a youthful Mars and drilled us in the weary manual of arms, was doubtless a fine fellow, but if we had been a squad made up of A.W.O.L.'s he could not have looked us over with a fishier eye. The boy officers were tyrants. After sixty years, I should feel it a benediction upon my old age if I could get my fingers on the throat of one young cadet lieutenant. On dress parade, when I was presenting arms for inspection, he loved to come up behind me and, under pretense of giving a correct slant to my rifle, run a pin into my buttock. Then would the West Point lieutenant frown and make a note of my instability. We marched and we countermarched, we practised the manual of arms till a musket became for me the devilish thing it is. Lessons, quite subordinated to military training, were scarcely palliatives. They were taught by underpaid and unhappy young men in coats worn shiny and ingrained with chalk. I recall but a single exception, the teacher of English, who encouraged me to recite "Ruin seize thee, ruthless King," in the spirit of romantic drama. Had the school been a place where gentlemen could exist, he would have been a gentleman. I bless him as I pass. I bless too an older boy, Gus Willard. If he still lives, I salute him. For on Saturday afternoons he would sometimes take me on a long ramble over the countryside, filling the clothes bags slung over our backs with stolen apples and half-ripened chestnuts. What bliss was in those intervals! They were the only respite except when with a long night's sleep ahead I would slip into bed whispering to myself the single refrain, "Eight hours till reveille!"

But very often there were not eight hours. Sometimes on the stroke of eleven I would be waked by a terrifying crash. No other noise in my experience has been quite like it — a sort of quivering, shivering, sliding thunder. The cause I learned later to understand. A group of desperate heroes would climb along the ledge of the topmost story, and breaking into the room where the extra china was kept, would bring out a rich assortment. Then when eleven o'clock struck and the last light went out, they would hurl the crockery down the long corridors, slop pails, basins, mugs, chamber pots, anything that would splinter and make a noise about it. The fragments would go slithering along the polished floors and bring up against the radiator at the far end with a crash devastating to a master's ear and infinitely satisfying to the perpetrators. A moment's utter silence would follow. The conspirators would dissolve into their respective beds, and immediately the trumpets would sound assembly. Out we would all rush in our nightgowns — pajamas were newfangled then. In every dormitory roll would be called. Never was a boy missing; never a boy who had not been obviously asleep two minutes before. Then and there the entire school would be marched to the basement for two hours' punishment drill. Oh the misery of it! Sleepy, tired little boys with uniforms half-buttoned would right-shoulder, left-shoulder, support arms, arms port, till midnight passed and one o'clock came. Then a little troubled rest till reveille and the old routine again.

But the worst thing about the school was the indefinable sense of corruption that hung thick over it. I was an innocent little boy. The works of the devil were quite unknown to me, but I was horribly conscious they must be very near. I felt them in the universal secretiveness, in the casualness with which whispered conversations were interrupted when I approached. Nine tenths of my fears were, I dare say, morbid fancies. But evil has its own nauseous smell, and that smell hung about the school.

My family tell me that when at the age of five I was asked the classical conundrum, "What was the color of Washington's gray mare?" I lisped the reply: "I am not suffithcently acquainted with histowy." Had I progressed far enough in my school days to understand the color of French history, I could have prophesied with accuracy the fate of that school. That blessed spring I left it, for a chance vacancy had turned up at Groton, but not long after my time, Revolution came. The boys broke into the armory, fixed bayonets, drove out the teachers, nailed the headmaster into his room, commandeered the butcher's cart and the baker's wagon, and proclaimed a republic. Liberty was short-lived, for parents and constables poured down on the school in an avenging flood. Supplies were refused, pocket money cut off, and the garrison surrendered at discretion. But none the less it was a famous victory.

This was the background against which I first saw Groton. Perhaps if her severer critics had enjoyed the same perspective, they would have painted a different picture. Anyway in this "rich boys' school" I found many boys as poor as I, and at the time my father was very poor. If the school was filled with snobs, I knew them not. Perhaps I was a snob myself, but to this day I cannot remember who it was I enjoyed looking down upon. What I remember clearly is that all alike had twenty-five cents to spend during the week, and that a nickel of that was earmarked for the plate on Sunday; and that the white collars we were obliged to wear at supper set off suits of much the same appearance. Of course Pierpont Morgan was President of the Board of Trustees, and there were a number of boys whose mother's names appeared regularly in the social column of the *New York Herald*, but I am mistaken if term bills were not of major concern to at least half the parents.

Groton was in its first youth then, hardly three years old. There were less than fifty boys, an excellent number. The

The Happy Profession

sixth form had just reached the first year of its existence. It consisted of one boy, George Rublee, who has since lived a distinguished and useful life. Many years after, when I was a trustee of the school, I remember remarking slyly to Mr. Peabody: "Well, of course, the school goes up and down." He turned to me with one of those Jovian looks of his. "What do you mean, *down?*" "Why," said I, "you began with George Rublee and have never done so well since."

Always Groton was striving to be an institution but always it was personality that made it what it was. The core of it, the life, heart, and breath of it, were the three young men who gave it being. That was a triumvirate without a parallel — those three men the eldest not far from boyhood. As I look back upon their confident young faces I remember that they were called the "Team," but to me it seems that the three of them made up the sum of human divergence. To William Amory Gardner was given the scholar's mind, imaginative and unpractical; to Sherrard Billings, the talent of the teacher and the preacher; to Endicott Peabody, the power of personality. Each was absolutely and utterly himself. We shall not look upon their like again. Personal affection and the compulsive ardor of religion bound them indissolubly, but in all their characteristics they were diverse as the elements. Gardner was a *lusus naturae* and looked the part. With Aeschylus or Homer doubled back in his pocket to keep the place, he would hover about the school he loved beyond all earthly things, kindling the brains of the intelligent to a pure flame, diverting the rest of us by the quaintness of his quixotisms, turning the order of classrooms into chaos, and contriving, in some esoteric way, to stamp on every boy an impression of what loyalty means to life.

It was Gardner who gave the school its other-worldly character. I do not mean the spirit of religion nor yet of unselfishness, although he was deeply religious and without worldly taint. Rather he seemed to be weaving fairy tales in a prosaic world. The most accomplished Grecian perhaps who ever came out of Harvard College, there was about him a fantastic quality which seemed in common touch with all the creatures of fancy from leprechauns to giant killers. He was full of theories and defended them in paradox. The approach of the holidays filled him with sorrow, and Black Monday was the brightest day of his year. There was something of Puck in Gardner, something of Ariel, and to all of us he gave in some measure the sense of living in an unmaterial world.

In perfect contrast, Sherrard Billings was the impersonation of law and order. He was a little bandy-legged man with an unfailing sense of dignity — and of the humanity of laughter. His bodily insignificance was a cross to him, and side by side with the physical magnificence of the Rector it was wonderful to see how much of a man he looked and was. What a struggle little men have in the world! Lucky for them that Napoleon and Nelson were in the five-foot class. It stimulates morale to think of them. Billings was a preacher of intensity and force. Somehow the pulpit seemed to add inches to his stature, and in the classroom he had the priceless gift of keeping boys on their toes. With what skill he brought us through the horrid complexities of indirect discourse! All that Caesar did to obfuscate the intelligence of small boys, he undid with an ingenious system of what he called Chinese boxes. Take a sentence beset with inner clauses, one tucked within the next. Billings would pick up a series of colored chalks. Writing an inextricable Latin sentence on the board, he would underscore the subject in white, and then, passing over half a dozen convolutions, would mark the predicate also in white. There you had your statement. Some man said or did something. Then for its modification he would underline the principal subordinate clause in yellow. It was quite easy to understand now you had got a firm grip on it. But at the heart of the sentence still remained an undigested clause, and within that some pernicious phrase invented for the devil of it. Mark these with green and blue. The sentence became intelligible. Caesar was licked.

There can be a relation between a boy and a schoolmaster unlike any other in the world. Each has so much to offer and to accept; knowledge for trust, enthusiasm for experience. For those who love the profession, which has no rival for usefulness save the physician, no call is so clear, no reward so certain. I too have loved schoolmastering but I have never been insensible of the shadows which hang over it. School generations are short-lived; four years, six at most, and the companions you have learned to love best are gone. And if you happen to be interested in ideas rather than in people, the long, long thoughts of youth give you little sustenance. The desire to live your own life, call it selfishness if you will, sweeps over you. What is the life of man? *"Les générations sont des haleines qui passent. L'homme respire, aspire et expire,"* as Victor Hugo says. You have one life to live. Then live it.

Such were my hesitations but no such doubts assailed Billings. He was a born schoolmaster but that overmastering passion could not save him from disappointment or from bitter sorrow. Any man of his capacities would have loved to be first; always he was condemned to be second. Under poignant circumstances he lost his wife and child. But courage and faith and duty, companions of a lifetime, stood by him to the end. At the close of his life he suffered a long and wasting illness. I was told that one of his few pleasures was to hear from old boys, and I wrote him at length. Letters for deathbed reading are not inspiring. I tried to strike a cheerful note. I reproached him for his lifelong tyranny as Senior Master, for the black marks he had given, for the midnight pleasures he had ruined, for the Latin traps he had set for the unwary feet of carefree boys, and I marveled how it was that these same Christian and forgiving children had continued to love him and to remember him with gratitude. Then one day he sent for me. His tiny shrunken body looked as Gandhi looks. He had no longer strength to raise his head from the pillow, but he laid both his hands over mine, and with the barest ghost of his familiar smile slowly withdrew one hand and from beneath the bedclothes brought forth my own letter and pressed it against my palm. Dear old Billings! There is no teaching like a good man's life.

The Caesar of the Triumvirate was the Rector. They used to call him the Sun God in his youth. He was the perfect autocrat with the power of life and what to small boys was much worse than death. On the playground you could do anything short of snowballing him. But in his vast study with room for the whole school in it, that was a different matter. To be alone there, on instant summons, with your heart open and no desires hid, was like cramming for the Last Day. I do not believe any boy, however crooked his tongue, however deep his sins below the surface, ever lied face to face with the Rector. There was an instinctive, comprehensive understanding about him. He never spied, but he always knew and you knew he knew. Out with it! There was no other way. Yet perhaps the most remarkable thing about him, the thing a boy could never guess and only the friendship of decades could discern, was the complete and disciplined humility of his spirit. Underneath the schoolmaster was the priest. God was all in all, to serve Him was to rule.

The Rector was the perfect example of the healthy-minded man. "Sick souls" he imperfectly understood. And though

The Happy Profession

he was tolerant toward ills of the flesh it was evident that he did not think well of them. A boy with a cold felt under a stigma and a leg twisted in football practice was little to be proud of. Born in the days when hopes of a perfected world seemed possible, never ill, with a wife lovely as she was beloved, knowing nothing but happiness, he looked on trouble as transitory and held it firmly underfoot. If ever in the freshness of his youth a man was born into eternal life, it was the Rector. In spite of the gaiety of his temper and the cheeriness of his talk, you were always conscious of his consecration, and in the chapel the sense of it became an undercurrent of existence. I am not what is called a religious man, but almost the strongest deterrent of evil I have known is the remembrance of afternoons in the chapel, the sun streaming through the painted windows, and the Rector's pleading voice: "Keep innocency, for that will give a man peace at the last."

The body is not made by men alone nor is the spirit. It would have been as anomalous to bring up a family without a mother as Groton boys without Mrs. Peabody. How else would the spirit of chivalry — and what is more important in a boy's education? — have entered into the heart of any of those young ruffians! Men can preach admirably about chivalry. They can quote you Sidney's ideal, "High erected thoughts seated in the heart of courtesy," but without the presence of the lady the lesson is idle words.

I am one of hundreds of Groton boys but I speak for the rest. To me, who is like Mrs. Peabody? Whose manners are like hers? Whose smile recalls more happily the memories of a beloved past? Whose laugh is gayer, whose affections look out more naturally from understanding eyes? In the world of most of us there are individuals, a few of them, and there is the crowd, but what old boy ever shook hands with Mrs.

Old School Ties

Peabody without knowing that her friendship was his own private right, his own personal possession. So long as time lasts for us, what is she to every Groton boy but "my Mrs. Peabody."[1]

Groton has been written about more than enough, but I think this testimony is not without consequence. Take me for one moment as exhibit A. I was a nonconformist by nature. I hankered for the individual life, I hated organized athletics and — heresy of heresies — utterly disbelieved in their beneficial effect upon character. I took a somewhat fastidious taste to be a safer guide than any law of morals, I was certainly not a "healthy-minded" boy nor an interesting one, and certainly I was secure from the temptations which come from being too attractive. I was in fact poles asunder from the Groton boy he approved, yet Mr. Peabody liked me and trusted me. He took me into his family life, made me a master of the school, and for thirty years liked to have me by him as a trustee. My point of view was certainly at variance with his. I do not understand it but I am grateful. And I am grateful beyond measure because he it was who rescued me from complete unbelief in myself and gave me a degree of self-confidence which through all changes and chances I have never quite lost.

There was more to be learned at Groton than knowledge and character. By example and very strictly by precept we were taught manners which I still think important as anything a boy can learn. They were not mere company manners, clean collars, ungrimed hands, and a smile for the visitor. They went below the surface. It is astonishing how glad you can be to greet an old acquaintance or to make a new one if you only behave as though you really were! Just as form is apt to be a

[1] This was written while she lived.

The Happy Profession

more permanent preservative for a book than substance, so manners, if not a substitute for virtue, at least make every virtue shine. Then on Saturdays and Sundays there was apt to be the greatest extracurricular advantage of them all — the presence of interesting guests. Not infrequently Phillips Brooks was there — our first school building was named after him. I remember his vast, benevolent bulk filling my study like Gulliver in Lilliput. When the Rector came in too, the host was driven to sit upon the bed. In the pulpit Brooks's torrential eloquence was all that tradition says, but after talking with him I remember wondering whether he did not love everybody too dearly to care especially for anybody.

A stronger impression was left on me by Father Hall, later Bishop of Vermont. He taught me to understand how necessary asceticism is to sainthood. In the chancel, his gaunt figure, looking strangely emaciated in the purple light of stained-glass windows, seemed to me a figure in some holy, medieval legend. Then at supper his deep infectious laughter made me realize that there must be fun in Heaven, despite the solemnities of circled angels and above the din of sackbuts and shawms. How he loved to tell a story! Clerical stories are always a solace to the clergy. The intonation of his voice comes back again as I hear him tell the timeless tale of the vicar, solicitous for the health of the entire family, who, after anxiously inquiring concerning each child, grandchild, aunt, and uncle, paused for breath, but noticing a long white hair on his parishioner's skirt took a long chance and with the voice of understanding said, "And do tell me, how is the dear old gray mare?"

But speaking of stories, the storyteller of the age was a frequent visitor. Theodore Roosevelt, beginning his battle for righteousness and the strenuous life, was attracted to Groton by the tradition of muscular Christianity which had risen

Old School Ties

from the Rector's acceptance of the moralities of Dean Stanley. These visits were occasions, and Sixth Formers were invited to Faculty Supper. While Mrs. Peabody scrambled the eggs and the Headmaster recommended the apples, the Commissioner would spin his boisterous cowboy yarns. We would shed tears of delight at the culmination of each adventure and just before the fatal stroke of ten, one of us with entire naturalness would stand before the telltale face of the clock while the rest would drown the ten minatory strokes with clapping or applause. All this was twenty years before "practical politics" had stiffened the Roosevelt face into a mask. Then he looked like the boy he was at heart and his falsetto voice had a vigorous, honest ring to it. Leonard Wood too came to see us and taught every boy what a soldier should look like, and John Fiske proved to our universal satisfaction that a philosopher could eat quite as voraciously as he could read. So astonishing was his appetite indeed that we boys made special inquiry concerning it, learning to our delight that at his own family table he received his full share of food by contriving for his personal benefit a reshaping of the dining-room table. At the master's end of the oval he had an ample concave hewed out of the wood and, still sitting at the head of the table, had access to its very heart.

Visitors to the school, apart from old boys who flocked about us each week end, were usually of that admirable class known as Leaders of the Community, men with a message, which they would impart to us in an hour's lecture on Saturday night, or preach from the chapel pulpit on Sunday morning. But also there were unobtrusive guests of whom we saw nothing "official" who had their indirect influence upon us. Many of these were guests of Amory Gardner. In the summer Mr. Gardner was accustomed to sail his ninety-foot schooner, luxurious winner of America's Cup, but during the months

The Happy Profession

of school he lived in a comfortable house of his own almost under the dormitory eaves. These guests of the Gardner house formed a shimmering background to monastic life. They gave us an impression of current fashions, but more important to a country boy like myself was the sense they brought of a world outside the school, a varied and delightful world where people lived at the foot of the rainbow and enjoyed themselves in ways wholly at variance with school life. I carried these glimpses round with me and built for myself little stories about them which I was much too shy to impart to my mates. Some of these whimsical dramas I recall to this day. Here is one that concerns two people not unknown to fame, but it will not be found in their biographies.

The time was a lovely Sunday morning in the late '80s. There were two hours before church, and I well knew the danger of running across a master and hearing his suggestion that there is nothing like a Sunday morning walk in God's sunshine. I had other views, and with a copy of *Ben Hur*, which had just burst on my excited world, I slipped into the gymnasium and, piling two wrestling mats, rolled them up in one corner, tucked myself securely behind them, and was lost to the world. For an hour I was buried in my book, when suddenly the gymnasium door was thrown wildly open and a woman's voice thrilled me with a little scream of mockery and triumph. Cautiously I peeked from my concealment and caught sight of a woman with a figure of a girl, her modish muslin skirt fluttering behind her as she danced through the open doorway and flew across the floor, tossing over her shoulder some taunting paean of escape. But bare escape it seemed, for not a dozen feet behind her came her cavalier, white-flanneled, black-bearded, panting with laughter and the pace. The pursuer was much younger than the pursued but that did not affect the ardor of the chase. The lady raced

Old School Ties

to the stairway leading to the running track above. Up she rushed, he after her. She reached the track and dashed round it, the ribbons of her belt standing straight out behind her. Her pursuer was visibly gaining. The gap narrowed. Nearer, nearer he drew, both hands outstretched to reach her waist. In *Ben Hur* the chariot race was in full blast, but that was eclipsed. "She's winning," I thought. "No, she's losing." And then at the apex of my excitement, "He has her!" But at that crucial moment there came over me the sickening sense that this show was not meant for spectators, that I was eavesdropping and, worse, that I would be caught at it. There was not one instant to lose. The window was open. Out I slipped and slithered to safety.

For me that race was forever lost and forever won. The figures go flying motionless as on the frieze of the Grecian urn.

> What men or gods are these? What maidens loth?
> What mad pursuit? What struggle to escape?

I knew not then whether it was lost or won. What I did know was that the Atalanta of that Sunday morning was Mrs. Jack Gardner and Milanion Mr. John S. Sargent. It was that same year he painted the famous portrait of her with her pearls roped about her waist, her beautiful arms glowing against a background that might have been the heart of a lotus.

How big a community should a small boy grow up in? If you believe as I do that there is no force in education like the impress of a personality, Groton's theory on the subject seems sensible, although I sometimes criticize her practice. From the outset it was determined that the number of pupils should be no larger than the headmaster could know individually and with a genuine degree of intimacy. In my time there were some fifty boys and the family seemed pretty complete, but when in after years the number rose to more than one hundred and eighty the bond between the headmaster and the new recruit became inevitably thinner. Everything grew more institutionalized, a little more metallic, a little less human. The old amateur spirit where teachers taught purely for the love of it had become professional. No doubt the teaching is better now, more methodical, more rationalized, but I wonder whether it is more exhilarating. There is more head and less heart in it.

It is a curious thing about size that many littlenesses do not make up bigness. A big school, a big company, a big town, is as different in kind as it is in size from what it was in its former smallness. Groton is still small as schools go, but it has come to have something of the quality of bigness about it. The family is a clan now. Graduates wearing the red, white, and black used to be brothers, now they are cousins. A Company of Cousins has hardly the ring to it a Band of Brothers used to have.

A journalistic professor unencumbered by firsthand knowledge, and feeling in his democratic bones that Morgans, Harrimans, and Whitneys cannot have passed through a school without defiling it, maintains it to be the veriest accident that so many men eminent in public life have Groton backgrounds. The ignorance of prejudice is a shade thicker than other kinds of ignorance and this is of it. From the early years of the school, in season and out, public service was held up to every boy as a shining goal. It is God's mercy that all of us didn't go into it! If we wouldn't be clergymen and couldn't be missionaries, what clearer call was there than a public career? An astonishing number of able young men responded. They all started from Groton, but Lord, Lord! in what different directions they have traveled since! Some have been all and more than all the school could have hoped. Others are re-

Old School Ties

membered in silence. A public office is a public trust but a public servant may be a public menace. Evil and good have entered into Groton careers in a proportion astonishingly similar to their proportion in any community. The eternal problem is as insistent in school as elsewhere. Can a good man keep his honesty? Must a blackguard be a blackguard still? As I write, I think of certain politicians, once Groton boys, whose careers have been as cynical as their ambitions. I think of others who have served their country with the single-mindedness which they once learned at school. No more than any other school can Groton make a man. The gods dispose, but Groton certainly has started her graduates with a powerful push in the right direction.

To make a school "tick," organized and compulsory athletics are regarded as a prime essential. Of course the normal boy — the boy to whom boarding schools are dedicated — dotes upon them. My only protest is that the odd boy, the boy who for some reason or other swims against the current and educates himself against sufficient odds, should be made subject to this tyrannous compulsion. Surely the pressure of school opinion is hydraulic enough without an official draft into universal service. If schools are a training ground for democracy, it must be ever remembered that democracy's real test lies in its respect for minority opinion. But as a practical matter nothing simplifies a master's duties like sentencing his charges to hard, daily, and universal labor. Two hours of football practice will take the starch out of the highest spirits. It may dull a boy's intellectual capacities, but it makes him docile as a sheep. Exhausted boys are good boys: that is no secret in any dormitory. But to be fair to masters, I do not believe it often occurs to them how useful compulsory athletics are to their professional convenience. They take them as

The Happy Profession

a matter of course, honestly believing that the school team is an embodiment of the spirit of the school. All for one and one for all seems to them the exemplification of the very ideal they strive for. And younger masters especially are apt to share the astonishing belief that moral courage is a by-product of the physical struggle, that it fosters all the nobler virtues. The probability that it may tend to atrophy the brain is never discussed at faculty meetings. Organized sport is the personification of manliness. The boy who seeks another road to his development presents to the master a picture of a shirker and not infrequently of a poltroon as well. And from the boys themselves, masters half accept the quaint idea that victory for the team is an added glory to the school.

I do not wish to be misunderstood. Teams should play and play to win. But boys to whom the whole idea of organized athletics is depressing should be allowed to go their several ways and no blight of recognized eccentricity should fall upon them. The records of after life seem to bear me out. It has not been my experience that boys who have worn school letters on their sweaters and whose names have rung out across gridiron or diamond at the end of nine hurrahs are a whit more likely to have the moral courage which active life demands than those nonconformists who have climbed their own lonely staircases to positions of responsibility. I will go further and say that even in physical courage the heroes of boyhood do not always put up a better front in times of later danger. Determination, character we call it, comes by devious and difficult roads. Many of these routes are unsurveyed and where is the guide who can lead straight to the goal that every father seeks for his boy!

Should it chance that these unfashionable ideas should fall for discussion in a group of learned clerks or Grotonians or both, they will exclaim in chorus: "Think of the elevation of

Old School Ties

the physical idea as the Greeks taught it." To this with great deference, I will quote the opinion of Socrates in Plato's version. The talk chanced to be on this very subject. Socrates remarks that while boys are growing up it is well for them to take good care of their bodies, to get a *base and support for their later use by philosophy*. Then, amplifying his opinion, the wisest of Greeks goes on to say: —

"They [boys after an athletic contest] come into motion slowly. Learning is hard for them as if they were numb, and when there is work for the mind to do, sleep attacks them and they are always yawning."

In those old Groton generations, once so familiar to me, I recall but a single instance of a boy who became the acknowledged head of the school wholly innocent of athletic supremacy and merely gifted with character and superlative intelligence. Bayard Cutting died before the world could know him well, but his name still stands among us as of the best which Groton has to offer.

Over every boarding school hangs the arch of experience. Never does the same boy return to the home which has been all in all to him. He has taken an infinite journey. He has picked up a new measuring rod. The old criteria are gone. Family judgment is no longer his judgment. Grotesque as his opinions may be they are his own, or he thinks they are. And the transformation has come during the most tremendous week of life — the first week of boarding school — when nostalgia has attacked him, and he has died and been born again. Homesickness is the estranging sea that each one of us must cross. He who has never felt it, trust him not, for he is without the bowels of compassion. It has been so since the beginning. Only yesterday I chanced to read the story of a Chinese Embassy setting out on a hazardous visit to Rome in the year A.D. 97. Never before had these Chinamen left home, and when they got as far as the Persian Gulf, they heard with terror rumors of a new pestilence, "a kind of homesickness which men have when they have been long at sea." Travelers died of it, they were told, and were glad to die. So wisdom came upon them. They turned their ship about and sailed back to the beloved port of their native land.

CHAPTER VI

Omitted from the Curriculum

IT IS WRITTEN that when the half-gods go, the gods arrive. but in the story of the writers of New England there is a reversal of that glorious succession. I was born when New England was in flower, but by the time I was out of corduroys and buttoned into my *toga virilis*, the oaks were going and the sap ran a little slow and thin in the second growth. The fact that the "Last Leaf on the Tree" was buried in Dr. Holmes's grave the year of my graduation from Harvard will give my date for any substantial purpose. Although wild horses would not have dragged it out of my undergraduate bosom, I will confide to my gentler readers that the criteria of Matthew Arnold were secretly woven into all my literary enthusiasms. The poet's "perfect line" was my private touchstone and, though I did not find it in magazines or even in books, I was as certain that come again it would as I was convinced that outside my own Stockbridge the Upper Classes were being materialized, the Middle Classes vulgarized and the Lower Classes brutalized, and that, while this condition existed, neither poetry nor literature generally could be born into an unpropitious world. In those days, as I looked up and down the decent village street, none of these three appalling Classes was visible. But Arnold had spoken of their crystallization in England and, before I went into the world, I took it for granted that this must be so in America.

At Harvard College I began to think differently. Freshman life in 1890 was not, to put it gently, conducive to a lettered education. But almost at once I saw with my own eyes that one stand at least of New England oaks still flourished. My family were old-time friends of the Jameses and at the outset I wandered into the classroom of William James. His very first lecture, almost his first words, changed my world. "Young gentlemen," he said (I garble the quotation but the idea still stands clear in my mind), "the more inquiring of you will ask why you have chosen a course in philosophy. I will answer you in a word. The object of philosophy, my friends, is to *learn to know a man when you see one.*"

As I went out Tommy Sherwin, the slender Mercury of the football team, threw his arm over my shoulder.

"There is something in that," he said. "Well," I replied, "that's what my education is going to be."

And so it was that within the limits of my boyish intelligence I chose my courses at Harvard not by subject but by the men who taught them. William James was essential to my plan; so was Francis James Child, "Stubby" Child to the students, scholar of scholars to those that knew. Professor Child was the husband of my mother's elder sister, and intimately beloved by my family. We thought of him as another M. Paul (if you know the most delightful of the Brontë novels) for, as with that unduplicated hero, deep and unsuspected within him blazed a romantic chivalry which would break out on occasion with surprising force. His labor and his learning were well-nigh incredible. I have heard President Eliot speak of him as the chief ornament among his band of scholars, but I like best to remember a tribute paid by his favorite pupil, Kittredge. Harvard has produced no more formidable exam-

Omitted from the Curriculum

ple of scholarship than Professor Kittredge. His beard — well he knew it — was carved precisely to suggest the omnipotent beard of God the Father, as Raphael conceived it. All my college days I feared him mortally, and the unrest his presence brought with it persisted with me for decades almost unimpaired until he broke the spell by the humanity of this tribute to his master, the first Professor of English in Harvard College.

It happened in this wise. Professor Kittredge was invited as a guest to an old Boston dining club of which I had long been a member. He was seated of course on the host's right hand and I as an appropriate sacrifice was placed on his other flank. Two or three times I deployed my skirmishers and advanced upon the frowning works. But each effort was repulsed with frigid dignity. Conversation was getting nowhere. It was not until our champagne glasses were filled for the third time that I launched a profitable attack. "Professor Kittredge," said I, "let me tell you a story. Some thirty-five years ago I happened to drop in on my uncle, Professor Child. The moment he saw me, he invited me to his study; it was an unaccustomed honor for his workroom was inviolable. 'I want to show you something,' he said, 'hoping you will remember it.' Such a desk! No brush or dustcloth ever intruded there and papers were piled a foot high in a confusion which seemed to me utter. Directly in front of his chair, however, was a narrow opening between the ramparts, almost a foot square, and there rested the open pages of a thesis. 'Look at that,' said Uncle Frank, 'it is worth your while.' I looked. The manuscript seemed to me remarkably like any other manuscript except that it was immensely long and without a single interesting correction. Uncle Frank offered his explanation: 'Here is a dissertation written by a pupil of mine, Kittredge, George Lyman Kittredge. The name will be worth remem-

The Happy Profession

bering.' He seemed to be thinking of far-off things. Then he added dreamily: 'Do you see those shears?' I saw them, but the reference was unintelligible and I asked what scissors had to do with the thesis of the young Mr. Kittredge. Uncle Frank seemed to be weighing his words. He replied slowly: 'I could take those shears and cut that thesis into equal halves and, if I did, common fairness would oblige me to give each half of it the mark of A.' "

Professor Kittredge was listening intently. An expression came over his face as if the heavens had opened and the Lord above had spoken. His arm stole round my shoulder. "Did — Professor — Child — say — that? Did — he — say — that — of — me? Sedgwick, drop the Professor. Call me Kittredge."

I felt then what scholar owed to scholar.

There were other constellations in my firmament. The Harvard skies were bright in those days. There were Nathaniel Shaler, Kentucky made, whose theories were, I imagine, a somewhat romantic and personal version of geology, but whose laugh, like the laugh of Boanerges, was a contribution to the humanities; George Martin Lane, purest of Horatian types; Royce and Palmer, the contrasted philosophers, Leibnitzian and Platonic; Charles Eliot Norton. They were the last of the Ancient Race, the last stand of New England oaks, part and parcel, though some had been transplanted in their youth, of the high tradition of New England literature.

From Norton a boy could learn anything except the subject of the lecture. For that you went to the Library, but to the lecture room you went for ideas and standards of an ancient world to which the universe of the '90s was wholly subversive. When, in Fine Arts 3, his modulated voice dropped off to something above a pensive whisper, you could just

Omitted from the Curriculum

catch the words, "There are handsome landscapes in our country but in America even the shadows are vulgar"; the very atrocity of the description stirred young minds to the consideration of certain elements in American life more substantial and much more disagreeable than shadows. And when Norton began a famous lecture thus: "Young gentlemen — and as I speak these words the realization comes over me that no one here has ever seen a gentleman," the corrosive inference almost started a riot. At the door I met Dan Shea, the papilionaceous son of a Boston barkeep. Dan was visibly explosive. "To think! To think!" he spluttered. "Why, that man never knew my father!"

Snobbery was, of course, the first thought in youthful minds as youthful ears drank in animadversions so preposterous. But they were the kind of extravagances that secure attention from three hundred impatient boys when the year's at the spring and butterflies flutter in and out of open windows. Later when one grew older and wiser and entered more fully into Norton's companionship, it is hardly too much to say that he brought to hundreds of our undeveloped spirits a new universe. Beauty became not aesthetic satisfaction merely but took her place high among Moralities. Looking backward over fifty years I believe the inscription written beneath his bust by his admirable pupil, Professor Grandgent, not extravagant but just and right: —

HE TAUGHT AN UNSEEING AGE TO SEE

In that New England grove the topmost oak was Charles William Eliot, towering above his fellows, standing apart. There was an austerity about him which extended to his administration, but which was misunderstood. Undergraduate opinion operates in a world where convictions, however arrived at, take the place of facts. Most of my friends were committed to the proposition that C was the perfect mark and we sang with enthusiasm a verse of the Examination Hymn.

> Shall I be carried to the skies
> On flowery beds of E's
> While others fight to win the prize
> And sail through bloody C's?

Most of us knew of course that A or even A+ would not be undesirable in the world beyond college, but that was a long way off. Meanwhile a "Gentleman's Pass" was the thing. It took all the energy of President Lowell and a radical change in the curriculum to eradicate that idea. But this revolution came many years later. It was President Eliot's theory to make knowledge interesting, to offer it in immense variety, and then, if a boy did not take advantage of his opportunities, to bid him a brisk good-bye. I still believe that the right course, but we have entered a new world. Specialization, subspecialization, is the cry, and Eliot's idea is an exhibit in the educational museum.

These were things the Class of 1894 certainly did not understand. We regarded it as the president's settled purpose to eliminate everybody but the grinds and to turn Harvard College into a factory for the working classes.

But it is astonishing how the vision changes, when in the third decade one is fitted with glasses. When I returned to Boston in 1908, Mr. Eliot was the Institution and Harvard University almost the pseudonym of its great president. He lived through an age of transformation. It is trite to say that he found Harvard a country college and left it a world university. Men who fought or even watched the battles of his reign may differ in judgment and some join in his dispraise. But there stands his work. His successor gave it material mag-

Omitted from the Curriculum

nificence but the real edifice rests upon Eliot's foundation. In spite of Mr. Santayana's trivial satire on the futile flickerings of a decayed philosophy, President Eliot will by New England generations be remembered as the Last Puritan.

It is hardly germane to my thesis, but it is entertaining to recall the effect of the austerities of the Eliot regime on officialdom about him. Until the humanizing discovery of Dean Briggs, which worked a miracle in undergraduate faith and morals, the Dean of Harvard College was one efficient and unjustly detested Smith. I still recall how, to the tune of

> The animals came in two by two,
> One wide river to cross . . .

we used to sing, as our elder brothers had sung before us: —

> If the Dean of Harvard College
> Had been there in the swim
> I wonder who in thunder
> Would have walked along with him!

I was more dependent, as I have said, a hundred times more, on the teacher than on the things he taught. My education was a thing of shreds and patches: no majoring, no perfect comprehension of a minute segment of the infinite circle, merely a shimmering understanding of what men are and do when they are men.

From a mature point of view it seems scarcely necessary, but college feels obliged to make room for boys as well as for professors. We entered the Class of 1894 some six hundred strong, but between a plague of deans and a pestilence of examinations, the mortality rate was high. In the extent and variety of what has been written of his exploits, the most notorious among us was Harry K. Thaw, whose career would have graced any Newgate calendar. But unhappily I never extended my education far enough to know him, and the

The Happy Profession

hard frost of examinations nipped him in his Harvard bud. Many others there were, less famous but more useful. Reading over our *50th Report*, it amused me to compare prognostications of the careers of our classmates with the records they left half a century later. One go-getter, certain of success in business, we all picked. Our choice never enjoyed an idle moment. He ran the *Crimson;* he ran most things that needed a brisk business mind, and I suspect he ran right past his education. Forty years later he called on me professionally with a line of pencils, desk pads, and erasers. The pencil business, he informed me, had the advantage of requiring no capital. You worked on commission. When his employment in the West had winked out he had bought a one-way ticket east and was peddling frantically to get cash enough to get his wife home too. But with all his disappointments something of the old standards stuck. After furnishing my desk with all the pencils and erasers it would hold, I said: "Let's heave together for '94. Here is fifty dollars." "I'd be glad to take it as a loan," he answered. I shook my head. Loans between friends are bad business. "Take it for old times' sake!" But he wouldn't touch it. No suggestion of repayment was ever made.

This trivial instance reminds me that this same moral principle was in force at the expense of another classmate. His sensible father, knowing that a "touch" between friends costs both the money and the friend, advised his son never to make a trifling loan. It is too easily forgotten. "Never lend a chap the five dollars he asks for. Give him twenty-five dollars." The advice was acted upon. On the way to a football game the son was promptly asked by a classmate, "Let me have a fiver till Thursday, won't you?" "Better take twenty-five," was the reply, and that was the last of the transaction.

But to continue more seriously. I notice also in the record a characteristic that interests me very much. Apart from the

Omitted from the Curriculum

scholars, and our class was rather radiant with them, collegians who were to make substantial names for themselves began for the most part very slowly. It took time to set them going. In college their mechanism seemed to mesh with deliberateness, and it was not until they got on to professional schools or felt the stimulus of active business that they began to shoot up in the world. I have noticed the same thing in shrubs and trees. Dig their pits deep as you will, compost them, manure them, water them, yet often for a second or a third year they will remain just so high. Then from God knows where, there comes a change. The sap runs more freely, the sparse buds begin to cluster, the tips shoot out and up. Something, as we like to say in this mechanical world, clicks. Nowadays men of science tell me that they get new light on human problems by studying parallel growths in nature. My personal philosophy, borrowed from the East, maintains that all life is one. A single river flows through all creation, and there is oneness in life if not in its manifestations. These things are worth a thought, for day by day college grows more impatient with slow beginners. Pretty soon they are apt to be excluded altogether, and my prophecy is that society will lose thereby both in solidity and in character.

It is of course an obvious difficulty with our system that in the twelve years of school, time is lost which a spurt of four years in college cannot make up. But I am thinking not so much of the way we educate as of the stuff we are educating. The growth of intelligence is not a continuous process, but a thing of stops and starts. In the cortex of the brain, the particles, whether they are material atoms or spiritual monads, go whirling round too rapidly for the educator to count them, but their timetable is not ours. All that we know is that in time the Tortoise will get very close on the heels of Achilles.

The object of college is to learn to know men and to think

The Happy Profession

as a man. Read any biography of a person whose life is worth a "Life" and almost invariably you will find in it reference to some one man or one book which gave your hero the precise stimulant he needed. I remember the evening when at fourteen I opened a volume of Buckle. That night I slept intermittently as though I had been touched with fever. Buckle, right and wrong as he was, was my man. The human electricity that makes the world go round is generated by the few. Decried by our economic determinists, the aristocratic spirit of one man living or dead is essential, however democratic the social method. Shoot a hundred citizens of Boston or a thousand in New York and the rest may as well be shot too, so far as improvement in the community goes. Still school and college struggle on as they feel they must struggle on, "educating" the masses. The old wisecrack of Viscount Sherbrooke, "Now we must educate our masters," is in everybody's mind. Bigger and solider and more impenetrable grows the mass, and the obvious danger is that the few will be lost in the quagmire. The quadrupling, the octupling of college enrollment is the pride of the nation, but for 70 per cent of the students, what profit remains to them for the four years they consumed in college? Bigger and Better will continue to be the cry, but Smaller and Better follows the law of nature. Pick your boys carefully, don't trust to written examinations a bit more than you do to personal characteristics. Take heredity as well as environment into account. Let two out of three go, and devote yourself with personal devotion to the rest. That way salvation lies, but to talk after this fashion is to sweep away the Atlantic with Mrs. Partington's mop.

Nowadays, Harvard undergraduates are vocal on the subject of politics. Radical Clubs have sprung up after the fashion of foreign universities. Speakers of national reputation are occasionally secured, and a thorough airing given to ele-

Omitted from the Curriculum

vated ideas whose enactment into law is fortunately postponed until the audience is old enough to vote. In my time, our political views came nine times out of ten from our paternal inheritance. We were born Republicans or Democrats and the *Crimson* was not apt to change our views; but as it happened my father was a mugwump — the political bird, you remember, with a mug on one side of the fence and a wump on the other. That was what its enemies said, but in Cleveland's time the most precious heritage of mugwumpery was enthusiasm. I was red-hot with it and a small incident of my sophomore year fanned my flame into a bonfire.

It was a lovely Sunday morning in spring and I was spoiling it by toiling over History I. The work was serious and I was hard at it in my undershirt when a knock disturbed me. I opened the door and there stood on the landing a most elegant young man in the sleekest of top hats. "I beg your pardon," said he, "my name is Sigourney Butler — 22 Holworthy used to be my room and I want to show it to Mr. Cleveland waiting below in a carriage." Mr. Cleveland! The angel Gabriel would not have been so welcome. On went my shirt and jacket, under the couch went everything that had to do with the Merovingians. The next moment there was a ponderous step on the stair, and in walked Grover Cleveland with Speaker Crisp close behind him. I stuttered out my sense of the honor of such a visit, and for twenty minutes we had a talk I love to remember. That was in 1891. Mr. Cleveland had lost the last election, but was certain, as I assured him, to win the next. He looked at the narrow shelf which ran opposite my bed. "That's where we belong, Crisp," said he, "it's not wide enough for me, but you would just fit." By this time every window in the yard was filled with gaping students. I put my head out and shouted reassurance. "What's the excitement? Mr. Cleveland has just dropped in for a

The Happy Profession

moment to call on an old friend." Mr. Cleveland had a way of laughing from his diaphragm and I loved to listen to the commotion within him. When he left me, I knew as I know today that of the Presidents of my time, Grover Cleveland was first in character, first in unpolitical performance of duty. A boy often makes up his mind for keeps, and I did then.

Let us turn to more profitable discourse. In thinking of what I might have learned at Harvard College I am wondering whether the oration is a branch of literature. I am uncertain but I submit that some knowledge of the difference between orating and oratory plays its part in the education of a young man. Taste, despite the professor and the moralist, is one of the deepest things in life. To my thinking it points out the cleft between good and evil; the chasm between Heaven and Hell: but that is a private matter. At any rate, at Harvard as at Groton I count it part of my education to have listened to Phillips Brooks and to have learned on many occasions how stirring the spoken word may be. And after I left college the process continued.

It was a famous day in New England history when there was dedicated, on Boston Common, Saint-Gaudens's monument to Robert Gould Shaw. The "Fair-haired Northern Hero" marches in bronze at the head of his "niggers" who fell with him at Fort Wagner. Every spectator at that great celebration knew how Colonel Shaw had been hissed from the windows of the Somerset Club as the black regiment paraded down Beacon Street on its march to death and immortality. On that day it was William James who spoke, and Booker Washington (and who is a more central figure in the traditional thought of New England than the founder of Tuskegee?) gave the moving oration. We realized then that the Negro had stepped on the first rung of the long ladder.

Omitted from the Curriculum

On a less memorable occasion I heard a Bostonian speak words which, in my ears, sounded like the very poetry of oratory. It was at a dinner in memory of "Billy" Russell, a Massachusetts Governor cut down in his prime, whom we thought the very type fitted for the Presidency. How I came to be invited to the dinner I have forgotten but the great and the near great were there and among them Patrick Collins, once our Consul General in London and a popular officeholder to whose Irish genius was mercifully added a probity which entitled him to the respect of all citizens. I dimly recall the toastmaster, who sat near, slipping behind Mr. Collins's chair and whispering that of course he would be called upon to speak. "Pat" Collins looked at his watch. He had two minutes for preparation. When he rose it was with the measured utterance of a man thinking of his lost leader. Slowly he began: "I have known many a politician in my time, many, aye, many a statesman, but it is my de – lib – e – rate opinion that *he* dwelt an arrow's flight beyond them all."

The effect was immediate and, on me, enduring.

I remember, too, at the solemn funeral of William James in the old Appleton Chapel, the impressive bulk of Dr. George A. Gordon standing at the head of the coffin. From some old-fashioned prejudice the mere thought of eulogy numbs my soul, but that resonant invocation to a great spirit gone still reverberates in my ears: "Teacher, Preacher, Follower of the Truth."

The most important fact for a parent to know about Harvard or any other college for that matter is never mentioned in the catalogues. College walls are not high enough to shut out the larger life which flows about them. Education aims at segregated experience, but experience like all nature abhors a vacuum, and the influences to which young men are subject are beyond calculation. As an odd instance of this I will tell of a curious incident which happened to me during my sophomore year. In bitter weather, after a late party, I had driven out from Boston in one of those ancient sleighs known, I know not why, as "booby-hutches." The characteristic of these eccentric conveyances was their discomfort. They were shrouded in leather curtains which flapped wildly in the wind and had an inanimate genius for intensifying drafts. After the heat of the dance, this particular booby-hutch did for me. I caught a heavy cold, pneumonia followed, and within a day or two both my lungs were seriously involved. Harvard had no hospital in those days, and there I was; my big room in Holworthy Hall heated by the coals of a single grate, with running water three floors below and two trained nurses to assist such chances of life as sick students had in those days.

Now as it happened the attack had caught me just as I was wrestling with a thesis on the character of Jonathan Swift, and turbulent incidents in the life of the ferocious Dean of St. Patrick's swam about me in my delirium. One of my nurses, distinguished by red hair and an angular figure, I called Vanessa. The other was to me the dearer Stella. She was a comfortable body, pink, plump, and motherly, and between us the happiest of domestic relations were soon established, in spite of my whirling head and the desperate pain in my left side. When I tried to throw myself out of the big picture over the bed which I took to be a window, it was Stella who made me all snug again. She it was who watched me with a nurse's intentness as I fixed my own gaze on a tobacco jar standing on the mantel across the room, and said aloud (as she afterwards reported), "I am too tired. That jar holds the elixir of life in it. All I have to do is to struggle up, walk five steps, and drain life from it. But I am too tired. The road back is rougher and longer than the way ahead." Then she bathed my hot forehead, whispered that she would bring that draught of life to me, gave me my medicine, and slipped me off to sleep. Stella's American name was Jane Toppan, and as the crisis passed, the bond between Jane and me grew strong. Some weeks after the crisis, Vanessa left, but Stella stayed to see me through my convalescence and many a confidence we exchanged during the long days and nights. We laughed together about how I had christened her my "Star," and I gave her a deal of instruction about the savage Dean and his inscrutable affections, and translated for her, whether correctly or not I can't remember, the famous inscription on his tomb: —

Ubi saeva indignatio ulterius cor lacerare nequit.

Then we would fall into more personal discourse. She asked me about my ambitions, and in return would tell me of the satisfactions of her own career, the passionate interest surrounding endless battles between life and death in the sickroom, and how it was in the nurse's lap that the destiny of the patient lay. As I grew stronger, I told her stories about the three: Clotho, Lachesis, and Atropos, who spin the thread, wind it, and cut it with the shears. She listened eagerly and explained in return how it was not the doctor but the nurse who held the shears and how she was ever conscious that the fate of a human being rested upon her. On Sunday evenings it had been her custom to go to church, but she hated to leave me and said it was better fun to settle me in an armchair at one side of the grate, while she threw on another scuttle, poked the red coals below, and made all ready for a good talk. When the time came for saying good-bye, we promised always to be friends.

The Happy Profession

For years I heard nothing of Jane Toppan, and then a strange history appeared in the newspapers. Jane Toppan had been arrested and charged with murder, not the indiscretion of a single homicide, but the massacre of thirty-one patients. Thirty-one only were proved victims but the doctors believed that the holocaust numbered nearly one hundred. After all, thirty-one is a sufficient number of indictments for murder. It seemed unnecessary to pursue the gruesome trail to the end. Many families preferred to let their sisters and brothers rest quiet in their graves and not to open the gates of speculation as to whether their deaths had been owing to natural causes. It seemed, and later evidence bore it out, that my Stella had a homicidal mania on an imperial scale. For three or four deaths she had been responsible before she undertook to weigh my own fate, and skipping occasional patients, as she mercifully skipped me, she put away the rest in a succession that grew more rapid with practice. Her method and the fascination of it gave me a tiny peephole into the deeper abnormalities. Jane would fight hard for a patient's life, but when victory seemed within her grasp and the doctor, confident that vitality was mounting, had left for the night, Jane would stand by the lonely pillow holding two vials in her hand. One contained morphia, one atropin. She would give a dose of morphia and, stooping over the bed, scrutinize the dilation of the patient's pupils as they expanded into a wide and vacant stare. Then with a dose of atropin she would watch the drama of the pupils as they narrowed further and further till they became pin points of light. To such treatment there was an inevitable end. The extraneous and unexpected symptoms would puzzle the physician. They seemed to transcend his experience, and it was not until a long line of patients collapsed, one after another, just as they seemed destined for physical salvation, that suspicion turned upon Jane.

Omitted from the Curriculum

And just at that unfortunate moment Jane did an imprudent thing. She had been the devoted nurse of two sisters. One had just died and Jane, like a decent body, went to the funeral. As the coffin was lowered into the grave, to the consternation of the bereaved family someone thought she heard Jane mutter: "It won't be long now before the other goes." Vague suspicion gathered about her but Jane was known as the best nurse in Cambridge and any definite imputation was too dreadful to be spoken aloud. It was only when four members of a single family in which Jane had been the competent nurse followed each other to the grave within the unreasonable interval of forty-one days that action was taken. Jane was questioned and arrested. A series of bodies were exhumed, stomachs were analyzed. Finally the whole terrifying story came to light. The nurse's mania was diagnosed. Her fifteen years in the assiduous practice of murder were reviewed by the court. She was convicted, sent to Bridgewater, and incarcerated in a hospital for the criminal insane, where I trust she found nurses competent and considerate as she. There, for thirty-five years, till at the ripe age of eighty-one her own time came, Jane Toppan revolved the story of the Three Fates.

Much that was interesting was said of Jane Toppan's career. I quote a pungent paragraph from the unpublished papers of Dr. Charles F. Folsom, Professor of Mental Diseases at Harvard.

"In the pleasure and excitement of crime," he wrote, "Jane Toppan seemed to find the criminal enjoyment of doing aesthetic work to which danger appeared to add zest."

But perhaps Jane's attitude toward life can but be summed up in words of her own, uttered during her trial. She had paused to recall the circumstances surrounding the murder of one of her particular cronies who had come all the way up from Cataumet on the Cape for a sociable visit. The women dined together. The dinner was prepared by Jane. The visitor was taken violently ill and a few days later returned to Cataumet in her coffin. Jane, who never failed a friend, had journeyed to the Cape for the funeral and thus described her sensations as a mourner: —

"When the people came down to Cataumet from Cambridge with Mrs. Davis's body and brought flowers and other emblems of sorrow, I wanted to say to them: 'You had better wait, for in a little while I shall have another funeral for you. If you will only wait, I will save you the trouble of going back and forth.'"

How much better they order these things abroad. Here was a champion of American murder without an equal, yet she was permitted to die in obscurity. Jack the Ripper in London, Bluebeard in Paris; how much had they accomplished? Jack the Ripper may have had half a dozen or perhaps a dozen killings to his credit; Bluebeard, eight or ten wives, yet their names are blazoned in the majestic history of crime. But this New England spinster who could have taught both of them their trade from the ground up has left no biographer behind. This simple tribute of mine is her unique reward.

What ought a boy to carry away from college? Facts are convenient but of little value compared with knowledge of how to read shutting out every avenue of consciousness except the single road which he is traveling; to understand just why two and two make four; to know a man when he sees one — all these are cheap at cost of three or four years. But there is something else, which if the student understands it, and few do, is a possession of great price. The boy has lived in a community free from the grosser iniquities of the

Omitted from the Curriculum

world, a society of scholars to whom learning is its own ample return, a republic where the crown of olive is the unmaterial reward. And if the young graduate is wise as well as knowledgeable, his diploma will tell him that in all this world there is no such fun as learning to understand.

CHAPTER VII

The Metropolis Against Me

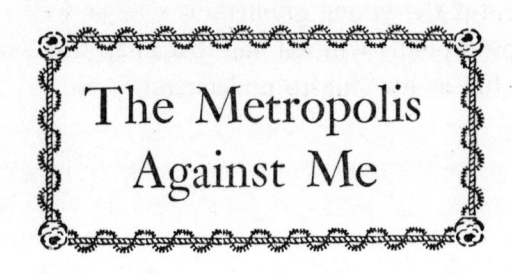

INCREDIBLE as it seems, people get used to New York and the perpetual drama of the city does not strike them in the face. In my mind that drama is always present, but never did it strike me so forcibly as on the first morning I went to work in the big town. In the business world of the city I had not one friend, and when I tumbled out of my Pullman berth and found myself standing on Forty-second Street at seven o'clock in the morning, I knew I was in for the fight of my life. The palisade of buildings scowled across the way as if each one were an active belligerent. It was the metropolis against me, and the odds were on the metropolis. I laugh now as I see myself clenching my fist and shaking it at the big bank opposite, muttering to himself: "Damn you, New York. I will wring a living out of you yet." I walked up to a newsstand. There were a hundred magazines on display but the one which I had come to edit was far too anemic to find a place in that tumultuous competition. I thought of the name and the horrible handicap it must prove in the struggle for existence — *Frank Leslie's Popular Monthly!* Frank Leslie had made a reputation for himself with his *Illustrated Weekly* of Civil War fame, but the name Frank Leslie was dead as a haddock and as for "Popular," that was not even funny as a joke. However, beggars aren't choosers, and

The Metropolis Against Me

through the kindness of Walter H. Page of blessed memory, who put in the necessary word for me, I had been given the job of reconstructing this magazine. So to its office I betook myself on the stroke of nine, that horrible morning.

I had had a single interview with the partners who were my prospective employers but that had merely given me a sense of the flabbiness of their support, very present with me still, as I pushed the door open and asked for the proprietors. The office boy had a scared look which was not reassuring. "Both gen'l'men are out," said he, and I felt in my bones there was trouble ahead. "Where's the editorial room?" I asked. The boy pointed silently across the hall. Following his direction I threw open the door of a singularly unprepossessing room. There in one corner was a big iron safe; in the center a huge old-fashioned desk and two chairs. In one of these sat a tall, rigid young man some dozen years older than I, and before him a mountain of papers. He gave not the slightest sign of recognition of my presence.

I spoke with the greatest politeness: "Pardon me, but may I ask where my desk is? I am the new editor." It was as though a bee had stung the stiff young man. He turned on me with a look of the utmost ferocity. "This is the editor's room," he said. "I am the editor. No new one needed. Be so kind as to close the door as you go out." Dimly I understood that I had entered on some quarrel respecting the ownership of the magazine and that my "proprietors" had felt it a comfortable time to be out of the way. But this was the first round of my fight with New York, and I was not ready to throw in the towel. Fortunately I kept my temper. I said civilly, "May I ask your name, sir?" "There's no need to ask it, but it's Tyrrell, if you want to know." "Mr. Tyrrell," said I, "there seems to be some question of legal authority here. You and I can't settle it. I will take a chair and start to work and you

The Happy Profession

can keep right on working too." I seated myself definitively at the other side of the desk.

You would have thought my courteous words an explosive insult. "If you want to try to be editor, try it!" With that he stretched out both arms, sweeping every paper into one monumental heap, got up, walked to the safe, stuffed every manuscript, letter, pad, pencil, paper, within, slammed the iron door, put the key in his pocket, and remarked, "Now you can try your hand at getting out the magazine." With that out he stalked, leaving me victor of a singularly barren field. Nothing was left to work with. There were no schedule, no manuscripts, no slightest aid to issuing a magazine, no suggestion of what the magazine was like, and nobody to turn to.

Now I had noticed that it is a frequent habit with executives to press a push button. There was one on the desk. I pressed it, and the scared office boy reappeared. "What is your name?" "William, sir." "William," said I, "I have immediate need of your services. Will you kindly go out and fetch a locksmith." The first dawn of a smile spread over William's freckled features. He touched his sleek forelock and disappeared down the elevator. Half an hour later he returned with a very handy workman who tackled the lock and opened the safe competently as any Jimmy Valentine. I unearthed the schedule, took out the manuscripts, ran my eye over page proof and galleys, and went to work.

It was not until afternoon that the proprietors came in and gave me a sheepish welcome. They were sorry to have been out when I arrived but absence was unavoidable. That day was merely the harbinger of all that was to come. The proprietors continued as they had begun, seeing trouble afar off and making a safe getaway before it arrived. But in some way or other they compounded their difficulties with the

The Metropolis Against Me

widow of the founder, who so far as I could tell had once held title to the magazine. I cannot recall seeing Mr. Henry Tyrrell again, but his patroness, Mrs. Frank Leslie, did make her appearance: a figure of fun if ever New York had one to show. She was a shriveled old lady, bedizened like a Dresden china shepherdess archly carrying Bopeep's staff with a shining silver hook, smirking and talking as if she had been Queen of Sheba. The partners fawned about her and she smiled with a flutter of her enameled cheek. That is all I remember.

Compulsion is the powerhouse of the world's mechanism. It is wonderful — the smoothness with which the infinite complexities of earning a living wage resolve themselves in the daily round. Nine o'clock, twelve o'clock, five o'clock, all is crowded confusion. And then suddenly the last slot drops into the last hole and all is orderly. My own special compulsion was three meals a day and an envelope every Saturday afternoon holding twenty-eight dollars. Just that. All twenty-eight were essential to me and I earned them. I kept at my job.

It was a comfortless job, but in it I found a friend and that made all the difference. The young advertising man on whom our precarious existence depended was able, courageous, and honest. We formed an offensive and defensive alliance. Robert Cade Wilson has since made his mark in New York publishing. So successfully has he cultivated the clients of his successive periodicals that now in his retirement he is cultivating roses, acres of them — and to turn twelve-time contracts into Mme. Quinards and Douglas MacArthurs is something to have lived for.

It is my constant advice to young aspirants of the publishing business that instead of joining some company solid, orderly, and regimented, they should sign up with a leaky ship, scrape down her decks, caulk her seams, refit her sails;

The Happy Profession

for it is on the slipperiest deck that adventure beckons, and a speedier chance for rising in the world. *Frank Leslie's Popular Monthly* was a hulk not fit for a crew in a ladies' breeze, and without a qualified skipper aboard, but she did give her apprentices a chance to learn a good deal about the difficult art of navigating in a storm.

What every editor does not know is the financial scaffolding which supports him. At the heart of the competitive system is a wild and whirling center, where dog eats dog, and throats are cut with suavity and dispatch. Very close to the heart of the tempest lies the magazine business. In travelers' tales I have read of a zone of blessed quiet, the vacuum nestling at the heart of the storm center, but I have never discovered a parallel to this in business. In any hurricane of course there are great galleons like the *Saturday Evening Post* or *Life* and *Time* which ride out the gale with hardly a tremor apparent, but for the LST's and their like, the small and unseaworthy craft, crises come thick as April gusts.

Editorial rooms are such gentlemanly places — or were at least in my time — and tradition is so strong that they should serve as drawing rooms for literary conversation, that a recruit gathers the impression he is entering upon civilized existence. My advice to him is to distrust appearances and occasionally to visit the boiler room and study the intricate mechanism that generates power for the machine. The price of paper, the net on subscriptions, the comparative value of newsstand sales, how advertising is solicited, and the delicate degree to which editorial co-operation can be properly applied; all this multifarious and complicated machinery, which in theory is no concern of the editor, in reality concerns him so nearly that without it he cannot exist. Of all this I have acquired little precise knowledge, but something of it I do know, and occasionally feel competent to form independent judgments.

The Metropolis Against Me

This reasonable power of appraisal has been of great practical value to me; especially valuable is an inkling of the dynamics of advertising. Often I have devoted a few days to intensive training in that romantic sphere, keystone to the arch of imagination in American business, and have accompanied the advertising solicitors on their trips, interesting clients with new ideas and trying to inspire the deadly round of advertising argument with exciting visions of a magazine's future.

On a rickety little periodical like *Leslie's Monthly* (as I insisted on renaming the magazine, wiping out the twin stigmas of "Frank" and "Popular") there was an abundant opportunity for the editor to make himself familiar with these manifold problems. The very crudity of the organization made it easier to understand. The beginnings of this course in my new curriculum, however, were painful. Very soon after my arrival in the office, dog had eaten dog. One proprietor had vamoosed; one was left, but he, being a gentleman uncertain of his own mind, soon began to consult my wealth of inexperience upon financial matters. This business my boss approached in a way singularly uncomfortable but well adapted to promote my practical education of the world.

The situation was this. My prime difficulty as an editor was not so much catching hold of ideas and translating them into acceptable manuscripts as that the prices which I was permitted to pay for contributions were between a third and a half of the going wages of writers, which in that nonprofessional era were low enough. My position was further complicated by the fact that the pittances I had to offer were apt as not to be held up at the end of the month. We were supposed to pay on publication. It was hard on a poor devil of an author to wait thirty or sixty days for his money, but when publication day came and cash was not forthcoming, the situation was desperate. I soon found that my prime responsibility was not so much to shake up an author as to shake down the publisher.

How I dreaded publication day, the black twenty-second of the month! The morning before I would take a firm position at my boss's elbow with the warning: "I shall need fourteen hundred dollars tomorrow."

The publisher would drum the desk with his fat fingers. "Fourteen hundred dollars; four*teen* hundred dollars," he would say, "and what are you going to do, young man, with *fourteen hundred dollars?*"

Invariably the conversation followed a routine. One month was merely a dress rehearsal for the next.

"To pay my contributors, sir."

"Aren't they a little grasping?" he would remark. "It isn't as if these accounts were overdue. Fourteen hundred dollars; fourteen hundred dollars. Now I'll tell you what, Sedgwick, if we are going to oblige these fellers by paying them *on the nail* they ought to come part way to meet us. You tell them that if they will give you a 20 per cent discount, you will pay them *spot cash*." The words "spot cash" always had an inspirational effect upon the Boss, as if they represented a burst of unrequited publishing generosity, and he would go on: —

"That's an offer they can well jump at."

Then I would begin to bargain. The discount would be shaded to 15, then to 10 per cent. In time of stress the Boss always weakened a little, and finally it would be agreed that in certain cases of absolute necessity the entire amount would be forthcoming.

Now this policy was more easy to formulate than to carry into effect. As his contribution the Boss merely waved his plump hand in a gesture of large encouragement. "I will leave the details entirely to you."

The Metropolis Against Me

Such was my problem. Solving it was exceedingly unpleasant. Of course every author knew that I was on his side, but friendliness shows wear under provocation, and I soon discovered a fundamental fact about human nature which I have never read of in the books.

Men are more reasonable when they are quiet. They are more quiet when they are alone. *Always interview your creditors one at a time.*

This truism was borne in on me after a day of tumult. Four creditors had been introduced into my office at one and the same time. The way they rubbed against each other's nerves and excited one another to speak louder and louder, more and more forcibly, taught me a lesson. Thereafter I made careful arrangements. William, the office boy with the sleek forelock, had strict orders to admit callers one at a time, and I contrived to have an exit quite separate from the entrance to my office. To effect this it was necessary to make use of the freight elevator. Callers would enter at the front and be slipped out at the rear with the goods and magazines. All possibility of collusion between any two of them was eliminated. In talks thus arranged it was astonishing how voices were kept within their natural range and how effective was my quiet assurance to one man at a time that I would see to it his interests should not suffer in the long run. But at best it was an odious occupation and well calculated to interfere with a regular night's sleep. Day by day it was borne in on me what debt is.

To tell the truth this was a lesson that I hardly needed. When I was ten years old, my father, who had augmented a comfortable fortune, had rolled down the top of his old-fashioned law desk, liquidated his partnership, and returned to the pleasures of retirement and family life. He had taken us all abroad while the Old House was being enlarged, and with a degree of confidence wholly worthy of the Vicar of

The Happy Profession

Wakefield had given a comprehensive power-of-attorney to a gentleman of six months' acquaintance. During our absence abroad, this friend, finding himself in urgent need, borrowed a hundred thousand dollars without informing the owner of the fact, and to recoup himself my poor father had to part peremptorily with solid real estate, thus well-nigh doubling his loss. For many years thereafter the black shadow of debt hung over the Old House, and the pile of promissory notes, each of ten thousand dollars face value, "with interest at six per cent," furnished by the thief in lieu of going to prison, and securely locked in an iron safe, offered less and less hope. Before I was fourteen I understood the extremity of the disaster and the word DEBT was a horror to me. The catastrophe had ruined my parents' lives, but as a sort of sardonic compensation it had made me. I had to get on. I doubted the capacity but I felt the necessity, and necessity triumphed, as it invariably will. One of the most satisfactory days I can recall is that which, after college, divided my youth from manhood. I was off to teach school at a guaranteed salary of five hundred dollars a year, expenses paid for nine months. My father remarked that I would need money. How much ought he to give me? I was ready with my answer: "Ten dollars," the price of my railroad ticket with some change over. My father had given me an education but that was all the money I had from him until after many somewhat better years he left me a substantial legacy in his will.

Against this background, the knowledge that my magazine was falling deeper and deeper into debt did much to help me toward maturity. Such as it was, *Leslie's Monthly* was my best hope. I was determined to sink or swim with it.

As the years went on my inadequate salary kept obtruding on my thoughts. Looking back through the old files I can see how present such rumination must have been, for my private

The Metropolis Against Me

thoughts constantly escaped into the pages of *Leslie's*. I quote a suggestive excerpt from one of my juvenile editorials.

> I have a friend a manufacturer. A year ago he hired a boy. For months the only noticeable thing about that boy was that he never took his eyes off the machine he was running. A few weeks ago, the boss looked down from his work to see the boy standing behind his desk.
> "What do you want?" he asked.
> "Want me pay raised," said the boy.
> "What are you getting?"
> "T'ree a week."
> "Well, how much do you think you are worth?"
> "I t'ink I'm worth four, and I've been t'inking so for three weeks, but I have been so blame busy I haven't had time to speak to you about it."
> The boy got his raise.

For all I know that may have been the genesis of my plan. True my salary had been intermittently improved and I was drawing eighty dollars a week. Of this I could save fifty dollars and my bank account was growing, but I had this problem on my mind. Every young man in New York realizes that in the market for services, the salary last received is regarded as index of his capacity. An eighty-dollar-a-week man looking for a new job has just 80 per cent as good a prospect before him as the candidate resting on a record of one hundred dollars a week. Not that I intended to leave *Leslie's*. If the magazine succeeded I would succeed with it. But if it failed I wanted as substantial a life preserver as my market afforded. After puzzling my brains over this for several careful weeks, I hit on a plan which has at any rate the virtue of originality.

I approached my employer. "Don't you think," said I, "that the magazine has improved? We have doubled our circula-

The Happy Profession

tion since I came." The Boss was expansive in his commendation, and this was precisely what I had hoped for. "And don't you think," said I, "that I am helping you to the tune of a hundred dollars a week?"

His expression changed. "My dear boy," he said paternally, "I should love to give you a hundred a week. Only I haven't got the money."

"Oh yes, you have," said I. He looked incredulous, and I sprang my plan.

"You may not have the money this morning." Then, watching the effect of my disclosure, I added, "But you can have it this afternoon."

"What do you mean?"

"I mean this," I said. "I will give it to you myself. I will pay cash" — then, happily thinking of his favorite expression — "*spot cash*, cash on the nail, and I'll take in return stock in the magazine." And, taking another leaf from my employer's book, I added, "At 20 per cent discount."

The Boss looked as Aaron looked when he struck the rock and the water gushed forth.

"You mean you are proposing to pay your own salary?"

"Yes. The bargain is this. You give me stock, 20 per cent off. I'll give you a thousand dollars, and beginning Saturday, my salary will stand at a hundred dollars a week."

I left the interview a hundred-a-week man, and I had a nest egg of stock which I subsequently enlarged and which, when a miraculous sale of the magazine subsequently took place, yielded me one hundred cents on the dollar and ultimately became the nest egg from which the *Atlantic* was hatched.

This highly unorthodox transaction seemed to confirm my employer's confidence in my business acumen. Afterwards he was accustomed to discuss his financial plans with me in greater confidence. One day he called me to his office.

"Sedgwick," he said, and those pudgy fingers of his started drumming. "It is absolutely essential that we put out twenty-five thousand dollars in advertising. I am a pretty old story to the bankers, and I want you to fill in for me. You go to Mr. N. W. Ayer in Philadelphia and arrange for a further loan of twenty-five thousand dollars. Make any concession you have to, but get the money."

It was all as clear as daylight. Mr. Ayer sat at the apex of Philadelphia banking and had other strings to his bow which might attach him to us: the Keystone Type Foundry and what was then about the largest advertising firm in the country — the N. W. Ayer Agency, whose slogan "Keeping everlastingly at it brings success" was implanted on the mind and heart of every advertising solicitor in the land. It was obvious that my employer's assurances were no longer received at face value in Mr. Ayer's office, but that the banker's known sympathy for young men might reawaken the dying embers of hope in *Leslie's* power to perform.

The next Monday I was off. I had never before talked with a great banker. I had never seen one except the great Mr. Morgan, Jupiter Morgan, who used to lend color to Sunday morning services at St. George's, as he stood at the corner of my pew waiting for my quarter. I was afraid my voice might show a tremor. Mr. Ayer was grave and kind. He heard my story together with my confident views of our increasing circulation, coupled with the suggestion that it might be of advantage to us both if *Leslie's* were dressed in type cast by Keystone Foundry. He seemed pleased, but my dawning hopes sank below the horizon when he pushed his button and asked for Mr. Bradford. Now Mr. Bradford was a warning legend to the trade. He was one of those meticulously careful bankers

The Happy Profession

whom the term "watchdog" is wholly inadequate to describe. Mr. Bradford entered and gave me a firm, cold hand. Behind his ear was a pencil, exquisitely sharp. Somehow that pencil seemed to me the very symbol of adversity. If ever he should go figuring with it I knew the count would go against me. I began very briskly.

"Oh, Mr. Bradford, I wish you had heard what I have been saying to Mr. Ayer. At *Leslie's* we have jumped our circulation twice over. A twenty-five-thousand-dollar campaign — of course your firm would spend the money for us, Mr. Bradford — would give us . . . would give us . . . why, it ought to put us up to over two hundred thousand copies by Christmas."

Mr. Bradford looked thoughtful. "Young man," he said, "you know how much you owe us now?"

This trend of thought was intolerable. I talked with all the confidence I did not feel. "That debt, Mr. Bradford, just think what that debt has done for the magazine. It has made you partners in our enterprise. We must make it succeed." I thought the slight suggestion of partnership in that sentence eminently helpful, and went on with a rush, "I wonder whether either of you gentlemen watched the Cup Races last week in New York. The way that *Columbia* stood up to that gale! What do you suppose caused that?" Both gentlemen seemed mystified by the turn the conversation was taking, and I continued, "Why, it was the lead on her keel, that last twenty-five thousand pounds that were added to stiffen her in a blow. Now, gentlemen, what lead is to a yacht's keel, debt is to a magazine's keel. Don't plan a boat for fair weather. Plan a magazine for a blow."

This unconventional argument seemed to amuse my bankers. They went into a quiet huddle at the desk and I came away with a precious little slip of paper which nearly took our

The Metropolis Against Me

shirts from our backs but gave us the resources for a twenty-five-thousand-dollar campaign.

Unhappily my financial improvisations were not always applicable. In this harsh world, there are times when there is no substitute for cash. A cruel incident occurred which left an indelible impression upon me.

It was a moment of transient prosperity, or if not prosperity, at least the semblance of a hope of balancing the books. A wild surmise that the red ink was running out flew through the office and I had gone home to enjoy a carefree dinner. Then at ten o'clock, just as I was tumbling into bed, the telephone rang violently. It was the proprietor's voice with a tremor in it: "Come down at once."

Twenty minutes later I was at the office. The scene would have done credit to Broadway drama. There in the cashier's room stood the Boss, pasty as unleavened bread, and there facing him stood the cashier, his normally cheerful Nordic countenance transfigured with despair. "The total! The total!" the Boss kept saying over and over again in a voice any tragic actor might copy with profit. A tidal wave of papers inundated the little office. Checks, subscription blanks, bills, receipts, covered the floor. They were piled in heaps on chairs, table, and desk; and burrowing among them, looking for he knew not what, the Boss kept repeating automatically in his toneless voice: "The total! Give me the total."

Nobody spoke to me, nobody seemed conscious of my entrance, but what had happened was sickeningly plain. Money had been stolen, how much nobody knew. Were we ruined? Was the balance sheet I had studied so carefully a juggled lie? The thing was incredible. I blinked at the scene but did not take it in. The cashier with his shock of molasses hair and his Scandinavian face had stood against me from the first day. To him I was the symbol of expense. I had thought

The Happy Profession

him mean but the rugged soul of honesty. Never could I screw from him an extra twenty-five dollars for a desperate contributor. Always he had served the Boss with doglike devotion, dependent on his slightest nod. There he stood now, his fingers twitching, his lips stuttering in monosyllables, "I don't know. I don't know." Then I caught a string of disconnected words as he gulped them out. I heard "Race track . . . subscription cash . . . luck was bound to turn . . . I meant to put it all back." Then he would run his hands through his lank hair in a gesture of ruin. All the time the Boss was standing there and I could see his knees were trembling. It is odd how a man looks in trouble. I remember thinking his mouth like the mouth of a trout as you laid it gently on the bank.

Bit by bit the story came out. For a year — more than a year — the cashier had spent his Saturday afternoons at the Jamaica track. It was a tale old as time. At first he won, then lost, always lost and always borrowed to turn the tide. Most of the money he had laid hands on was in bills, enclosed with subscription orders; sometimes advertising checks were cashed and the figures entered at their face value in the books. It was all simple enough, clumsy enough, but what the total defalcation was we never knew. We guessed at ten thousand dollars and the cashier was sent up the river for seven years.

I don't know that the money loss proved serious to me personally, but what I saw bit into my conscience. A man who had been honest forty years, visibly there before me was thrown into the pit of hell. A sudden fierce hatred for gambling and the race track, for all sharps and touts and jockeys, for the crazy excitement of crowds, for Canfield's, for poker and table stakes — even for bridge — possessed me. What was I, to be proof against suffering the same horror that had possession of this wretched little thief with shaking hands and agonized eyes and that unnerved this fat terror-stricken publisher who thought himself ruined, just because temptation to cheat had never occurred to me! The emotion of it was stark and crude and primitive. If Billy Sunday could have caught me I should have hit the sawdust trail that night. The picture I was staring at affected me physically like a cramp. Since that moment I have not played cards for money. It may be sentimental and silly but some things burn into the imagination and as I think that night over I feel comforted for the pleasures I have missed by the very practical reflection that when I gave up bridge and poker and long sociable evenings round the card table I put out my time at interest and grew richer by at least a full year of my life.

Before I leave these financial recollections, I must mention an occurrence which took place some years later, an event whereby many people of far more consequence than I enlarged their experience at the expense of their cash accounts. When I came to New York my accumulated capital was just five hundred dollars. An account of this dimension seemed hardly an acquisition to any bank, and I was grateful indeed when a Vice-President of the Knickerbocker Trust Company consented to house my fortune, assuring me that it would grow and the time come when I should be a valued client. The uptown office of the Knickerbocker, all marble and bronze, at the corner of the Avenue and Thirty-fourth Street, became my personal symbol of the Rock of Gibraltar. I liked to feel the magnificent solidity of it as I walked past, conscious of my stake, then mounting to past six thousand dollars, tucked safely away in its steel vaults.

One morning I was hard at work when the telephone rang and a friendly broker through whom I had made some infinitesimal investments gave me a disquieting message. "Haven't you an account at the Knickerbocker?" he asked. Yes I had.

The Happy Profession

"Well, get it out this minute." If he had informed me that the Treasury had collapsed I should not have been more surprised. I consulted my bankbook, wrote out a check payable to cash for $6,243.50, wrote my name on the back of it, clapped on my hat, and ran to Thirty-fourth Street. Such a sight! From within the marble doors of the Knickerbocker an overflow of depositors stretched far up the Avenue. I joined the queue and then had time to reflect. This was a panic, and I had read much about panics. The way to quiet them was for the bank to pay, pay, pay, quietly and methodically, and pretty soon the excitement would die down. I looked along the line. I thought of the respectable businessmen putting their deposits in on Friday afternoons, and of the well-dressed women shoppers taking those deposits out on Monday mornings on their brisk trips betwixt Lord & Taylor's and Altman's. None such were in this line. It looked to me like an unbroken column of tramps waiting for a handout. The idea that many of them were place-warmers never crossed my mind. What obsessed me was the lack of dignity in my position. Here I was come to New York to make a decent living. I had my own little reputation to sustain, and what would an acquaintance think were he to see me in a galley of that kind at nine-thirty o'clock in the morning, doing my tiny bit to augment the panic.

For two hours I shuffled along in that procession, every minute more horribly self-conscious of the shabbiness of the part that I was playing. I had reached the marble portals. I could see the paying teller at his window, mechanical and imperturbable, handing to each depositor his little pile of notes. All was orderly and methodical. The run on such a bank as the Knickerbocker was simply idiotic nonsense. The sense of shame was too much for me. I left the line and went back to the office, to receive the jeering compliments of my

The Metropolis Against Me

mates. "Well, is your fortune safe?" Hardly had I sat down when my telephone rang again. It was the broker's voice: "Have you got your money?" "No." "Better hurry." Again I grabbed my hat. Again I joined the queue. It had taken on a more respectable appearance. The place-warmers all were gone. These were principals and the long file wore a look of responsible anxiety. Hour after hour I shuffled along. By two-thirty I had reached once more that marble doorway. By two-forty I was within a dozen paces of the teller's window. Just then something happened. From a neat briefcase, a gentleman who had reached the window produced a check and presented it with an air of consequence. Along the line the rumor flew that this check was for a million dollars. The teller stared at it, reversed it, scrutinized the face of it as if it were a curiosity. Then he turned and consulted one of the Vice-Presidents forming the second line of the bank's defenses. Suddenly I watched him raise both his arms high in the air. Down came the wicket. The bank was broken.

It was a scene for Hogarth. Women were crying hysterically, men looking about them in blank despair, and I saw one burly fellow shake his fist at the shut wicket. Then we all tumbled out into the street.

All this was some time after I had set up housekeeping. Rather grimly that afternoon I told this history to my wife. We counted cash on hand. I remember that balance. It was $17.55. We decided that this money was not to be touched except for carfares. We would give the credit system a chance. I crossed the street and broke the news gently to our grocer. He was true blue and promised that supplies would not be stopped. With our chops and potatoes secure I got out a bottle of wine and we made, my wife and I, a gallant attempt at dining. Neither of us was hungry and it was not a lively occasion. When I had finished my cigarette I tried to put a little punch into our festivities. Getting out a volume of *Vanity Fair* I read aloud the chapter on "How to Live Well on Nothing a Year." Thackeray had never fallen flat before, but in all that chapter there was not a ripple of mirth. Next morning I found on my desk a check I had drawn two days before. Across it penciled in blue were the letters "N.G." This was my first experience in such matters and my last. That N.G. left its stamp behind.

It was as I remember three or four years later that I got back my money — I think without interest.

CHAPTER VIII

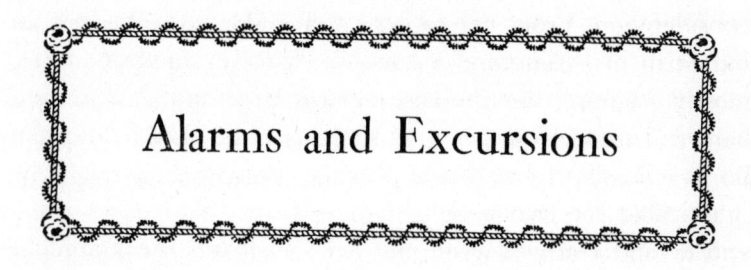

Alarms and Excursions

MEANTIME my work on the magazine had grown quite beyond my power to handle. I needed a reader. After very careful inquiry I learned that the young daughter of the Librarian of Columbia University desired employment, and it did not take great discernment to discover that Miss Dorothy Canfield was a pearl of price. She joined my staff; rather she became the staff, for at the time, she and I did all the work. She was not so many years younger than I but, long before twelve months had passed, her talent and imagination as well as the admirable education she had received were very evident to me. The bits of writing she showed me confirmed my judgment. I knew she was at the threshold of a career.

Late one day after a long manuscript session, she asked with that quiet little look of hers whether she might consult me very personally. Her problem was not wholly simple. A young Mr. Fisher, employed by the F. A. Stokes Publishing Company with which I had intimate relations, had asked her to marry him. She cared for him, but the prospects of the young people did not shine brightly. He was a year or two younger than she. Neither had money and her confidence was clouded by the fact that even then she was manifestly growing deaf. We had a long and sympathetic conversation. I asked whether she had no resources. She answered that she had nothing in the bank, but one hope might be taken into consideration. From her father's father she had inherited an old farm at Arlington, Vermont. "Mostly stumps?" "Yes, mostly stumps." But the acreage was large and a house and barn still stood from her grandfather's time. Could the place be let? Possibly: but for a pittance. However, it might be practicable for two people to live there. "You can write," said I, "and you will write; but he?" That was the stumbling block. Fisher was no farmer, and even if he were, the six meals a day required for two were not to be wrung from that thin soil.

Who would not bet on a Dorothy Canfield! I asked whether Fisher would not join our deliberations. He did. I liked and trusted him. Dorothy outlined her plan and I reinforced it. If they were married and went to live in the remote country, would she settle down to an undeviating routine and write for four hours every morning with another spell in the afternoon when she felt the inspiration upon her? In that case she must be absolutely carefree. The exigencies of housekeeping must not bear down upon her. She must keep her mind steadily on her work. Would he, then, make the sacrifice, give up his position, and make his career as the necessary partner of her existence; do the chores, tinker with the motor, stop the leaks in the roof, stand between her and all the world? He would do everything, and moreover he was clever with his hands and wholly competent to fulfill his side of the bargain.

So they were married. But it was her dearest wish to have many children and those children must have as good an education as their mother. This was certainly a complication. But Dorothy took it in her stride. Every year that a baby was expected, as she wrote me long after, she would plant on her

Alarms and Excursions

hillside ten thousand young pine trees. It was done German fashion; a scoop of earth, a tiny hole, six inches of pine tree pushed in and tamped down. Then two paces along a string line; another hole, another tree, and so on, acre after acre, till ten thousand minute sprigs of green stood in their geometric rows. Eighteen years later rows of tall pines were fit to be harvested, and off went a child to college. A few years ago I walked through those groves with Mrs. Fisher. Thousands of pine trees had been sawn down, trimmed, and sold to the mill, but thousands still stood. As a long-range educational system, the Fisher Model stands pre-eminent as its namesake in the field of automobile bodies. "Bodies by Fisher" is a famous slogan, but for energy, perseverance, and downright intelligence, "Education by Fisher" stands not a whit behind.

Of course I could not foresee the full achievement of Dorothy Canfield; her novels, her stories, her books on education. But I knew enough then to stand by the experiment and I take my tiny share of the pride in it.

In my little world, as in the big world outside, the old order was changing fast. For a generation, three monthly magazines had been reckoned of consequence, the *Atlantic* included by deference paid to the poor and distinguished. Their aristocratic price of thirty-five cents a copy defined their constituencies and they were later reinforced by *Scribner's* at twenty-five cents. Then in 1893, appropriately the year of panic, *McClure's* was founded, and with its brisk competitors, the *Cosmopolitan* and *Munsey's*, all priced at a dime, the ten-centers began hustling their dignified elders out of the road. The mass movement had begun. With cheap prices and the advent of illustration direct from the photographic plate, monthlies sprang up like mushrooms on a warm night. Whereas the *Century* with its elaborate dress

The Happy Profession

expended some five thousand dollars a month for plate engraving alone, a tenth of that sum provided competition by new illustrated magazines appearing freshly every morning on the newsstand. Starting a magazine was like stocking a pushcart. *McClure's* began when the total resources of the partners scarcely exceeded seven thousand dollars. Competition was murderous and we all lived by our wits. One day *Everybody's*, which had been almost as inconspicuous as *Leslie's*, catching the flying coattails of Tom Lawson, a speculator who had a way with him and scores to settle, plunged into muckraking and presently soared to the zenith while the rest of us were still glorifying the self-made heroes of the trusts. Next *McClure's* called the turn while *Munsey's* made hay beneath the shining sun by lively mediocrity and mass advertising. As an example of the crude impudence of Mr. Munsey's methods I recall an issue of his magazine which sold out to the last copy, thanks to a simple facsimile of his handwriting on the cover: "This is the best magazine I have ever published. — Frank A. Munsey."

Wedged in the ruck among the also-rans was *Leslie's Monthly*, without capital and without character, depending for its very life on an occasional hit. One morning startling news seemed to offer a chance. It happened that I was negotiating for an article with a Norwegian explorer, one Borchgrevink, who had achieved notoriety by leading an expedition bound for the South Pole which marked him as the man in all the world who had been farthest south. The possibilities of an article from him were moderate but respectable, when they were transformed by a terrific burst of news. Mount Pelée, the overshadowing volcano of Martinique, had erupted. An avalanche of flaming lava had swept over the city nestling at its foot and flowed out over surrounding waters, overwhelming the ships in the harbor in an ocean of fire. One American ship was rumored to have escaped. For the rest there was universal ruin. No such spectacular horror had occurred since the burial of Pompeii and to work my feelings up to editorial pitch I reread the younger Pliny's account of that memorable disaster. What a model for a magazine article that was! I hoped for such another.

Borchgrevink agreed to go as our representative on the Relief Ship immediately fitted out in New York. I telegraphed the Navy Department, received a sort of reply the Navy keeps on file to answer civilian requests, telephoned emphatically and got a berth for our distinguished correspondent. I was on the pier to see him off. The Norseman was a likable fellow, but such a touse as he made getting off you would think him just packed away to his first boarding school; no baggage but a shirt and a toothbrush, and the spirits of a boy at the high tide of human existence.

A mountain of crates, food, clothing, medicine, disappeared into the hold. The first toot of "All ashore going ashore" announced that time was short. Borchgrevink clapped his hand on his breast pocket. "I have no money!" he exclaimed. I gave him the hundred dollars I had extorted from our cashier. "But I need another hundred just to live," said he. So commanding was his figure, so illuminating his gestures, that he had become the central object of interest on the pier. Everybody was guessing who he was. There were five minutes to go and a hundred dollars to be raised. I climbed on a box and made an eloquent appeal: "Attention, gentlemen. This is Commander Borchgrevink, hero of the South Pole. *Leslie's Monthly*, in conformity with its policy of helping the distressed, is sending him to suffering Martinique. He needs another hundred dollars. *Leslie's* will repay it, and the editor will give you his receipt." I took off my hat, dropped into it my last ten-dollar bill and a dozen visiting cards and passed it round. In less time than it takes to tell it I had the money. Borchgrevink grabbed it and dashed up the gangplank. The whistle tooted for the last time, ropes were cast off. Thank God that's over, thought I, and on the very instant there was Borchgrevink leaning over the deck rail, his hands waving high above his head in a frantic gesture of despair. Evidently some terrifying thought had struck him. "My wife," he cried, "I had forgotten her! What shall I do? What shall I do?"

"Do with her?" I shouted back. "Where is she?"

"She's at Hotel Netherland."

The tug was puffing alongside and the relief ship edging into the Hudson. It was pretty late to arrange family matters, but the countenance of *Leslie's* distinguished correspondent took on a look of consternation.

"What *can* I do for her!" A wave of sympathy from the crowd made the drama very poignant. I threw my arms wide in the largest gesture of which I was capable and screamed "Give her to me!" Instant applause from the crowd!

"Swear that you will keep her safe and send her back to Norway," and I bellowed in return, "I swear."

I should like my chivalrous readers to know that my pledge was meticulously kept. My first duty that afternoon was to repair to Mme. Borchgrevink's apartment with a bunch of roses in my hand and in my pocket a ticket to Norway. But to return to my story.

Good humor is infectious. "I'll help you!" cried one man, and another shouted, "I've only one at home." "How many have you?" came from all parts of the dock. Borchgrevink grinned in recognition of American humor. He was off and had forgotten nothing.

A week passed. The tragedy of Martinique grew to hideous proportions. An entire city boiled in lava. Uncounted thousands had been burned to death. Every ship in the harbor had

Alarms and Excursions

been overtaken by seething flame, all but one; the bark *Roraima*, ablaze from stem to stern, had inched away, and before her own destruction had transferred what was left of her crew. The captain, Ellery S. Scott, who had been first mate till the master was burned to death, the purser, and a black steward had survived and would be shipped to New York.

The kidnaping of these distressed mariners the instant they put foot on shore was no easy matter in the world of newspaperdom. All credit then to my coadjutor and lifelong friend, Fred Hoppin, whom I had dispatched to the dock. Hoppin was a genial and sympathetic soul who knew his way about the waterfront and enlisted the aid of a series of friendly barkeeps to bid the visitors welcome.

Borchgrevink I knew could not hope to return for another week and, in any case, a correspondent without a chance to talk with the survivors was no answer to editorial prayer. That was obvious. What was essential to round out Borchgrevink's narrative was the personal story of those survivors. They had seen a sight no man had witnessed for two thousand years. In the teeth of competition they must be kidnaped, their stories must be taken down at first hand, and then they must be shipped off to some remote country asylum for the week that can be counted on to separate news from history. That was the job and we did it. The three sailors were nourished on much brandy and a little milk and all day they lay about my office, their eyes still dazed with the revelation of hell. They were like hurt children, moaning and whimpering with the ghastly look which horror brings to a man's face. I pieced and patched the story, putting in every authentic detail and signing the captain's name. That night off they went to the country in comfortable Pullman berths. I saw to that.

The trick seemed turned. But nowhere else on earth I think

The Happy Profession

is there so close a hookup between one trouble and the next as in an editorial office. Our story was rushed into page proofs without bothering about galleys. Within three days' time *Leslie's* would be on the stands and then, as I left the office that last frantic morning, I read an announcement in a newspaper that the complete story of the wreck of the *Roraima* told by Captain Scott would promptly appear in the *Cosmopolitan* magazine. It was a blow with a trip hammer. That story, I knew, would be a fake, made up of rumor and newspaper clippings woven together by some industrious editor. But that made no difference. The whole value of our advertisement would be irretrievably ruined. The *Cosmopolitan* was the whale and we the littlest of fishes. Our single hope was to stop the enemy in his tracks.

I rushed back to the office and into the publisher's room. The Boss had a gift for despair. He looked numb. "Is there anything to be done?" he asked feebly.

"Get out an injunction."

We called the lawyer, made the deposition, found the judge in his chambers, and got the writ returnable twenty-four hours after *Cosmopolitan's* publishing day.

"Now," said the Boss to the lawyer, "give that to the process server."

"Yes," said the lawyer, "and have the process served when the magazine is out on the stands and the harm done. It must be served tomorrow morning, and it must be served personally on John Brisben Walker. He will dodge any process server you can send."

Thick gloom settled on the group. Then out spake Brave Horatius: "I'll serve it myself," said I, "and I'll serve it tomorrow."

"Deliver it into his own hands," the lawyer said, "and do it quick."

Alarms and Excursions

Hardly had I heard my own words when I felt a violent constriction of the heart. If there were giants in those days, John Brisben Walker was an admirable specimen. He was eccentric but he was impressive. He it was who had first cut the magazine quarter in two and offered the *Cosmopolitan* at twelve and a half cents a copy, a revolutionary though singularly inconvenient price, squeezed down to ten when *Munsey's* took the final inevitable step. His extensive printing plant stood at the gates of his mansion house at Irvington-on-the-Hudson. His *Cosmopolitan* sold and deserved to sell four copies to *Leslie's* one. He was rich. He was feared. It was rumored that he was the stiffest man in New York to work for, and certainly he looked the part. Six feet odd inches tall, straight as an athlete, he would not have lacked for backers in any prize ring. All sorts of picturesque legends surrounded him. On each birthday past his prime, he would jump a four-barred gate and remark that he was good for another year. All this ran through my mind as I walked home that night, thinking the thoughts of David when he picked up those smooth pebbles of his in the brook bed in the Valley of Elah.

Betimes the next morning I was off for Irvington with the warrant crinkling in my breast pocket. I walked up the handsome driveway that led from printing plant to mansion house and rang the bell. It seemed not to tinkle but to peal. So loud it sounded, I thought I had set off an alarm. It was impossible to imagine that the butler would not see at the very first glance that I was a process server. But when that discreet functionary appeared, he merely waited for my inquiry.

"Is Mr. Walker in?"

"Mr. Walker is out riding horseback."

"When will he return?"

"Sometime before lunch."

The Happy Profession

"My business is urgent," said I, just as if I had come to close a friendly deal profitable for both of us. "I will wait," and, staying for no further encouragement, I sat down on a chair facing the front door.

God knows how long I waited there. Weeks seemed to pass. Certainly it was hard on lunch time when I heard a quick, firm step on the porch. Mr. Walker appeared in riding breeches, a crop in his hand. He looked at me, as I thought, quite casually.

"Mr. Walker," I said, "I have a document of some importance which I am bidden to give into your hands."

He seemed to sense trouble. "What do you mean?" he asked as though something had nettled him.

I held out the paper and instinctively he took it in his hand. Then I spoke out. "That, Mr. Walker, is an injunction to prevent you from stealing the story that belongs to *Leslie's*. I am the editor."

Mr. Walker's face was a study. It turned from white to red and he threw the paper on the floor.

"Do you mean you have the damned impudence to tell me — " he said and broke the sentence off, "you miserable little — little — "

"Editor," I suggested.

Then his rage exploded. "I'll break you," he said, "I'll destroy you. I'll drive you out of town."

I was angry too. What a wonderful help anger is when it comes at the right time! What a substitute for courage! What a support in time of trouble!

"That can all be attended to later," I said. "Just now the important thing is to stop those presses."

He raised his crop. I thought he would strike me, and I had grown so hot that I rather wanted him to. But he felt the danger quite as sensibly as I.

Alarms and Excursions

"I bid you good day, Mr. Walker." There was a surge of triumph in my heart as I walked down the steps.

The next day in came Mr. Walker to our office to eat his humble pie. I did not see him. That would have been indiscreet, and my door was tight closed, but I heard a voice with which I was very familiar. Some arrangement was made which composed our differences much to the advantage of *Leslie's Monthly*. Our *Roraima* edition was completely sold out.

CHAPTER IX

Yellow

THERE ARE times, or there used to be, when nothing seems to happen. A couple of world wars and an atomic bomb or two have done away with this sort of tedium, but once upon a time there were days very quiet indeed. My mind went blank. I went to dinner parties. I scanned the papers. But there was no excitement anywhere, and in the office despondency reigned. It was hard to bear, and my morale suffered visibly. It was then that I was tempted and I fell. I made the descent into yellow journalism.

Yellow journalism has no law. It lives by two simple rules: first, when there is news, transform it; second, when there isn't, make it. There was no news so I made it.

One spring day when all the world seemed asleep I had an entertaining visitor. Mr. David Buffum was a horseman. There was no doubt of that. He knew horses and he bred horses and he was full of horse theories little and big. I asked him whether he could breed equines up and down. How big could a horse be, and how little? Mr. Buffum loved theory and was eloquent on the subject.

The horse, he told me, could only be bred to perfection in a temperate country. Make the temperature extreme, up or down, the horse deteriorates in size. His frame will grow smaller. Let horses run wild in the Arctic or the tropics, and

Yellow

a few generations will reduce them to the size of ponies. I pressed Mr. Buffum to continue his argument and he gave me these interesting details. The tendency to diminution, he said, is greater in a mountainous country than in a level one. It is accentuated by heat, also by a damp climate. Therefore it may be briefly stated that those conditions which would naturally bring about the smallest breed would be a mountain country accompanied by damp heat. Theoretically, it might be said with equal truth, a mountain country accompanied by extreme cold — but there is a degree of cold in northern regions in which horses cannot thrive. There is, however, no region in the world so hot that horses will not easily be acclimated thereto. Therefore if in the tropics the same degree of heat existed on mountaintops as in the lowlands, ponies would become excessively diminutive. But in tropical lands the temperature is in inverse proportion to altitude and nothing except causes more or less out of the ordinary can produce in a mountain region a temperature as hot as that at sea level.

The words "causes out of the ordinary" are good editorial words. To the crowd the normal is not interesting. Neither is theory. It might be absorbingly interesting to the editor to discuss an hypothesis whereby the size of a horse could be brought down to the level of a Newfoundland dog without sacrifice of his delicate and beautiful form, but the normal subscriber would sniff and toss the article aside. If Mr. Buffum could translate his hypothesis into some semblance of experience and brighten up his text with pictures portraying race horses gamboling about on equal terms with dogs and cats, then and then only a great many people would be diverted.

"Mr. Buffum," I said, "supposing you were to write the story of how you bred these kittenish horses and proved it

The Happy Profession

with photographs of race horses brought down to plaything size by tricks of the camera, it might be entertaining; and if you take your pictures from Mr. Belmont's stud, you will give your sporting readers a sense of class. It will amuse ordinary readers too. What I want, of course, is a stunt, but not a hoax. There's a difference there. You make it all just as realistic as you can and I will tip our readers off by calling the story 'A Modern Voyage to Lilliput.' That will put everybody wise."

The difference between a stunt and a hoax — it seemed a proper measure of the gulf dividing *Leslie's Monthly* from yellow journalism — not for worlds would I bridge that gap, but to keep the story from falling flat it must be absolutely realistic. Readers must be half carried away by its exceeding naturalness and then pull themselves up short and remember that after all they have been reading a fairy story. But slippery are the slopes of Avernus.

When Mr. Buffum brought in his manuscript, upon my soul, I was very nearly convinced that the story was true, so matter of fact it was, so professional the knowledge shown in every detail. Defoe could not have done better. If one of the midget horses of the romance had turned out a centaur it would not have been much more startling. The realism was complete.

Mr. Buffum had selected "Lliani" for his adventure. There is magic in the name. Whether it comes from geography or fairyland beyond, I do not know to this day. The syllables tickled my ear. The isle of Lliani, so the left lobe of my brain told me, must be somewhere in the latitude of the "Flying Islands of Laputa," but the right lobe, intent upon the narrative, agreed that it was somewhere off the coast of Haiti. It was, it seemed, a giant columnar mountain, broken off from the mainland by some mighty operation of Nature, and shoved

Yellow

slightly seaward. This mountain showed marked individuality. Its sides — there seem to have been no slopes — were precipices of rock, but the top was a flat plain. Here were the tropics. Here was altitude. Here were profuse rainfall and ample pasturage. Nature positively cried aloud for a toy horse and Mr. Buffum gratified Nature.

Into this paradise no man had penetrated, for it was one of those spots "so frequent in the West Indies, which the Negroes believed to be haunted by *duppies* — a duppy in the voodoo worship which prevails there, being a spirit or ghost." The intrepid explorer with one bold companion had made the ascent with ropes and the support of a light ladder, and after two days of perpendicular rock work had attained the mighty rim. Here, to a man even of Mr. Buffum's experience, came a great surprise.

"Instead of finding ourselves," he wrote, "on the edge of a giant's table, we were, so to speak, on the rim of a teacup, for a vast depression extended over the whole top, like a crater of an extinct volcano. I am inclined to think this is what it really is, though it is comparatively level at the bottom and is not circular in shape, but oblong; being, as I roughly estimated, about five miles long by two broad. . . . The surrounding walls shut out the breeze, and it was suffocatingly hot. There were few trees, and even in the shade of these the temperature stood considerably above a hundred degrees Fahrenheit. The grass — the 'pimento' variety of the tropics, but shorter and finer than usual — was scanty and partly dried up, and near the center of the plain was a natural pond, apparently very deep and about an acre in superficial area.

"I give this exact description because I believe it has exact bearing upon what I found there."

What he did find there was truly astonishing. Frisking

about was a herd of miniature horses about the size of Scotch collies, weighing perhaps fifty pounds apiece. There was no suggestion of the pony about them. They were unquestionably blooded stock, show animals with all the points, beautiful and perfect.

From wonder to wonder the story went on. After infinite difficulty Mr. Buffum brought his prizes home — three stallions and four mares — and domesticated them on his farm at Wickford, Rhode Island. The tale was told in painstaking detail, factual to a degree, and documented with the evidence of a number of fictitious horse fanciers. The photographs, as photographs do, bore lying and emphatic witness.

"Heaven above us!" I exclaimed. "This is too persuasive. Put in just a little fiction. Take your pets to a hotel and make a paddock for them with a couple of towel racks in the bathroom."

But that seemed to us really to border on the make-believe, and we compromised by introducing a thief who was caught running away with a stallion under one arm and a mare under the other.

I knew the credulity of the American public but I thought that incident would put a sufficient strain upon it in the face of any testimony or any statistics. I remembered that there are three degrees of prevarication — lies, damned lies, and statistics. The preposterousness of the whole tale seemed to me to shriek aloud.

"It's too airy-fairy," said I, "we must weight it down a little." And so with very sober faces, we added a lengthy legal attestation from the "State Committee on Livestock of the State of Rhode Island," certifying to its correctness. Anyone would guess, I supposed, that no such body was in existence, but there in print it did seem to tip the scales toward a moderate authenticity. Finally seeing I had gone too far

Yellow

in the other direction I appended a seriocomic warning which I thought adequately in the Gulliver vein.

> While Mr. Buffum's story was under consideration in the office, one of the editors, more or less learned in subjects connected with natural history, expressed some incredulity, not unreasonable in view of the unusual character of the manuscript. He even went so far as to compare it with Gulliver's Voyage to Lilliput and declared it nothing more than the dream of a stock-breeder. We wish, therefore, to put the story clearly before our readers, hoping each will weigh carefully the interesting evidence laid before him.

Was CAVEAT EMPTOR ever put into plainer words than those? So I thought, and I reflected too that the strain of humor for which the newspapers tell us Americans are famous would rise to the surface. Not a bit of it. In the deluge of letters that followed, there was not a suggestion that the story was a "spoof." The writers were deadly serious and desperately interested. The Lord knows we had given them statistics enough but they cried for more. The prices which we had quoted of recent sales, thirty thousand dollars for a mare, and thirty-two for a stallion, seemed to these professionals bargain rates. Men who had lounged about fancy stables for years were fascinated by visions of making the race track an indoor sport to compete with ping-pong and battledore.

Nobody seemed to harbor a doubt. When letters from the Blue Grass of Kentucky began to come in, then I thought we were safely beyond the limits of credulity. But no. They only showed a more detailed and scientific interest. Had we only had stock in hand I verily believe we could have opened a mail-order business then and there. The stunt was certainly a hoax.

Never before had a doubt occurred to me that Americans

were gifted with a sense of humor. Now suspicion crept in. True, the "funnies" have never struck me as mirth-provoking even before they took on romance as a substitute for humor. But then nobody, even partly sophisticated, is a fair judge of what is generically amusing. Funny stories, of course, are popular. Their popularity is apt to arise after the author's reputation is made and newspapers refer to him as an inimitable fellow. When a reader knows a thing must be funny, if he is an average man, he really enjoys the joke. But a funny story has to have its trade-mark. If there is a mother-in-law in it, that labels it at once. And if it is ascribed to a famous jokester, a hearty laugh ensues, for that, too, is a practical test. Many men of many minds have torn the gossamer web of humor apart to find what is inside. Certainly a jostling of discordant concepts plays its part. Concepts are ideas and you have to have other ideas to compare them with. The enjoyment of humor then is a by-product of education, but it cannot be taught.

> 'Tis never by invention got,
> Men have it when they know it not.

Yet if there is a single test of the quality of a man I think it lies in his sense of humor, or more surely, perhaps, in his sense of the just proportions of it.

But to finish my story. One letter and one only we received from a disillusioned reader. Four pages of it were filled with sound and fury. It was postmarked Lexington, Kentucky, the horse's natural home, and I opened it with expectations. It exceeded them. The writer was a breeder to whom horse-knowledge, from mane to hock, was an open book. The information given him by the magazine was new knowledge. It had fascinated him. Miniature horses became the single topic of family conversation. His wife longed to see them; the boys

Yellow

thought of nothing else. "Relying solely" upon the editor's reputation, the man had drawn money from the bank and bought four tickets — Lexington, Kentucky, to Wickford, Rhode Island. Bursting with excitement these very horsy people reached the farm to find — the truth. The final page of the letter was one long splutter. The party had arrived on a Saturday. There was no train back till Monday noon. The week end had to be spent in Wickford, Rhode Island. The trip cost close to three hundred dollars and the writer begged to be damned if he wouldn't make *Leslie's* pay for it.

I made an editorial resolution: —

> And since, I never dare to write
> As funny as I can.

CHAPTER X

Friends and Crooks

ANY young man in a hurry to get on pays little attention to the limitation of working hours, but juvenile editors in search of ideas are so many boys chasing butterflies. They pursue them all day and at night they hunt for moths! Ideas have a way of taking any shape, any time. The editor's business is to catch and domesticate them and to put them to hard and useful work. Any story is grist to his mill. One morning a friend confided to me that coming to town on the train he had overheard a discussion between two railroad clerks as to the proper subclassification of guinea pigs as an item of freight. I knew the happiest humorist of my acquaintance would appreciate that. At the time, Ellis Parker Butler was editing a magazine devoted to the interest of wallpapers. Now there is little in life less congenial to the moods of humor than wallpapers, and I was forever prodding Ellis to turn to a more expansive vocation. This was my chance. I asked him to lunch, embellished the tale here and there with the slightest touches of fancy, and turned it over to him. Within a week he had transformed it into a thing of beauty and a joy forever. Three months later "Pigs Is Pigs" was recognized as a classic. *Leslie's* had sold out to the last copy, and the story republished between covers made Butler

Friends and Crooks

famous. Wallpapers knew him no more, and the satisfactions of life became intenser for all of us.

I like to recall too that about this time I served as a sort of step-grandfather to the celebrated Mr. Tutt. The famous firm of Tutt & Tutt was not then born to the humane and profitable practice of the law, but the future author of its being had graduated from college a few years behind me. Once installed as an Assistant District Attorney, Arthur Train discovered the fascination of the melodrama daily enacted in his office. It was to *Leslie's* he brought his first story, "The Maximilian Diamond."

Thinking with sorrow the other day of Arthur Train's death, I reread the story and was delighted to recognize there his first collection of the inimitable stage properties which he enlarged and exploited through the decades.

I have spoken of the gullibility of the public. The American mouth is always open. The monstrosities it gulps down outstrip the confines of credulity. When Orson Welles described the World's End, he had only to augment the horror with a few of his vivid touches and the public swallowed it wholesale. Ask any Better Business Bureau. The hundreds of millions of dollars which Americans part with when smart alecks offer their preposterous bait would make a nursery governess weep. Or, more simply, stop on the sidewalk and, merely remarking "How extraordinary!" point to vacancy. Then watch the crowd discern the marvels they see in a passing cloud. All this an Assistant District Attorney knows far better than I, but even Arthur Train surmised that credulity in this enlightened country had its limits. He was in error. In thirteen volumes he had recounted the fictional adventures of Mr. Tutt. In the fourteenth, *Yankee Lawyer*, Mr. Tutt's acumen rose to great heights. Working upon a case of his

The Happy Profession

own, a certain attorney-at-law who had become his enthusiastic admirer felt that Mr. Tutt was just the man he needed as a witness. When the summons was disregarded, the attorney's dander was up. Forthwith he brought suit in the Supreme Court of New York making Arthur Train and his publishers, Messrs. Charles Scribner's Sons, joint defenders in a case of fraud. Mr. Tutt's failure to materialize constituted the fraud. Fortunately Mr. Train came to his friend's defense. He rested his satirical argument upon the manifest fraud of which Daniel Defoe was guilty when he represented Robinson Crusoe's story as his own, and further buttressed his case by summoning Dean Swift into court to answer a similar charge for publishing *Gulliver's Travels*. Let us hope that the fillip this notable case gave to the sale of *Yankee Lawyer* served Arthur Train in lieu of heavy damages.

It was not often that ideas flew into the butterfly net as easily as Butler's pigs into their correct category. As a matter of routine I began to make acquaintances at both ends of the social scale. Dinner parties on Park Avenue were rewarding but not less so the slum which Jake Riis had rescued by Mulberry Bend, and supper with Miss Lillian Wald on Henry Street was always an event. From her genius for understanding I picked up some knowledge of what to have not means in education for life.

Likewise I found the Hapgood family exhilarating. Norman stretched your brains, Hutchins strained your sympathies. It was through the latter that I formed my first intimacy with a burglar, for this acquaintance quickly ripened into familiarity. Jim Caulfield was an old hand at the game but he had found it singularly unprofitable and was now eager to get into some securer line of endeavor. I got him one honest job after another, but three consecutive weeks never elapsed without the escape of his secret and then there

Friends and Crooks

was always a new job to be found. It is very discouraging, the bad name you give to a dog, and I have reflected much upon it. Jim and I had many talks over cheap meals on the East Side, or at night in my own room. Fourteenth Street was the deadline for crooks, and in the daytime Jim would never accompany me south of that well-fortified line of defense.

Jim had done three terms in State prison and enough was enough. On the first two occasions, as he was free to admit, he had got what was coming to him, but of his last incarceration, three years and six months, counting time out for good behavior, he spoke with extreme bitterness.

"That judge was a God damned snide," he said. "I was no more in Brooklyn that night than you were."

The disclaimer did not impress me. "Alibis are easy to come by if you have a right to one," I remarked.

Jim became passionate. "Alibi, alibi!" he exclaimed. "My God, that alibi was just my bitch luck. It was a pal of mine that did the Brooklyn job. I knew all about it, but of all the damned crisscrossing!" (At times Jim was very genteel in his expressions.) "That very night I was on a piece of second-story work in West Orange and that judge asking me where I was! I suppose you think it was up to me to tell him!" His face flushed. His innocence of that Brooklyn crime was very close to his moral nature.

I learned a good deal of life as it is lived in professional circles. Jim asserted he never knew a man get as far as one story up without a pistol in his pocket. The heavier penalty for a burglar caught with arms was no deterrent. If things looked like five years ahead for you, it would be a fool who wouldn't risk another five by using a gun to make a getaway. As in all crowded professions, the apprentice makes his way by easy stages. There is usually pocket-picking to begin with or just snitching from a pushcart, then a bit of porch

The Happy Profession

climbing while the family is at supper, but you learn your trade most thoroughly by serving as lookout for a senior professional. You are a helper on the job. I pressed him for some of his more glamorous experiences and he told me a story I have not forgotten.

The scene was in the Oranges. Jim was in business with an old Sing Sing pal of his. They had watched the house for three weeks on end (burglars have the lawyer's propensity for careful preparation), and they had worked out a comprehensive plan of the premises. One or the other would loiter about across the way or in the field behind, and they both became familiar with the owner's routine. He was a man of method. He would come home at five-fifty, and every night at ten would make the rounds, locking the windows and putting out the lights; but on Saturday nights five friends would come in just after supper for a poker game. The back curtains were up and the watchers could see a bottle going around between jackpots. At eleven-thirty the host would rise. There was a last drink all around. The chips were put back in the box and the guests would crowd out, every man of them, as Jim said, obedient to the wife's injunction to be in before morning.

The partners pondered the case. The earlier the bed the lighter the sleep, they argued, but the later the party, the deeper the slumber. So they judged, and picked on Saturday night.

Professional burglary makes chronic demands upon the nerves. It is a good deal as it would be in Worth or Wall Street if panic were endemic whenever a business deal goes through. Both men were taut as the strings of a violin. Behind the house was a little garden framed by a picket fence, and behind this the pair lay prone on their stomachs peering through the slats. By ten o'clock they were in position. By eleven, although it

Friends and Crooks

was a fresh autumn evening, their bodies were streaming with sweat. By half-past eleven their tempers were strained like halyards in a gale. They watched the host rise, pick up a bottle, and pass it right to left. There came a rattling of chips, much shaking of hands, and a string of good-nights — five of them — as the host showed his friends out of the front door. Then one by one the lights went out and at five minutes before midnight the bulb in the corner room on the second story was snapped off.

Outside there was light still, till the moon went under a smoky cloud. For forty-five minutes by the watch they lay motionless. Then, slipping over the palings, they wriggled toward the house. There was a trellised porch. The rear door was beneath it and above a shingled roof ran up to the window sills of the second story. Under the shadow of this porch both men waited.

Ten minutes passed. They took off their shoes and, with a signal to Jim, his partner rose and began to shin up the corner column, hand over hand. He was five feet from the ground when Jim's strained ears caught a tiny rustle. It might have been the wind blowing over the grass, but Jim was on edge. Involuntarily he put his finger to his lip and whispered "Sh-h." The climber dropped to the ground like a cat, and for an appreciable time they lay motionless. It had been agreed that the senior partner should edge up the porch roof to the hall window, jimmy it, step downstairs, and open the back door to his confederate. His was the opening move, and after the spell of perfect quiet, up he went again. Precisely as his head came parallel to the lowest row of shingles, again Jim heard that tiny rustle. "Sh-h," he whispered once more, and again the climber dropped. They huddled in absolute silence. There was not a breath of wind now, and the only sound came from hearts beating like drums. It was all imagination. The older hand was exasperated: "God damn you!" he muttered. "If you do that again, I'll do for you if it's my last act on earth." He got to his feet, and for the third time shinned to the roof's edge, pulled himself over it, and crawled up to the window. Taking a jimmy from his back pocket, he slipped it beneath the sash. The window was thrown up violently. There was a report like a giant cracker, and the man crouching outside rolled like a bundle down the slope and pitched to the path.

Jim was reliving the story as he told it. "Think what you like of me," he said, "say I'm a dirty coward if you want to. I knew he was lying there with blood all over him. He might be dead for all I knew, but I didn't wait to see. I left him there in a heap and ran like a scared rabbit."

Lights were on now upstairs and down and two voices shouted "There are two of them. Get the other." Jim heard them as he vaulted the fence and cut across the field. In fifty yards he reached a road, turned right, and then left at the next corner as if the devils in hell were after him. He turned into a third street lined sparsely with houses, then into another, running till his ribs were bursting. He was tired now but his ears caught voices a hundred yards behind him. "He went this way," cried one, "I saw him." Jim called up his final reserve. He turned two corners. His ribs were splitting now, and his breathing racked him. He passed a driveway. At one side of it stood a kennel. There was a huge dog within, fastened he thought by a chain. On the instant Jim was on his knees. He threw his arm round the beast's neck and pressed his face against the soft neck. As he crept inside the dog licked his cheek. There was a rush in the roadway. "He went in there!" he heard, and the answer, "No he didn't. I know that dog." The men passed. For five minutes Jim lay there fondling the Saint Bernard. The beast seemed to recognize

Friends and Crooks

a friend. He had been awaked from sleep, but by one of the miracles that save bad men and good he did not bark, but licked and licked as though he had found a new master and liked him well.

Full five minutes passed before Jim got to his feet. With the most fervent prayer of his life he blessed that dog. He left the kennel, turned into the road, and walked — it was safer than running — in the direction from which the chase had come.

Safe enough now, he thought to himself; and then he knew better. He was in deadly peril. He had no hat, no shoes. What conductor would fail to remember him if he took the trolley toward home? Just across the street there was a little frame house. It had a kindly look. Jim walked round it and found the kitchen window. All his courage was gone, but one more break he had to make. He jimmied the window. It went up as though the cords were oiled. In he climbed, walked through a passage to the hall, mounted the stairs, and listened at the first door. Whoever it was that lay there in bed was snoring. Jim opened the door noiselessly and entered. The bed, he knew, must be opposite, and the closet over against the inner wall just across from the window. Softly he turned the handle and bent low. Yes, there was a row of shoes. He ran his hand along them to make certain they were man-sized, then picked up a pair and crossed to the dressing table. A watch lay on it. The ticking bothered him. Jim slipped the watch into his trouser pocket and stowed away beside it a roll of bills that had been pinned to the cushion. The change he did not take, for silver can ring. Then he groped for the hallway and crept downstairs. At the front entrance was a hatrack. Jim slipped a coat over his arm, took a derby hat from the peg above it, tried it on and, two minutes later, walked down the highroad neatly dressed. He caught a five-

The Happy Profession

thirty bus, patronized the ferry, and shortly after six reached his hangout in the city.

"I was all in," said Jim, "in, body and breeches. The woman who looked after us gave me three little pricks with a dope needle and it was three days before I left that bed. When I got round again, they told me that my pal was in the hospital. The doctors gave him one chance and the cops were standing by to see whether he took it. That's all I know."

Jim had more time on his hands than I, for he was retired from business and I active, but we found many a half hour for talk and I got from him much of the know-how of his trade. Above and below the line which divides the upper from the under world, it seems, society is ranged in circles, each a little higher than the last, and an accomplished cracksman hankers for the society of a porch climber not one whit more than a gentleman of the Union Club for the companionship of his white-collared clerk. Scattered through the city, as the police well knew, sometimes in a slum alley, sometimes cheek by jowl with respectable uptown residences, were friendly hangouts where a man might go after a night's excitement or a few years in stir, get a bed and a welcome, something to drink, a shot of cocaine when it was needed, and, most refreshing of all, companionable talk from fellow travelers along the same road.

So much I heard that I wanted to see, and I asked Jim to take me on one of his rounds. We fixed on an evening. I dressed for the part, left my watch and wallet under my shirts in the bureau drawer, slipped just three dollars into my waistcoat pocket, told a discreet friend (as the simplest of precautions) where I was off to, and boarded a Fourth Avenue car going south. Halfway down the Bowery I alighted at the designated street. Midnight was striking. Timing it to the minute, there was Jim sauntering north as if he had not a

Friends and Crooks

care in the world. For five minutes we strolled in and out of streets and alleys and stopped at what seemed to me a singularly uninviting spot. We were opposite an unlighted tunnel, perhaps five yards long opening directly on the street, and at the further end I could see a flight of steps disappearing to the second floor. "A mousetrap," I said to myself, as we entered the hole, mounted the stair, and found ourselves in a large dance hall completely hidden from the street. There were rows of chairs and tables along the wall, in them a long string of sailors, half a dozen roustabouts, and a few men in blue shirts and bright cravats, with a girl or two in every group. The proprietress, a lady of formidable dimensions in a red wig, topped with a commanding comb, was seated at a big desk just across the room. "The fence," whispered Jim. "She does the trading," he added as he led me to the only empty table. A waiter came up. I ordered a brace of whiskies and handed the man a two-dollar bill, saying distinctly, "That's two dollars." Presently he returned with the drinks but not the change. I was a boy at my first party, but I knew this was the test. No gentleman of standing in this community would let a waiter get away with that. I called out sharply, "Change please," and got it.

Then Jim and I fell into a most interesting conversation. Never pointing, never looking in any particular direction, he gave me a who's who of the company. He seemed disappointed that I should be so unfamiliar with famous names, but with a spark of fire in his eye whispered of certain dramatic happenings I had noticed in the newspapers, never affirming but suggesting that a good many actors in famous casts were here present. The talk absorbed me and it was almost by accident I looked up. Instantly a comely young woman, pink and trig in her dotted shirtwaist, who sat chatting with a sailor on the bench opposite, caught my eye with hers. I looked down;

The Happy Profession

glanced again. Her eyes were still fixed on mine and with the same understanding stare she rose and walked across the room straight toward me. "For God's sake!" I whispered. "Who am I?" Jim was quick as thought. "Pittsburgh, six years, forgery," he said in syllables I could just catch as the lady came alongside. "Have a chair," I said, "and a drink." She turned to Jim: "What's his line?" But I gave the answer. "Penmanship." She smiled and sat down. "So I guessed," she remarked, and I felt that my clothes suggested an adroit rather than a rough profession. I did not care for the personal turn the conversation was taking, and merely grunting, "Six, in stir, Pittsburgh. Just out," carried the attack to the enemy. "How's business?" I asked. "Brisk," she replied. "Last night I turned a curly-headed sailor boy on his head and frisked him sixty plunks' worth." And then she told me how sweet the boy had been on her. The conversation grew intimate but Jim was uneasy. "Got to be going," he said, and I admit it was refreshing to pass through the black tunnel and see the stars shining overhead.

In and out we walked through streets and alleys. Jim stopped before a door. There was a diamond Judas in it about five feet from the ground. "My club," he said, and put his face directly in front of the tiny window. All was black inside. Jim rang the bell. In a moment there was light within and I caught plain sight of a very steep flight of stairs and at their top another door with another Judas; a man's face was looking through it. Jim pressed his own nose against the pane in the street door, and a lanky chap in a waiter's apron came down the stair and unshot two bolts. "Friend," said Jim hooking his thumb toward me. The waiter threw the door open, let us in, shut it again, and slammed both bolts. We climbed the stairs and I found myself in what seemed an ordinary restaurant of the cheapest sort. A succession of high-backed

Friends and Crooks

settles ran the length of both walls of the long narrow room, giving a sense of privacy to the tables between them. In the cubicles on both sides of the passage sat the "members" of the club in twos and fours bending over their beer and ham and eggs. We took an empty table, ordered, and bent forward to hear each other's confidences so that our heads came close together. Our table, in which Jim seemed to feel a sense of proprietorship, was perhaps two thirds of the way up the line. "See those lowest tables?" he whispered. "Riffraff, second-story men and such. Just above are fellers in business, penmen like you and chaps like me. And you notice that slick little article opposite? He's a lawyer with quite a trade. There up beyond us are the real boys, cracksmen, and that top table, those are yeggs. They blow the banks."

It was a model of a well-ordered society. Nobody disputed authority. A man was content to wait until his talents were recognized and his turn came. Everyone knew his place and everyone understood the way that led up in the world.

Poor Jim! His heart yearned for a career, but he knew he was through. His nerves had gone flabby. On our way uptown, we stepped on a car just as a burly cop brushed roughly by on his way out. Jim's face turned white as milk. He had nothing to fear. He was squared with the world, but he shook violently and his jaws began working. "I've seen so many of them!" he said simply.

It was useless trying to get work for Jim in New York. I wrote to a friend in St. Louis and eventually found a job for him running an office elevator where he could ruminate and take his ups and downs more philosophically.

CHAPTER XI

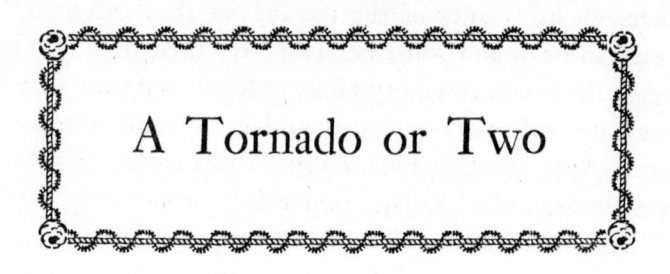

A Tornado or Two

WHAT's in a name? Everything. To Bob Wilson and me the name *Leslie's* meant wish-wash and failure. The proprietor, accustomed to think his trademark a large capital asset, was reluctant, but we needled and nudged and worried him till finally he consented that henceforth we should be the *American Magazine*. We registered the new trademark in Washington. A week too late, Mr. Hearst, thinking of his Sunday Supplement, applied for copyright on the name, but we had it — the *American Magazine*. That small piece of luck filled me, somehow or other, with great expectations. There was no hope animating Mr. Micawber which I did not nurse in my own bosom — and something did turn up. A revolution — I had seen it coming — occurred in *McClure's Magazine* and the most brilliant staff ever gathered by a New York periodical left Mr. McClure in a body. Some outlet they had to have and one miraculous day they signed a contract assuming the burden of debt under which we had been staggering, throwing in a little cash beside, and taking over the magazine. Blessed be the word "American." The name has salvation in it. Just what the price was I forget, but it topped half a million in debts assumed, inventories accepted, and cash paid, and it secured my precious savings. Of the whole, some sixteen or seventeen thousand dollars were coming to me from my small holding. My last interview with the proprietor dealt with that detail. It was painful to both of us.

"The money goes for the debts," he said, "when printer and paper man are paid, there's little enough cash for the rest of us, but of course we must all share and share alike. It means about 80 per cent discount I'm afraid."

The Businessman with the heart of Bessemer steel! I had often published stories about him, and now I took a leaf from his copybook.

"My stock is for sale at one hundred cents on the dollar," I said. "I paid a hundred for it and it's worth that to me. Could I talk fairer than that?"

Had he been a real partner to me I should have taken a different tone, but all I could remember was his scrouging and whimpering and encumbering me with help. I stood my ground. The Boss's face took on the expression he had turned on the cashier one night I could remember. It looked as though someone had sprinkled flour over it. "After all our struggles together! After five years!" But I was in no sentimental mood. I merely asked whether he would buy my stock. For him the whole bargain depended upon it and he did. I never saw him again.

Whoever it was that listed the Deadly Sins took little note of human nature. The Seven bear down too hard on the positive side. It is the negative sins which when we are miserable have done most to bring on the misery: acts not criminal but short of honesty, conduct inert, devious, and false.

A young man out of a job is a young man in a hurry. The talent had left *McClure's*. There was room for commoner stuff. I applied there for a job and found it, but what that job was I never knew. When I began one task I was sure to be switched to another. I began to think myself a problem child.

A year at *McClure's* was an adventure of quality. It enabled me to watch at close range a very remarkable man. Mr. McClure had genius, there was no doubt of that, genius with all its coruscations. But his genius was an amalgam. Something I do not like to call charlatanry but which certainly was dross was mixed in with it: perhaps that is an invariable concomitant. No man's flame burns wholly pure. But somehow Mr. McClure's word was not like the word of other people. It was spoken in enthusiasm. It was reviewed in an atmosphere where new interests had arisen and ardor had cooled into indifference. After all, few colors are fast when winds and rain have beaten upon them.

I do not think that Mr. McClure ever thought he lied any more than a greater man of somewhat kindred temperament whose word was often questioned, Theodore Roosevelt. The thought of both men was tinged with emotion. The emotion they remembered long after the dry and literal words of talk crumbled into forgetfulness. What is truth has troubled historians as well as philosophers. Is literalness the test? Is it the genuine feeling, the hot enthusiasm, which registers veracity, or is it the analytical dissection of a bargain in cooler weather and in other circumstances? Men like McClure think so fast that precisely what they say seldom registers. After all a thing is said in one mood. In quite another it seems reasonable to retract it. These are all nice questions. What I can affirm is that people who made a bargain with McClure were not invariably apt to find that the terms which remained in their minds completely tallied with his recollection. I recall the office one melancholy day. Mr. McClure was away and a lady of obvious consequence came in, leaning on her ebony stick asking sharply where he was to be found. It was Mrs. Humphry Ward, and through the office went the rumor that on

A Tornado or Two

Mr. McClure's latest trip abroad he had heard of a forthcoming serial of hers and had offered twenty thousand dollars for it, but that when the manuscript arrived and the readers called it a disappointment — a washout was, I believe, the term used — Mr. McClure had written to Mr. Phillips, his partner, kindly to see to it that the manuscript was returned and the matter explained to Mrs. Ward.

A man cannot be the sum of all the virtues. Mr. McClure had many, and I like to dwell on them. One which I prize highly was his enthusiasm. That was a burning force. He never liked the word "crusade" but when he went crusading, he might have given points to Peter the Hermit. Everyone about him caught fire and he would inflame the intelligence of his staff into molten excitement. The mood would be too hot to last but would bring results. Should anyone object that another magazine had printed an article on the very subject he was suggesting, the chief would run his hand through his electric hair and shout: "You say other magazines have told that story. You are wrong. A story is never told till McClure tells it."

He had a Napoleonic belief in his own star. Small wonder! That star had led him out of the Irish bog which had once been home. It had guided him to America. It had shown him how to pick up an education of sorts. It had pierced the blackest night of poverty and had brought him to success. More than all, when he was a farm boy in a hand-me-down suit it had encouraged him to ask a professor's daughter, a girl far above him in station and in accomplishments, please to wait for him for seven years while he proved himself worthy of her, and, in the very teeth of her father's natural opposition, to marry her when the time was out.

Mr. McClure's mind embraced everything an editor needs to store there — and nothing more. It was purely eclectic. Of the past he knew nothing, but every contemporary idea seethed promiscuously in his brain. He professed to have read Homer and Virgil, too, in his youth, but they were the only dead authors in which I ever heard him evince the slightest interest. Asked once by Mr. Kipling how he liked *David Harum*, McClure replied: "Never read him. He's dead." And quick as light Kipling commented: "The mark of genius, McClure, is to eliminate the unnecessary."

Eliminate the unnecessary he certainly did. His brain traveled light as a man's should when he is constantly on the move. Its cargo was living writers, living ideas. It never occurred to him that the dead past had something to do with them, the dead who are so living to us. On the other hand it never took a reputation to attract him to an author so long as the author was producing. With talent, he made electrical contact. Stevenson, Meredith, and Kipling he may have taken for granted, but that was only because they were friends and gave sustenance to him, Sam McClure, whose infallible divining rod was his personal enthusiasm. And always he gave in return. Pick up Stevenson's *Wrecker* and see the gay portrait of Sam McClure in the delightful guise of Jim Pinkerton. Conan Doyle had not emerged from obscurity when McClure swooped down upon him, bought twelve stories, and recklessly paid him sixty dollars apiece.

"I had but one test for a story," he said, "and that a wholly personal one — simply how much the story interested me. I always felt I judged a story with my solar plexus rather than with my brain; my only measure of it was the pull it exerted on something inside of me. Of course sometimes one is influenced by his own mood; if one is feeling more than usually vigorous he is apt to transfer some of his own high spirits to the story he is reading. To avoid being influenced by this, I always made a rule of reading a story three times within seven days to see whether my interest kept up. I have often been carried past my station on the elevated, going home at night — reading a story I had read before within the same week." As every sound editor must, Mr. McClure talked to everyone he met. Never, he declared, did he pick up an idea sitting still. Notions came to him from everywhere — from everywhere but the past. He was forever on the move to the future. Seventeen successive nights in a sleeper did not terrify him. He seldom wrote, for he had small gift for expression and could employ plenty of men who had. One paragraph borrowed from his recollections sums up his tumultuous existence.

"From 1890 on," he wrote, "I was overcome more and more often by periods of complete nervous exhaustion. When I had to get out of my office and out of New York City, when I felt for my business the repulsion of the sea-sick man for the food he most enjoys in health. Crossing the ocean would relax this tension. New interest would take hold of me in London or Paris and before I knew it, I was picking up ideas again. Good editorial work can only be done out of spontaneous personal interest; it cannot be forced. To lose his enthusiasm is the worst thing that can happen to an editor — next to having been born without any. In Europe I always got a renewal of power to be interested; and that for me was simply the power to edit an interesting magazine."

The blessed quiet of those days when McClure was abroad! The dove of peace descended upon the office and every man took up his own life.

Poor McClure! His misfortune was to have had his career before an Atlantic crossing squeezed six days into twelve hours. His tempo was always beyond the speed of the old universe. The aeroplane would have helped the world to catch up with him and would have spurred him to higher

The Happy Profession

bursts of celerity. His was a toy copy of the tragedy of Napoleon, who never had the atomic bomb to play with.

I should have understood Mr. McClure better had I then been more familiar with his past. He was a trafficker in ideas; by education as well as by instinct a peddler. His history is all of a piece. At Knox College he had stretched his course from four to seven years through constant pauses to peddle kickshaws through the countryside. For hundreds of miles he traveled from door to door. When he could, he drove. When he couldn't, he walked. If a farmer's wife refused to buy, at least she would not refuse to gossip, and young Sam never left the kitchen door without adding some new quirk of human nature to his stock in trade, to be retailed in after years through his newspaper syndicate or his magazine.

To sum up: a week in the McClure office was the precise reversal of the six busy days described in the first chapter of Genesis. It seemed to end in a world without form and void. From Order came forth Chaos.

Executives are self-made, and spare God the responsibility. Never, I affirm, in American business, was there a brighter talent than McClure's for disorganization. If the chief did not originate a design, he could at least obfuscate it. One day he found me working assiduously at some task assigned by a minor authority. Mr. McClure, striding through the office, happened unfortunately to glance in my direction. "What are you doing?" he said sharply. "No matter what it is, put it away. Go home and lay on my desk at nine tomorrow a list of twenty ideas, twenty good ones. Now get on."

The staff worked under some natural law of desperation. The chief was forever interrupting, cutting every sequence into a dozen parts. He would foster ideas of his own, sitting on them like a mother hen till they hatched, but with the process of other people's business, he had small patience.

A Tornado or Two

There were despondent attempts at self-protection. Schemes were constantly made to circumvent his activities. Since the office could not harbor a quiet desk, so by collusion with the cashier, the staff would hire a secret room in some hotel and then until the hide-out was discovered, a systematic effort would be made to finish an article before the deadline. The device never served for long. All New York was within too easy reach, and there were occasions when staff articles would only be written in the precarious security of a Washington bedroom.

Yet with all his pokings and proddings the fires he kindled were brighter than any flames his staff could produce without him. The sun will burn up anything that comes too near, but it remains the source of life and light, and the intensity of McClure's enthusiasm would bring any project to a white heat. Extraordinary as it was in a man so comprehensively devoted to disorder, his word was *thorough*. He would have Steffens or Stannard Baker work two months or three on an article to ensure absolute accuracy. Miss Tarbell toiled for three years on her serial history of Standard Oil, but when it was done, the work was invulnerable. No abler group than the McClure staff ever labored in an American vineyard. But in journalism the standard is everything, and the standard was set by McClure himself.

For that I honor him. Slipshod work, even in tiny details, he would not tolerate. Strange in so romantic a man, but (Mr. McClure was full of contradictions) to him, a fact was a fact to be scrutinized, attested, indubitably fixed. Of course in this scrupulosity the law of libel played its minatory part, but McClure's passion for accuracy (in everything but his own assurances) was a noble trait. In the office of the old *New York World* there used to hang a placard, ACCURACY, ACCURACY, ACCURACY, but that seemed a mere safeguard against damages. In *McClure's*, accuracy was a moral force.

Mr. McClure had a standard for writing quite as high as his standard for facts. The staff accepted it and lived up to it. They gave him something beyond their best. It was not style McClure taught. Tradition, so living to the rest of us, meant nothing to him, but he knew that what interested him would interest the world and the thing he demanded was its expression in clear, logical, intelligible, hard-hitting form. He had also the artist's instinct against exaggeration. He reverenced the power of understatement. "Always," he shouted, when in one of his excoriating articles Lincoln Steffens pilloried Tom Platt, "understate the facts. Always understate the facts. When *McClure's* calls Tom Platt a moral leper, *McClure's* understates the facts."

It was miraculous how in that incandescent office the forces of attraction and repulsion were kept so nearly in balance; that with all the subterranean rumblings and occasional little spurts of flame, the explosion was so long postponed. But come it did, and one day John Phillips, the office seismograph, measuring the tremors and apparently controlling them, Miss Tarbell the historian, the dynamic Steffens, Stannard Baker, fairest of reporters, Henry Siddall, the handy man, and Bert Boyden, assimilator of rancors, dearest of companions, walked away, recruiting the pungent Mr. Dooley on the way, and, to my own blessed relief, taking over the *American Magazine*.

To turn from Mr. McClure to his minion, that parade of all the talents from *McClure's* to the *American Magazine* meant to me twin blessings in one. It took the burden off sore shoulders and it gave me a fresh start. I had taught myself what I could and it was time to study under a master of the trade. Besides, my pride was stirred. The very name, *McClure's Magazine*, had an irresistible attraction for any young man

A Tornado or Two

who believed the American world susceptible of improvement and wished to be counted in as a "helper" on the job of improving it. The magazine had been yeast in the ferment of the era of Theodore Roosevelt. True it was that the President, in one of his astute oscillations to the Right, had borrowed a pungent phrase from Bunyan and stigmatized McClure as the Man with the Muck-rake, but that charge had been political and unfair. *McClure's* hunted alone. It never joined the pack of sensationalists; when it indicted a man or an institution it gave chapter and verse. It never murdered by innuendo nor massacred by invective. Its onslaughts were coherent, cogent, lethal, but the general policy of the magazine was constructive. It supported orderly progress. It had become an American institution of which multitudes had a right to be proud.

So it was I started with high hope and for an uncomfortable year I served Mr. McClure, constantly to his dissatisfaction. He was too unpredictable to be a good teacher, but there were fitful opportunities for education, and through the miserable months I did not altogether want for content. New stars went flashing through the office. Will Irwin, Sam Adams, and the rest, came, quarreled, and went their way. Only Miss Cather, secure in her respected genius, remained apparently unmindful of office thunderstorms. The magazine grew more and more unsettled. New changes were in the air. My own services, quite obviously to me, were not indispensable. To this day I think that when Mr. McClure turned me off, he treated me scurvily. That may be owing to my self-esteem, but it certainly was worth a month's salary to be free and able to tell the chief, face to face, the good and evil I thought of him. When we parted with a little rising temperature all round, he certainly expressed very moderate confidence in my future and I had my own chance.

The Happy Profession

"Mr. McClure," I said, "I admire you for your accomplishments and for the tenacious enthusiasm which has brought them about. And there is one thing you have taught me I shall never forget. The money you have made, you take at its real value. You never hug a dollar. You use it as a counter to buy opportunity. You never regard it as anything but a tool." He seemed pleased with this, and in a burst of candor I ended: "You could do anything, anything, if the truth were in you. *But it's not.*"

These were severing words, words angry and perhaps unfair. I was party to a quarrel and Mr. McClure may have been more right than I. I flushed and walked out, expecting him never to speak to me again. But whatever his faults, Mr. McClure did not harbor rancor. Two years later, when I sat at the *Atlantic's* desk buried in manuscript, I realized that a friendly hand was on my shoulder and looked up at Mr. McClure's smiling face. He had come in to wish me well — and possibly to pick up some stray idea that might be lying about the office.

Twenty years passed, sad years for Mr. McClure. Long since, he had sold his magazine to Mr. Hearst, and with the magazine, his name. His newspaper syndicate was dead or very sick. A dozen grandiose plans had come to nothing. He was desolate and alone. One day walking up the Avenue I caught sight of a familiar figure ahead of me. It had lost the old confident walk and moved wearily. It was a cold autumn day and I noticed Mr. McClure had no overcoat. My old feeling of admiration welled within me. I quickened my steps and touched his arm.

"Mr. McClure," I said, "you look depressed, and you look cold. I'm sorry." He shook my hand. "Yes," he said, "they've got me down. They've taken everything. They've taken my money. They've taken my magazine. They've taken my *name*."

A man pays the price of his talent. It throws his weight heavily on one side. The cry for justice is the rebellious cry of mankind. In nature there is no justice nor semblance of it but there does seem to be a sense of balance, and if some exceptional quality overloads a man on one side, there is likely to be an exceptional defect on the other. Defects there always are, but it is the positive things that count. The Ten Commandments have got us all into the habit of thinking what we ought not to be and do, while the New Testament has never got us altogether out of it. Mr. McClure may have paid a high price for his talents, but they were wonderfully worth having, and while he kept them shining, they were an inspiration to the rest of us, and lighted a bright candle in the world.

CHAPTER XII

Sunny Weather

A GREAT and a glorious thing it is to be free and slave no more, but after the first exhilaration of it, the counterbalancing alternative of learning to live on nothing a year dampens one's satisfaction. Shortly before my dismissal from *McClure's*, like the hero of any other story, I had made a superb gesture and, withdrawing all my savings save four hundred dollars, from the bank, had purchased a corner house on upper Park Avenue. On top of my slender equity was piled one mighty mortgage after another, but I was the owner and, for all my neighbors knew, might be enjoying an income of thirty or forty thousand a year. But when on the afternoon of my deliverance I went home, those mortgages took visible shape. There they were, weighting down the roof, and to sleep beneath them was a strain on the nerves. Before a week was out, freedom had gone where freedoms go, and I found myself working as a book editor for the ancient firm of D. Appleton and Company. In its day Appleton's had been a mighty house, but had crashed in a panic and was now in the hands of bankers. It is my considered opinion that bankers are not much in the publishing line, but this group was fortunate in selecting as their representative Joseph Hamblen Sears. Sears, scion of a line of sea captains, had been a hero and still looked the part. When I

Sunny Weather

was a freshman his glory had not faded from the Harvard Yard, for had he not been fullback of the '89 team, and what was then the extremity of Harvard hopes had *almost* beaten Yale. His was the dawn of that bright day in '90 when Arthur J. Cumnock actually led a Harvard team to victory. Him, history remembers: —

> *Arma virumque cano*
> 'Twas Arthur J. Cumnock you know.

But Sears had played his part and I went to work under him with a will.

It was a hard-bitten office but not unpleasant, and what was for me a prime factor, many of its clients were interesting people. Theodore Dreiser used to barge in and out. His was a drab and heavy figure, drab and heavy as his novels. He was a castigator by profession, but I looked at him with admiring wonder, for it was he who had written *Sister Carrie*, a novel with more uncontaminated pathos than any book of the day. *Sister Carrie* remains a landmark too in the history of Convention. It deals resolutely with facts and its appeal to the emotions lies in its perfect candor; but as the century began the horror Society displayed when reminded of its weaknesses was a thing to marvel at.

Doubleday's was under contract to publish the novel, but its heroine was a lady of such easy virtue that the publishers were appalled. It was the height of the Comstockian era.

> Anthony, oh Anthony!
> Don't mind the people's roars.
> We'll cover up the table legs
> With cotton flannel drawers.

I omit the final stanza as more inelegant.

So we sang, but none the less, Anthony Comstock's ghost

The Happy Profession

stood beside every editor's desk shaking a minatory finger. Everybody felt the influence of that stern warning. Doubleday begged the author to reconsider, and when he would not, the firm issued the novel in felt slippers, without a word of advertisement. The book died its foreordained death. It rose again and today, in spite of the unadulterated journalism of its style, *Sister Carrie* remains a study of deep and unfeigned emotion. The other day I reread it. The style is the style of a country newspaper, but Carrie, with her tinsel ambition, is a living person and the pathos of the story still strikes home.

Dreiser was at continuous odds with the world, but as he went beetling about seeking where to bite it, there was one weak spot in his own carapace. Ask him about dramatic criticism and he would react with violence. To enemies and friends the reason was famous in those days. He had started life on a St. Louis paper and when as an eighteen-dollar-a-week reporter he was appointed dramatic critic at a salary of thirty dollars, he seemed to have reached the heights. But Dreiser was ambitious. His predecessor had reviewed one play a night. He would triple the score. He would review three plays a night. Of course the criticism had to be written from handouts before the theatrical openings, but all three of them were polished off to the critic's satisfaction and set in type for the morning paper. Now vaulting ambition overleaped itself. A great storm arose. Three trains were late; three companies stranded; three theaters remained dark that night, and in the morning criticisms of three unperformed performances were there for all to read. Rival newspapers did not keep the secret. The critic did not wait to be fired. He accepted a reporter's salary on another journal and returned to his accustomed eighteen dollars a week. The distrust of the world which beset him his whole life long was not lessened by this incident.

Sunny Weather

As sunrise to sunset in comparison with the lugubrious Dreiser, there was Joe Lincoln; dear Joe, with his hardy annuals from Cape Cod. No *Sister Carrie* for him. Decency was decency on the Cape. And in the end right was always might; no shadow of doubt about that; never a trace of smut sullied the white walls of his cottages. Many a long afternoon have I spent with Joe in a Sixth Avenue restaurant, answering every chuckle of his with a comment or suggestion on the manuscript lying before us. Lincoln was what publishers love to call a "property." The sale of his books was certain-sure and their royalties could be clipped like coupons.

Perhaps the gayest of our visitors was Robert W. Chambers, then at the height of his delightful reputation. His books, regular as clockwork, were worth betting on. They were big business and might be very big business indeed. Chambers was master of a single magic formula. The dashing, lovable hero always had the lady at a disadvantage and, as Joe Sears used to say: "He always could, but he always didn't." It was the embodiment of the moral tradition of the Republic, and Chambers deserved every dollar he made. Each autumn he would bring in a new novel, and every spring a fresh volume of short stories.

A singular and impressive figure often came to the office. David Graham Phillips was a handsome young man inches above six feet, powerfully built, but with an air of austerity about him and a marked disposition to quarrel which made any casual greeting one might offer a little formidable. Of publishers he thought, just naturally, as rascals. At a freshwater college he had chummed with Albert Beveridge and both young men had gone into the world with the determination to transform it to their liking at any cost. Phillips thought it a bad, black world and wrote about it long, somber novels not devoid of power and chock-full of purpose. All night

The Happy Profession

long he wrote them, standing upright at a lectern borrowed by way of an antique shop from some tabernacle to keep himself alert. Reform was his mistress, but he wanted to transform her into a slave to do his bidding in the world. He lived novels as well as wrote them, and his life, we were told, was filled with violent encounters of love and hate. To women he was mysteriously attractive, and in the course of highly intimate conversation one lady has confided to me that her passionate admiration led her to write him the most candid and engaging of notes, offering to fly with him to parts unknown. Fortunately his answer was in the most scrupulous tradition. He, like young Werther,

> For all the wealth of Indies
> Would do nothing for to hurt her.

She told me that her father, whom she adored, had been violently opposed to the whole project, but I judged it was with profound regret that she had acquiesced in the decision.

One morning the newspapers carried a tragic story. David Graham Phillips had been found dying on the sidewalk with four bullets in his chest. The murderer, who promptly did away with himself, was apparently under some illusion the novelist had used his sister as a model for one of his realistic studies of the fair and frail.

From that little world of Appleton's many figures slip to and fro on the screen of my remembrance: one remains constant. Mr. William Appleton was a tranquil, quiet man, a little proud and reserved. He sat at a desk next mine outside the rail dividing employers from employed. A tall and singularly handsome man, he had seen days of greatness. Once he had been a partner in an opulent firm. His brother Daniel was Colonel of the Seventh Regiment, and his family had always been accustomed to accept the best as theirs in the

Sunny Weather

gracious order of nature. I am not sure that his capacities were more than modest, but character he had. Day after day he sat there, a pensioner at a living wage for his name's sake. The bankers thought it fitting that one Appleton should justify the continuing use of the firm name, and Mr. William Appleton trod the daily round with memories and without hope. His hands I remember were always beautifully white, making me horribly conscious of the state of my own fingernails. Never have I seen a man of more habitual courtesy. There was a gentleness about him, and a delicacy, which bore strong contrast to the rough-and-ready company peopling the office. I think of him as a candle in the world of neon lights. He was always quietly cheerful, never letting fall a word that could be interpreted as a call for sympathy, though God knows I was ready enough to offer it. I never heard him suggest an idea serviceable to business, but the whole office was conscious he was sitting there amongst them and was the better for it. Everyone knew that it had taken many generations to make him the gentleman he was.

Always I had been faintly bored with the sentiment of Thackeray's *Newcomes*, but when I came to know Mr. Appleton, I entered with my whole heart into the famous paragraph which sums up the book: —

> At the usual evening hour the chapel bell began to toll and Thomas Newcome's hands outside the bed feebly beat time. And just as the last bell struck, a peculiar sweet smile shone over his face and he lifted up his head a little and quietly said "Adsum" and fell back. It was the word we used at school when names were called; and lo, he whose heart was that of a little child had answered to his name and stood in the presence of his Master.

If nothing else gives enjoyment in this world, hope will. And through all those New York years, hopes buoyed me up

The Happy Profession

from day to day. But one embracing hope transcended them all. I had tried a good sampling of employers and found them not altogether to my liking. What I wanted was an employer whom I could trust as a child trusts his mother. I hankered for a kind, sympathetic, considerate, intelligent boss, a boss who would take special interest in me — the kind of man I could respect and understand — and it seemed to me I might never be wholly satisfied until I took the job myself. Gradually my determination was fixed. I would be my own boss and thence it followed that the business of my new employer must be a very modest one. The idea took root long before I left college. If by hook or crook I could get hold of the *Atlantic*, I would make a go of it. This ambition did not seem immoderate. When Walter H. Page took the magazine into his vigorous hands (it was during the time of my college life) the magazine did not number five thousand subscribers, and from what I could learn, the annual deficit, always expected and as readily realized, was charged to advertising by the owners, Messrs. Houghton, Mifflin and Company. Divorced from this substantial house, the *Atlantic* would be just the type of diminutive business which I thought I could handle. The magazine was long on tradition, and I liked tradition; it was short on realization, and that, energy could supply. According to my diagnosis, what the magazine suffered from was its position as the very small fifth wheel of a very cumbersome coach. What it needed was the individual devotion of a small and compact organization. One day, as I have been reminded — I must have been a college junior at the time — a Yale contemporary came to see me. We exchanged confidences. What was he going to do? He was not sure. Had I plans? Yes. I proposed to edit the *Atlantic*. "Gee whizz," said he.

This idea was a notion prudent to keep to oneself. I cultivated the benevolent acquaintance of Mr. Horace Scudder,

Sunny Weather

who had long been editor. He was a dear, devoted old man, much put upon by the firm. The *Atlantic* seemed the least of his duties for he was always working at his "knitting" as he called it — his green bag full of notes for school editions of copyrighted and profitable classics. To me he was the kindest of friends, asking me often to his house where I loved to hear him talk with admiration of New England Gods. He thought of editors as acolytes serving the altars of literature and often said to me, "Ellery, one thing I have never done. I have never *invited* a contribution to the *Atlantic*. If it is offered, I receive it. If it is good, I print it." This advice came quaintly from a distant past, but I loved the old gentleman who gave it.

Page succeeded Scudder. There was no nonsense about Page. Scudder would lead off the *Atlantic* with an admirable paper on the Upanishads, but under Page, the old magazine jumped forward a full century. A young man could not have had a more exhilarating tutor, and when I dared to send him a little contribution or two and they proved acceptable, I knew the privilege it was to hear him hold forth on the modern world. When I graduated, he asked me if I would come in as his assistant. It was not an appropriate time to confide my ambition to the man who held the job and I told him nothing of mine. But I did reflect that the road toward it should be more roundabout than the one that he suggested.

"Mr. Page," I said, "I'm afraid the *Atlantic* raft won't hold two." He laughed and agreed.

No man ever gave me more valuable hints on editing than Mr. Page. Any boy would have been excited by his energy and courage. The self-confidence of his vigorous mind was a thing to wonder at. I remember remarking to him: "Mr. Page, when you are elected Pope, of course you will accept."

After Page came Professor Bliss Perry, who gave the maga-

The Happy Profession

zine a warmth, a friendliness and a charm it had not known. He presided over the *Atlantic* for ten years, and in the tenth confided to me an important secret. He was going to retire. That was my chance. I felt it in my bones. The subsequent letter which I wrote to Mr. Mifflin offering to buy the magazine was only two pages long, but it took me a fortnight to compose it. No offer of marriage was ever formulated with a greater infinitude of pains, and when the answer came to say that Mr. Mifflin was interested and would see and talk with me, my soul was lifted up.

All through that winter our talks went on. Every other week end I would come on from New York. If I was enthusiastic, Mr. Mifflin was cautious, and I particularly dreaded the influence of his partner, Mr. Kay. Mr. Kay was a Scotch gentleman, dour and determined, whose pennies had come one by one, and one by one they certainly were paid out. When an expense of any kind was proposed by a junior, Mr. Kay's answer was ready: "Young man, I came to my office this morning with a single purpose, and that purpose is to say NO."

But despite all obstacles, dismal fears, and extravagant hopes, Mr. Mifflin and I did come to an agreement. Before he gave his consent to the sale of the magazine he offered me a junior partnership in the general firm, but when he saw that my heart was fixed on paddling my own canoe, he gave me his blessing.

I was to find fifty thousand dollars, and the *Atlantic* with all its tradition, its circulation of fifteen thousand copies, and its annual deficit of five thousand dollars, was to be mine. Here was my chance.

The last deficit had been entered on the *Atlantic* books.

My predecessors in the Atlantic Seat of Judgment had one and all been distinguished men. In a Brahminical community theirs was recognized as an Apostolic Succession, while my reputation was the better for being unknown. All through that winter of eternal conferences I wondered that Mr. Mifflin should be so wary, so very circumspect. Now I marvel at his temerity and the foolhardiness with which he closed the bargain. Throughout my life I have loved every man who has amused me. Mr. Mifflin amused me, but he terrified me too. He was the most genial of men but subject to sudden bursts of anger and even of truculence. He was a rigid believer in the established order. Born to comfort and position, from the day he left Harvard College the pride that was in him fixed his determination to come up through the ranks by the hard way. He went straight from the Porcellian Club to the printing shop at the Riverside Press and deviled at it there as grimily as any boy on the premises, often, as he liked to tell me, flat on the floor under the case mending an injured rack. By his own diligence he climbed the ladder and by his own right sat down in the president's chair of the most famous publishing house in America. To his printing partners, the Houghtons, he left, I imagine, the larger share of the swag, but after all, they remained printers; he was the publisher of great books. His library was lined with them, beautifully printed, admirably bound, but there is no scrap of evidence to show that he ever read one of them. He had a gift for telling a book by the look of it. The colophon of the House bearing the superlative initials "H. M. & Company" was enough for him. That did for a book something beyond any merit of the author. It transformed what had merely been a manuscript before into an achievement of pride and permanence. Mr. Mifflin handled a book with reverence. That was his perfect tribute to its excellence.

When I started work in the little live room that looks out so trustfully on the permanently dead in the Old Granary

The Happy Profession

Burying Ground, I felt that Mr. Mifflin's eye was upon me. I must show myself to be serious. I must wipe off the insouciance of New York. I must associate myself with some enterprise of obvious importance. For this I was primed. It was a full year before that I had heard of the existence of a diary kept by Gideon Welles, Secretary of the Navy in Lincoln's Cabinet. Seward, you remember, had determined to keep a needed checkup on his chief by jotting down each day's event and each day's evidence of the folly of the President in a journal of his own. That experiment as I remember lasted for three days, or was it two? The rush of life was too much for it. But Welles was a journalist by profession; he wrote easily and well. Gifted with all the prejudices of a cantankerous nature, he loved to set down proofs of human perversity. But he was honest, he was able, and his record of the rough material of history must be, I knew, of large importance. Nowhere else were set down the continuous firsthand reports of Cabinet meetings. Nothing else was known of the diary except that it was in the possession of Edgar T. Welles, son of the Secretary, and that he lived in New York.

During the months that followed the receipt of this useful information, I approached the prize with circumspection, but the progressive tantalization of the quest was hard for a young man to bear. Mr. Welles was pleasant, Mr. Welles was moderately communicative, but Mr. Welles would never, never make up his mind. Indeed three visits passed before he would so much as let me clap my eyes on the chest which contained the precious papers. It was only on my fourth call that I was permitted to enter Mr. Welles's chamber. There beneath the bed was a solid iron box with a huge padlock on the hasp. The key was on the chain in Mr. Welles's pocket. It was like the first act of a play in the spirit world. The medium was there in the flesh. The spirit was in the wardrobe always about to

Sunny Weather

materialize and always prevented by some malignant influence in the audience. After that day every call of mine was rewarded by a good look at the iron chest but never did it budge from beneath the overshadowing bed.

I had a game of chess on my hands, and there were few gambits I did not attempt. I appealed to history. I saluted the pride of the Welles family. I called upon the son to make the father famous. I talked like a confessor of "the wrong done to unborn generations" by depriving them of their natural inheritance. I even urged, though I did not think it a question of money, that the great Diary could command a price.

Mr. Welles was a shut-in. He spent his days in his comfortable apartment. Apparently he enjoyed my visits but the winter passed and I was not an inch ahead. Exasperated and determined, I went on another tack. I asked him about his boyhood in the Washington of Civil War days. Then I knew I had touched a spring, for he talked with animation and in his talk I seemed to discern the reason for his obduracy. Mr. Welles, it seemed, was an intimate and lifelong friend of Robert Todd Lincoln, son of the President and in later years Ambassador to the Court of St. James's. The two had been boys together, Robert in the White House, and Edgar serving as special assistant to his father, the Secretary of the Navy. The pair were about the same age and the tremendous impact of the war years made them almost brothers. In after time, Edgar had officiated as best man at Robert's marriage, and to the wedding of Edgar, Robert had brought the ring in his vest pocket. Although Mr. Welles never told me so in words, I was morally certain that it was to Mr. Robert Lincoln that he had referred the all-important question of the publication of the Diary, and I surmised that Mr. Lincoln had said "No."

The Happy Profession

After all the negative was very natural. Secretary Welles had been famous for his sharp tongue; there was always gall in his ink. Mr. Robert Lincoln was aware of that, and he remembered too that but for the magic of his father's name, his own substantial career could not have been achieved. His father's name! How marvelous had been the apotheosis of the martyred President! Descent from him partook of the nature of divinity. No new evidence could raise it nearer to heaven; conceivably, fresh facts might drag it closer to earth. Legend has the seeds of growth in it; disclosure has a way of whittling reputations down. There could be no question of the proper reply to Mr. Welles. The iron chest was the right place for the Diary.

All this was inference, but I felt its force. In any case, I determined to get all I could from my association with Mr. Welles. Here I was talking with a man who had seen history. He had run in and out of the White House during its heroic days. He had talked with Lincoln not once but often and familiarly. And — to me it seemed important — Edgar Welles, still under the astringent influence of his own father, could speak objectively of Father Abraham.

One experience of Mr. Welles's youth was graven on his recollection. He recalled a Sunday morning — I think it was during the operations against New Orleans to open the mouth of the Mississippi — the Secretary had gone to church, and Edgar was bidden to stay at the office in case there should be news. News there was and of the best. A telegram from Admiral Porter announced a great victory. Edgar knew its importance, but what to do with it? How casual were those old-fashioned habits! Sundays were days off, and business was entrusted to boys. Edgar hurried to the church door. The minister had not finished his sermon. He looked in upon the lairs of one or two old sea dogs. Nobody there. He ran to

Sunny Weather

the White House. The President was out, the doorman knew not where. Then in a flash he remembered having seen in the newspapers that General McClellan, back from the Peninsula, was in town to rest and report. By this time it was going on two o'clock when he rang the bell of the General's house. A darkey servant opened the door. The despatch was important? Well, the General was at dinner and did not wish to be disturbed. Would the gentleman please sit down and wait. Within the old brownstone house the hall was dark. A single gas jet at the further end made a solitary pin point of light. Edgar groped his way to a chair backed against the wall and sat down. In the corresponding chair across the hall was a shape, gaunt and black. Its outline took Edgar a moment to discern. He could make out that it was big and angular, and on its knees there rested some object that caught a faint line of light and seemed to be edged at the top with white. The boy's fancy played about the mystery. Gradually he recognized that the protruding white was a long envelope, the sheen, the light on a beaver hat. Suddenly the revelation came. McClellan was home from an exhausting campaign. Unwilling to disturb the General's dinner, the President of the United States was waiting on his convenience. What a scene! The humility of it was utterly out of place, absolutely wrong, but wonderful and infinitely touching.

Another story Mr. Welles told me which concerned Mrs. Lincoln. He remembered it in every detail, and what boy could forget it! Edgar was standing outside a shop on Pennsylvania Avenue when an open barouche drew up at the curb. In it sat the President, his features rigid as a graven image. Beside him, her voluminous hoop billowing about the carriage, sat Mrs. Lincoln. The darkey coachman stopped the horses not six feet away. The listener could hear every word of the conjugal conversation.

The Happy Profession

"I ask you one last time," Mrs. Lincoln was saying, "will you appoint him?"

"I will not," replied the President.

Mrs. Lincoln's voice seemed to burst with fury. "Abe," she said, "you appoint that man or I'll get right down on that sidewalk — and *roll*."

There was an instant's hesitation.

"All right," he said, "I'll appoint him."

The biographers have made a god of Father Abraham. They have bestowed upon him more humanity than is the right of mortal man. Yet from some strange sense of the proprieties they have drawn a quiet curtain over a supreme exasperation of his life and the full magnificence of his conquest over circumstance remains incomplete. No other President has so suffered, although the control of an imperfectly disciplined family has occasionally upset their equanimity. "I can do either of two things," Theodore Roosevelt would exclaim: "I can govern the United States, or I can govern Alice. I can't do both." But in speaking of Mr. Lincoln's tragic marriage, no lighter note should intrude. Mrs. Lincoln was a termagant and a horror, yet how is she remembered? The other day I turned the pages of a biography which made her the sweet heroine of romance, and even Carl Sandburg is so charitable that he thinks of her as a poet should think of every woman.

God knows Mr. Lincoln was great enough without the obscuring mists of legend. Another fifty years and his true lineaments will be lost in the fog of adulation, such as has eclipsed the great Washington, I fear, forever. The Father of his Country has become a togaed statue in white marble: its Preserver will be the brooding bronze of Saint-Gaudens's figure. Think in human terms of the virago with whom Lincoln was compelled to live. Think of that camel's straw atop

Sunny Weather

of burdens too great for human bearing. Then it is that Lincoln's humanity emerges.

You will say I exaggerate, but the case is worse than this. Not only is evidence ignored but for the sake of the proprieties it is sometimes suppressed. Damn the proprieties! I can recall reading in its original manuscript form a chapter excised from the Memories of Carl Schurz as improper to publish. It told of a trip on the Potomac which General Schurz made in company with Mrs. Lincoln and set down verbatim a conversation on her part so vulgar and so venomous that it can fairly be described as outrageous. I have also seen with my own eyes a group of three letters written in Mrs. Lincoln's hand not three months after the murder of her husband. They were addressed to collectors on behalf of a fund for the benefit of the President's widow. Now is the time, she wrote, to secure subscriptions when the tragedy is fresh and feeling most poignant, and she begged her correspondent please to remember that they were at liberty to subtract 25 per cent from all moneys collected to reimburse them for their time and trouble. Are there lower limits to the despicable than that?

I read the letters and thought of the cross Mr. Lincoln had borne, with a lump in my throat. "What will be done with them?" I asked their owner, my kind friend, the late Mr. W. K. Bixby of St. Louis. He, too, knew Robert Todd Lincoln. "Of course," said he gravely, "the family would suffer. They can never be published."

I do not mean to say that some biographers are not as forthright as they are conscientious. While Albert Beveridge was at work on his stately history of Lincoln, I came to know and like him well. One day in my study at Beverly he brought me a sheaf of his opening pages. Beveridge was absolutely convinced of Lincoln's illegitimacy, and his first chapter so stated in set terms. It was my turn to be horrified. Not that his argument failed to convince me but that the case did not seem to me absolutely proved, and I dreaded lest the overpowering bluntness of the statement arouse a universal prejudice against the book.

"For heaven's sake," I exclaimed, "print the truth, but print it in fine type! Footnotes are privileged from Gibbon down. Drop your discussion to the bottom of the page, and the dignity of history will be upheld."

Beveridge acquiesced, and neither truth nor history suffered from the decision.

One other unforgotten story comes to me. I heard it twice and twice only from my father, who felt a lifelong repugnance in referring to a memory which, try as he would, he could never quite obliterate. It was on February 27, 1860, that Mr. Lincoln gave the address at Cooper Union which left so ineffaceable an impression behind it. Putting up at the Astor House the previous Saturday, he spent the next two days in extending his New York acquaintance. It is recorded that he called at the office of the *Independent* but historians have not been able to chronicle with precision the minor events of the visit. The Union League Club was not to be founded until three years later, but the need for it was everywhere in evidence, and on one of these crowded days, Mr. Lincoln was induced to drop in upon a spontaneous gathering of young Republicans. Among the passionate young men who composed it was my father, and when Mr. Lincoln entered, he was startled like the rest by the lubberly figure, but recognized the wise and kindly smile, and, like the rest, was on fire with expectancy for the Word for which they had waited so long, the Word which was to be their divine command — and Mr. Lincoln began with a story so foul I cannot put it on the paper before me. Worse than that, it was a Rabelaisian version of his first meeting with Mrs. Lincoln and the scene was an

Sunny Weather

outhouse. There were volunteers for death in the group and this was the message given them. There was horror in the dismay the young men felt. Not until the very end of the war could my father discern in its clarity the vast and noble outline of Mr. Lincoln's humanity.

I am carried far from Edgar Thaddeus Welles. Our talks went on and on. If ever the famous drip wore down the granite underneath, that was an authentic instance. It was a year before I secured the precious manuscript, but when I finally showed it to Mr. Mifflin, he smiled with pleasure. Confidence was on the rise.

CHAPTER XIII

Manners and Customs in the Hub

PHYSICIANS, as is notorious, cannot cure themselves. The lawyer who attends to his own business has a fool for a client. The businessman, tired or untired, has to live another life when his day's work is done; for what family would welcome a discussion of the merchandising problem he has been busy at, or yet the interest charges? Not so the editor. He does not live in separate compartments. His life, morning, night, Sundays, and holidays, is all of a piece — one succession of adventures in human nature, a series of close-ups of people of all sorts and stations. The clergyman indeed may know men's souls better for he is a traffic cop on the routes to Heaven, but the roads men travel on earth and the kinds of men who travel them are best known to the editor. All this, when I came of editorial age, I dimly understood and felt due gratitude to my profession. I was grateful, too, to practise it in Boston. At least I was grateful after the first few weeks of wonderment in a place which, as the wits said, was not a city at all but a state of mind. How anyone could think as Bostonians thought was for a time quite beyond me. Of course the Boston I speak of was not the Boston of population and statistics, of State and Federal Streets, of the wool trade and of cottons, fine and coarse. It was the Hub much as the Autocrat had left it, with Beacon Hill as its axle.

Manners and Customs in the Hub

For more than a century it had been the pleasant custom of Boston gentlemen of a certain position in life to form themselves into dining clubs. These social and succulent gatherings lent an intimacy to society which I found highly agreeable, and it seemed proof to me of the constancy of Bostonian nature that on the rolls of the first club I was privileged to join still stood the names of Paul Revere and Charles Bulfinch.

How well I remember my first dinner. Brooks Adams, *frère de son frère* who believed only in the god of the Adamses, and Barrett Wendell were my neighbors. Across the table was James Ford Rhodes, a brother-in-law of Mark Hanna and once a steelmaker who, his modest fortune made, had come to Boston to write history. The talk ranged high and wide, but I noticed never, as in New York, was money mentioned, nor markets, nor taxes, nor income, nor expenses. That was a relief to me. Often the conversation detached itself from earth and almost from time and space. It dealt with ideas, and what ideas! I had always connected champagne with an instantaneous confidence in a bright future, but the future that Adams and Wendell looked forward to was that Pit to which the Rhadamanthine doctrine of the Degradation of Energy inevitably consigns us. The doctrine itself is untarnished by a gleam of hope. Its high priest was of course Henry Adams, to whom Poincaré and other mathematicians had pointed the way; among Boston intellectuals it was received as gospel. The world of manners, of cultivation, of all that makes life worth living, being but the other face of the world of matter, was degenerating too. The future was bleak and black as coal in a wintry bin. Extinction lay ahead. All change led downward. Each day universal doom came inches closer. The little a man could do was to dig his heels in and stay for a fleeting instant the drop to perdition.

Now this sounds lugubrious. But the miracle of the Boston

dinner was that it was not. The oysters went down. The champagne went round. Amusing experiences were told. Witty things were said. We were all astonishingly cheerful although the golden age of slave labor was behind us and aristocracy but a memory. To be sure the hourglass was running out. Chaos and universal night were ahead. But the wine was good, the chairs comfortable, the table circled with agreeable people. *Dum vivimus, vivamus.* Chaos could wait!

When I got home that night words failed me. My wife was sitting up eager for my impressions, but all I could say was: "I'll be damned!"

I have never been totally overwhelmed by the conclusions of science. Somehow or other, they are always penultimate. The ultimate is something different, something quite unproved, and I felt in my bones that the timetable of all the horror to come would be shifted. Even a reprieve of five hundred thousand years or so affects the spirits, and by next morning I had recovered my equanimity.

The gods of Boston had gone in those days and the half-gods come, but as I look back, the good town seems to have held a remarkable society. Its brightest ornaments were men and women grown old, but the embers burned brightly and I felt myself warm and comfortable.

There was one group which, in long retrospect, still seems to me unique. As a matter of fact it was not a group at all, for each member was separate as an individual planet. But all alike were ancient widows, ladies beyond threescore and ten, their lives behind them, yet not one had lost her brilliance. Mrs. Gardner, of course, was the sun in that heaven. Among the ladies of the Renaissance you might have found her exact parallel, but hardly, I think, since. She had been, though it was long forgotten and never mentioned, the daughter of one David Stewart who had engaged with success in various com-

Manners and Customs in the Hub

mercial enterprises clustering about drygoods, and who represented a material world where aesthetic considerations were rather elbowed out by matters of fact. His daughter was sent to a polite school for young ladies and there chanced upon a friendship which had lasting consequences. Among the substantial families of Boston there is a certain lingering anemia which greatly benefits from the stimulation and sparkle of New York. To profit by it a young Miss Gardner had been sent thither for her education. She was immensely taken with the animated Miss Stewart and brought her home for a visit. It was Boston's opportunity and the young lady's brother, Mr. John L. Gardner, laid his name and fortune at Miss Stewart's feet. But to us Isabella Stewart had been forever Mrs. Gardner. She lent an unaccustomed shimmer to a staid and respected family, solid as the rock of Beacon Hill. Adam had been the first Gardener and, as for Stewart, it was a commonplace of legend that when she had picked up a great Stuart portrait, right under the collective nose of the Royal Family, and had been reminded by the King's chamberlain that His Majesty would be grateful for permission to take it over for family reasons, she had merely reminded him that she too was a Stewart!

Her taste seemed infallible. Of course she had the advantage of the wisest advisers of her time, Whistler, Sargent, Berenson, among them, but to take the best advice is as rare as to give it, and in the making of every choice she was the guiding spirit. Had she not picked out Berenson himself when he was a poor boy struggling through college and helped to educate him? Surely, then, she was entitled to his advice. I inquired of her once whether her first purchases were still among her favorites. "I asked that question of Mr. Frick," she replied. "His are in his cellar. Mine are on my wall." What other collector could say as much? I think, for example, of the late Mr. Jules Bache, who had a marvelous eye for a picture. "Come with me," he said when the same query was put to him, and he led me to the third-floor bathroom where hung two little genre pictures of dogs and hoops. Mrs. Gardner, I think, could have appraised the pictures on her nursery wall; but this I know, for it was told me by Mrs. Henry Higginson who in her girlhood as Ida Agassiz had studied in Italy with her dear friend, Miss Isabella Stewart. The young ladies were seventeen or thereabouts, and confided to each other their girlish ambitions. "I mean," declared young Miss Stewart with the decisiveness which never failed her, "to make a collection of the best pictures in the world and hang them in a palace worthy of them." This conversation must have taken place after Miss Stewart had visited that most delightful of galleries, the Poldi-Pezzoli Palace in Milan, for it was there, so Mrs. Gardner told me, that the vision came upon her.

Of course her hope, like every other hope in the world, was too bright to come quite true. Mrs. Gardner had millions, but not millions upon millions, and picture for picture, her masterpieces are hardly the equal of Mr. Frick's or Mr. Widener's. But it was her peculiar genius to make of what she had a whole more glorious than its separate elements. In all the world her palace is unique.

I have spoken of her inheritance direct from the Renaissance. The Lord, I verily believe, had not shaped another like her these four hundred years. She was profoundly, sometimes ecstatically, religious and she was without a worldly scruple. Her favorite saying: "Don't spoil a good story by telling the truth," had in it more than whimsical significance. What she wanted, that she would have. When the laws of Italy stringently forbade the exportation of works of art, a way could always be found to circumvent those laws, and,

Manners and Customs in the Hub

as we Americans love to think, an Italian tempted is an Italian lost. She loved physical pre-eminence, the grace and symmetry of young athletes. One day when she did me the honor to dine at my table long after she was seventy, she told me the history of the day before. She had risen at six, caught a football train for New Haven at eight, watched the thrilling game, applauded the victors, returned in a crowded coach of rollicking, hurrahing boys, and then had refreshed herself by going out to supper. There was no sacrifice she would not make to Beauty. She would pinch herself to the extremity of economy. She would go without her carriage; she would live on the top floor of her palace almost on a diet of herbs, but the magical canvas, the inspired bust, the glass of Chartres, the ruby that men must have died for, and the three great ropes of pearls which hung to her waist; these things she enjoyed, she adored, and out of the fullness of her joy would thank God for them, and in His Holy Name make offering to His Church of the intricate loveliness of a marble reredos.

The other ancient ladies, whom I knew much better than Mrs. Gardner, lived unsupported by magnificence of achievement. There was Mrs. George Howe, on whom I often called to hear once more her stories of Mr. and Mrs. Browning and of a carnival life in Venice which seemed to me hardly to have changed since Goldoni's time. She had been a close friend of William Morris Hunt, and there hung in her parlor noble sketches of his for the greatest of his achievements, the wonderful ceiling installed in the Capitol in Albany and destroyed in what was artistically the most tragical of American conflagrations. And only half a dozen doors below my house on the Hill lived Mrs. Bell, child of genius, daughter of Rufus Choate. The friend of countless Choates, I asked where the family hailed from. Before their Salem days, was it really

The Happy Profession

Hog Island, the huge whaleback rising over Ipswich marshes? "Yes," she said, "you see the transition — Hog, Shoat, Choate; only it was the other way — Choate, Shoat, Hog." Her humor bubbled like the Pierian Spring, and her talk took on the quaintest terms of fancy. Her native drollery bore no likeness to the wit of her dear friend, Dr. Holmes. There was no premeditation behind it. Never was it privily hid, to be furbished and polished and exhibited at the effective moment, but it sparkled of its own nature like a hillside brook. Mrs. Bell had read widely and thought largely, but there was never a hint of the bluestocking about her. She was a town mouse, never without expostulation to be carried off to the countryside where books give place to flowers and libraries are lost in the trees. "Slap Nature's green face for me!" she would say to a rural temptress, and the phrase would trickle through the Hub. Someone spoke to her about a young man whose face and manners were his fortune, and who often exhibited them in society. "Does he know anything?" asked a close friend. "Know anything!" exclaimed Mrs. Bell. "He doesn't even *suspect*." Her happy phrases were current coin. Every caller it seemed would bring away fresh gold from her mint. Of a lady come from Cape Cod she remarked: "She ate so many clams that her stomach rose and fell with the tide." No Bostonian but knew by heart her prophecy made upon the advent of the automobile. "It will divide," she declared, "all mankind into two classes — the quick and the dead"; and in more intimate vein to Mr. Justice Holmes, who expressed some surprise that Bostonians should take so kindly to the Valkyrie where heroes fall in love with their sisters, she exploded: "Isn't that just what you Jacksons and Cabots have been doing for years?"

Men come and men go in Boston. But women defy the

Manners and Customs in the Hub

tables of Life Insurance. Mrs. Bell, a widow herself, lived with her widowed sister, Mrs. Pratt, in a cozy little house not too far from the Library of the Athenaeum. Had Doctor Johnson's Circle lived again, how famous would have been those little ladies, but it is the glory of Boston that their inner history is their very own.

Amongst this delightful company, my own nearest friend was Mrs. James T. Fields. Her husband, dead long years since, had been the second editor of the *Atlantic*, and that of course made a bond between us. It had been Mr. Fields who brought into relief the real significance of the name "Atlantic" by making English writers quite as much at home in the pages of the magazine as Americans were. Of his achievement I was very conscious, and almost every week I made my way to Mrs. Fields's Charles Street house, stored with memories of the Augustan Age. There the Autocrat had held court. There Thackeray had stayed. There Dickens had shown himself her devoted friend. In the long parlor, its western windows looking over the far reaches of the Charles, I would find Mrs. Fields lying on her sofa, still lovely in her soft gray gown. How lovely she must once have been when, as Annie Fields, a wife decades younger than her bewhiskered husband, she welcomed talent and genius to her table. Just over her couch, still hung the portrait of himself, given her by the young Dickens, beardless and glowing with Copperfieldian glory. With Mrs. Fields the past was the present, and as she relived it I became half conscious that I myself had known those undying friends of hers.

An almost constant inmate of the house on Charles Street was Miss Sarah Orne Jewett, beautiful in feature, but to my thinking a little classical, reserved, and cold. She was still in fullest command of her entrancing gifts, but in talking to her, one never thought of the mistress of the Pointed Firs, but rather of a lady of wider horizons and more conventional domain.

One dinner at Mrs. Fields's I cannot forget. There were but five of us round the little table, bright with the red and white straw of Chianti flasks. Mrs. Bell was there, and George Woodberry, teacher of beauty and poet of involuted cadence, and the guest of honor, President Taft. The two ancient ladies were like players of swift badminton; good talk, winged retorts, quips, jests, and stories flew back and forth between them, and for two hours I watched tears of laughter stream down Mr. Taft's substantial cheeks.

In those days the burly figure of Edward Everett Hale no longer shadowed the Garden where Bela Pratt's gigantic bronze of him now stands, the human approximation, children must think, of a gorilla on his hind legs. The talented, agreeable, and lazy Aldrich had passed on his way, but "Marjorie Daw" was still very much alive, and the Bad Boy still romped and capered through the old Portsmouth House. Aldrich's quips, too, still brightened everyone's remembrance. Referring to his successor in the *Atlantic* chair, whose laborious days were in heavy-footed contrast to his own unscorned delights, he had muttered, "What a world, with Scudders in it!" and his remark on his own alien youth is still quoted. "I'm not real Boston, of course, but Boston-plated."

It was amusing living in the Hub of those days. J. S. of Dale, who was Frederic Jesup Stimson, yet to begin his diplomatic career, was in the background, distinguished and aloof. Old Thomas Wentworth Higginson, "Twigginson" as the irreverent called him in differentiation from the other Higginsons, still lived on in his abolition memories.

Perhaps the bulkiest figure in the literature of those years was John Fiske, who wrote philosophy for all to comprehend,

Manners and Customs in the Hub

and history for all to read. To an editor he was a lure and a triumph. Invariably behindhand as he was, if the deadline were a Monday, serial postals would come from him deprecating, promising, swearing that copy would come on Wednesday, on Friday, on the following Tuesday: a great chronicler, a magnificent interpreter, and as a procrastinator, a nonpareil.

I should like to write of Dr. Crothers, pastor of a Unitarian flock and President Eliot's favorite preacher. Admirable in the pulpit, a discursive essayist without contemporary equal, he was his own encyclopedia of quotable prose and poetry, and the errors in his copy were almost as versatile as his charm. Was ever appearance so disarming as his? His great head was an oval, perfect as an egg, and from out it peered the eyes of an unweaned child. In those days Lawrence Lowell, Judge Grant, and Barrett Wendell were among the famous men about town. Lowell often, Grant occasionally, would discuss the value of revolutionary change. Wendell never. "Did you," he inquired of a friend on a street corner, "ever hear me admit of an improvement in the world?" "Surely not." "Did you ever hear me imply that progress did not lead downhill?" "No, certainly." "Thank God!" said Wendell, and strode off.

I have paid tribute to the widows in Boston. Let me close this chapter with a toast, respectful and affectionate, to the literary spinsters of New England. Good cause have I to be thankful to them. I think of Miss Amy Lowell of impossible manners and a golden heart. Her imagist verse was an appeal to the eye, whereas only the rhythmical memory of the ear can transmit verse to posterity. Her poetry may have been temporary, but it was talk wherein her real genius lay. She talked for victory, the rest of us to save our skins; endless disputation broken by hilarious laughter, while the smoke of

The Happy Profession

her Olympian cigars breathed incense over the field of battle. Neither of her famous brothers could talk her down: always resolutely and discreetly they avoided the fray.

I think of Miss Florence Converse, the best friend an editor ever knew, poet, dreamer, picker-up of dropped stitches, whose theology is ancient as her social theories are novel, but whose intense beliefs never cloud the clarity of an editorial judgment. When other workers fled to the hills or seaside for refreshment, Miss Converse would bury herself in some book of Christian economics, or spend three days in a religious Retreat, finding new life in meditation from Matins to Evensong. Radical and uncompromising in her social ideas, in faith she is a traditionalist. A dozen times I have told her that had she been born of a Tuesday instead of a Monday, she would have been a Tory in politics and a Come-outer in religion. But the Lord understands how to mingle his materials, and I, for one, made of other clay in other proportions, would not have had her changed by the ninth part of a hair. With her we still have Miss Alice Brown, fashioner for fifty years of human stories, never trite and full of accurate portraiture. Then there is Miss Alice Gould, who scans history as her father, the famous astronomer, scanned the skies, self-exiled to Spain, rescuing one by one scores of sailors from the *Santa Maria*, the *Niña*, and the *Pinta* from the ocean of oblivion, giving to each the background and the individuality lost centuries ago, and attaining her own immortality through a hundred footnotes. Think, ye mariners, of finding America and being forgotten, and bless the name of Alice Bache Gould.

Here is my last toast. To the dear memory of Miss Louise Imogen Guiney. Born a Catholic, living in pitiful poverty, she early repudiated "the black arts of mathematics and sewing." Every hour that she could steal from her employment she would squander upon the origins of English poetry, com-

Manners and Customs in the Hub

ing to rest at last in the sixteenth and seventeenth centuries. Her own exquisite, gay, but not unintricate verse attracted quiet attention, and, at the behest of a group of famous men, Holmes, Gilder, Stedman, and Aldrich, she was appointed to the singularly unpoetic office of postmistress of Auburndale, Massachusetts. The good Protestants about, in fear of their souls, refused to take mail from her Papistical hands, but the storm of anger arising from this incident ended it. Finally Miss Guiney struggled to England to find her Paradise in the Bodleian. "I came to England," she wrote, "not for excitement, not for gold, but for the velvety feel of the paths underfoot like moss of a forest floor to a barefooted child."

All these years she had lived a New England life and loved it. But now she had gone home, and at home she rests.

CHAPTER XIV

A Hero, a Heroine, and People in Between

WHEN IN 1857 the founding fathers of the *Atlantic* baptized their offspring they dedicated its uncertain life to Literature, Art, and Politics. James Russell Lowell was the editor, and under him — those were the tense days before the Civil War — Politics rather led the procession though more perhaps in spirit than in actual performance. His successors, Gentlemen of Literature and Leisure (I take the title from the bylaws of an old and typical Boston dining club), embraced Literature. Art remained somewhat as a foster child in the family, and Politics rather languished till Walter H. Page laid his revolutionary and invigorating hands upon the magazine. When I came along I gave full rein to an intense political interest born at the age of ten, when first I bolted the Republican Party, and burgeoning through the years. My earliest political memories cluster round the burly figure of Grover Cleveland. It must have been in the summer of '82 that, in corduroys and crimson tie, I made vocal the streets of Stockbridge, shouting: —

> I'll bet my bottom dolger
> That Cleveland will beat Folger!

Beat him he did, and two years later came the campaign of the century, political education enough for any boy, when

[*178*]

A Hero, a Heroine, and People in Between

"The Armed Knight, the Plumed Warrior" was unhorsed by my hero to the merry tune of

> Burn, burn, burn this letter

in tribute to Mr. Blaine's Mulligan correspondence.

Eight years passed. Cleveland was again up for re-election. My treble was becoming a bass: —

> Grover, Grover. Four more years of Grover
> Out they go
> In we go
> And then we'll be in clover.

So vociferous was my enthusiasm that our delightful friend and neighbor, Joseph H. Choate, whose politics were of another persuasion, congratulated me in the street. "You are quite right, Ellery," he said. "Grover Cleveland *is* the greatest all-round man in the world."

These trifles I recount to show how natural it was that, in preparing to take over the *Atlantic*, I found myself looking about for a hero. Heroes had been slow in coming and were in the years that followed for I remember my later hopes for Joe Folk of Missouri, for Brand Whitlock and Newton Baker of Ohio. But one night in 1905 the revelation came. To this day I recall the experience minute by minute. A Groton dinner was to be held in New York. Something in my interior arrangement always gags at reunions and I declined. But presently the voice I was accustomed to obey came over the telephone. It was Endicott Peabody saying he counted on my going, for the guest of honor was to be the President of Princeton. "You know, Ellery, he is very eloquent and is making a notable fight for college democracy." Now the Groton of those days was something of a club itself, and I felt in my bones that this Saint George slaying club life on the Princeton campus would not be a popular performer at our dinner. He certainly was not. Of the half hundred fortunate young men at that dinner, forty-eight by count were hostile, but two of us felt differently. The Woodrow Wilson of that night I cannot forget: the ascetic figure, the uncompromising features, the scrupulous courtesy, the perfection of utterance, the cogency of argument, the passion behind the word. He spoke as I had never heard a man speak before. Isaiah might have been at his elbow — and was for aught I know. Anyway, my heart and mind seemed tuned to his discourse and that night I went home a burning disciple. Rushing up the steps of my house and throwing open the door, I shouted upstairs to my wife, "I have been listening to a great man. I know it! I know it! Wilson will be famous."

Next morning the embers of my enthusiasm were still glowing. I took the train for Princeton, and called on its president. I must have spoken too excitedly, for never was blanket so cold, so clammy, so all extinguishing as that with which he promptly enveloped me. Not one trace of satisfaction did he show in the effect he had produced on one ordinary young man. Perhaps it was too common an experience. I took my leave, older certainly, wiser perhaps, but with my chastened purpose still undeviating. I might be the rawest recruit of the great army that he would summon to follow, but follow him I would.

I was a young man in search of a hero. Of that I have no doubt; but my faith was fixed. In spite of all the professors in Columbia, economics doesn't make history, history is made by a man when the spirit calling to him blows round the world.

As time went on I was able to do for Wilson, now President of a larger community, services small but recognized, and learned my way to the White House. The first two years

A Hero, a Heroine, and People in Between

of his first term I thought then and still believe to have been the most permanently useful in the modern story of the Republic. Then came the tornado which unroofed the world.

It was in the last days of March, 1917; *Annus Terribilis*. I had gone to Old Point Comfort for a brief rest. Editing was strenuous work. For two full years, before the war had seemed to approach our shores, more than a twelvemonth before other magazines cast overboard the safe principle of "Wait and see," the *Atlantic* had preached earnestly and persistently that the war was ours and that we must fight it. Now time had run out. The crisis had come. The air was black with rumor. The President would address Congress that day, the next, the next. Back I went to Washington, left my bag at the Shoreham, and hurried off to see the President's secretary. All the world knew Joe Tumulty, with his pink cheeks and yellow curls above them, perfect portrait of a political cherub new-risen from Irish soil. All devotion himself, he knew enthusiasm when he saw it and welcomed it in me. "When will the President speak?" I asked. "Nobody knows. He doesn't know himself," he replied. And then, in answer to my longing look, "You can't get in. You can't possibly get in. Why the demand for tickets" — and without finishing the sentence he threw his hands wide to express the vastness of the crowd. And then, seeing my involuntary dejection, he said, "No, there isn't a chance, but come in early tomorrow."

The next day was April second. As early as was decent I was in the secretary's office. The day had come, but nothing was decided except the immensity of the demand for tickets. "Why," said Tumulty, "McAdoo has just been here to get one for his sister, but not one was to be had. Not *one* I tell you. Congress will sit straight through. The gallery is plumb crowded and will sit it out, dinner or no dinner." And then, with that wan half-smile which an Irishman has in reserve for a friend in distress, he added, "Miracles do happen. They won't this time, but go back to the Shoreham and don't you leave the telephone, not for sixty seconds on end all day long."

Hopeless but alert I sat by the receiver. At 3 P.M. the bell rang. Tumulty's voice: "Come instantly!" Hardly had I closed his door behind me when I saw by the crinkles round his blue eyes that he had hopes. "No room. Not a chance," he said. "But there's the Secret Service. Are you a candidate?"

Thus it was I was accredited to watch over the President on the most dangerous night of his career. "Be on hand at six o'clock precisely," ordered Tumulty. "Dark clothes and none of your gay ties."

At six I was in the anteroom of the secretary's office. On a lounge against the wall were two heavy-set men, and bolt upright at the table sat another. "So this is what a Pinkerton looks like!" thought I, and we glanced at each other with the quiet breeding whereby gentlemen detectives come to know one another.

Three quarters of an hour passed. Our silence was growing intimate and I could feel pressing over my heart the police badge which was not there. Then an inner door opened and the rosebud complexion of the confidential secretary was disclosed. He beckoned, and conscious that the eyes of my companions were boring holes in my back, I closed the door on them forever. What part they played in the drama that followed I have no idea.

For a long time we sat, the Private Secretary and I. He spoke in monosyllables, drumming noiselessly on a table. Suddenly he looked at his watch. "Time!" We slipped out on the drive, Tumulty in his glistening topper, I in the slouch agreeable to my profession. We climbed into a car, second

A Hero, a Heroine, and People in Between

in line, and just ahead under the great porch I saw Mrs. Wilson and the President stooping to enter the motor bearing the arms of the United States. Up Pennsylvania Avenue we went, the crowds about us silent, ahead the outline of the Capitol dome ablaze with light. "Oh but it's beautiful!" Tumulty kept saying. "What a night for *him!*"

We entered by the door of the crypt at the back of the Capitol. As I jumped out, I caught Tumulty's last words, "Cling to him, don't leave him for one instant." The orders were ringing in my ears, but in front of me the President was already engulfed in the crowd. It closed behind him like waves astern a liner. I ducked and twisted under one man's arm and over another's leg, weaving my way roughly through the multitude in spite of cries, "Not so fast! Quit your shoving! Mind your manners, young feller!" On I went ruthlessly and hard, just in time to see the President's gaunt figure step into an elevator. Up he shot while I rang and banged the gate in a tempest of apprehension. The elevator returned. "What the hell do you want?" I heard the operator say, and in a stage whisper I replied, "Secret Service." The word was pure Sesame. In a twinkling I was shot up, and at the third landing, I think it was, the man flung the door open and jerked his finger to the right. "Quick!" he said.

The President's stiff outline was silhouetted not ten yards from me through an open door leading to a private room in the Capitol. The crowd had been herded to the left and seethed tumultuously about the corridor leading to the House of Representatives. Doubtless my professional friends of the Service had seen to that. At any rate, Mr. Wilson was absolutely alone. He entered. I followed. But of me and the whole world without, he was totally oblivious, conscious only of the intolerable burden he was condemned to carry alone. I understood the intensity of his suffering. Throughout the

The Happy Profession

Capitol cynicism was rampant. Isolation, utterly selfish in itself, had found strange allies in the humanitarian impulses of good people like Jane Addams. But the political bitterness about was unadulterated venom. The morning before I had spent in the office of the chairman of a powerful Congressional Committee, grower of a thousand acres of peanuts — and peanuts are profitable in peace. I had watched him stride to a southern window and shake his clenched fist at the White House. "That man," he almost screamed, "has got us into war and by God he shall get us out of it!"

That scene flitted through my mind as I watched the President. In the corner of the room were great piles of pamphlets, copies of the address he was about to make. I picked up one, now bound in the bookcase next my chair. Mr. Wilson's back was turned. He walked to a little fireplace over which hung a large mirror. In it was the reflection of a face which Dante might have borrowed. The features were twisted with pain. The chin was sensibly awry, the flesh deeply drawn and flushed in agony. He placed his left elbow on the mantel and looked steadfastly as on a vision at his distorted countenance in the glass. "It is a stroke!" I whispered to myself. I am witnessing the culmination of a tragedy. Then the President raised his hands, the left to his brow, the right to his chin, violently moulding it into place and smoothing the deep corrugations of his forehead. Over his shoulder I saw it all in the glass. Minutes — I suppose they were seconds — seemed to pass as I watched him with fearful expectancy, but gradually as under a sculptor's hands the contorted features fell into their natural shape, fixing themselves into the resolute rigidity which bars all suggestion of compromise. I might have been staring at the bust of John Calvin.

Three minutes by my watch he had stood there. Then he turned and strode into the hallway leading to the House of

A Hero, a Heroine, and People in Between

Representatives. Quick as I was to follow, the crowd swirled about him, cutting me completely off. I pushed and squirmed and struggled, but almost as I reached him, he disappeared between the swinging doors of the House. Instantly they banged behind him. Then my mission came full upon me. A picture of Ford's Theater rose in my mind. This was my Captain and my business was to be beside him. I threw myself against the double door, banged, and shouted. "What the hell?" inquired the guard as he opened the doors a few inches. That second my foot was in the crack and the magic words on my lips: "Secret Service." In I slipped and took my stand not six feet from the President on the second step of the dais just as Speaker Clark, hating the occasion, loathing the war, execrating the President, announced, "Gentlemen, the President of the United States."

The great address began. In front of concentric circles of Senators and Congressmen was ranged the Supreme Court, and dominating it, the huge figure of Chief Justice Edward Douglass White, famous for his Rule of Reason, English born, wholehearted American. After what I had seen I was fearful lest the President would hesitate and his tone lose its resonance. But never was his voice sterner, stronger. The sentences marched like fate: —

"It is a fearful thing to lead this great, peaceful people into war, into the most terrible and disastrous of all wars, civilization itself seeming to be in the balance. But the right is more precious than peace, and we shall fight for the things which we have always carried nearest our hearts — for democracy, for the right of those who submit to authority to have a voice in their own Governments, for the rights and liberties of small nations, for a universal dominion of right by such a concert of free peoples as shall bring peace and safety to all nations, and make the world itself at last free.

The Happy Profession

"To such a task we can dedicate our lives and our fortunes, everything that we are, and everything that we have, with the pride of those who know that the day has come when America is privileged to spend her blood and her might for the principles that gave her birth and happiness and the peace which she has treasured. God helping her, she can do no other."

One universal shout filled the chamber. I saw the Chief Justice pounding the arm of his chair like a boy at a football match. "The Stars and Stripes" broke out everywhere. In the melee the President disappeared, but I was at his heels till he stepped into his motor. Then I caught the sheen of Tumulty's beaver hat and dived in beside him. The pink cheeks were wet with tears. Choking with emotion, he kept saying over and over and over, "I knew he was a great man! I knew it! I knew it! And now they know it too!"

Who could sleep that night? Tumulty and I sat up in his office. Row on row of stenographers were still at work in the next room, and Tumulty whispered to me: "The Governor [he had been secretary to Governor Wilson in New Jersey] can't tell whom to trust. He writes his secret messages on his own typewriter. Now look at that second row in there. The third man from the left is Austrian born. He may be loyal, but who knows?"

My race of heroes died with Wilson. It revived again in a brief but violent flame with Al Smith, and after the *Atlantic* had given form to the great debate which culminated in Al's famous Apologia pro Vita Sua, I had my reward. The reporters were crowding round the Brown Derby. "Gentlemen," said Al with a broadening grin, "you think all of you together nominated me. It wasn't you. It was this High Hat from Boston." Al came and went, and after him my line of

A Hero, a Heroine, and People in Between

heroes disappeared forever. Not with a telescope have I caught sight of one since. A hero is a man whose self is forgotten in his victories.

After all, the staff of the *Atlantic's* life is not politics but literature. In fact it is precisely because the magazine's tastes are quiet and literary that its occasional political forays have created sound and fury. I struggled hard to understand what it is that makes writing good. At Harvard they had taught me a sovereign recipe — three preservatives warranted to keep literature fresh till opened like any prime food product. Clearness, force, elegance: these were the invincible triad, proof against rust and time. I could see their value and never shall be caught saying a word against them. But they are not enough. The simple essential ingredient which leavens any mass is *interest*, inherent, inescapable interest. And how does interest come: from without, owing to the tyrannous compulsion of the subject? Or from within by conscious or unconscious artistry which makes some trifling episode memorable as the fall of kings?

If interest is the nub of it, how can interest be gauged? Pick up a book. If, after a reasonable interval, you stir in your chair, fumble with your watch, grow conscious of gentle intrusions, the sense of errands undone, letters neglected, then your book is imperfectly interesting. But if children cease to distract and the dinner bell to interrupt, and you two, the Book and you, are alone in a timeless world, then the interest is real. When I was reading the manuscript of *Mutiny on the Bounty*, I recall that the pantry faucet sprang a leak. In all his voyages Captain Bligh was seldom wetter than I when the noise of many waters called to me twenty minutes too late.

Of course, real books, books that buy oblivion of all else,

The Happy Profession

are seldom to be found. I have merely given you a thermometer, with Blood Heat the only marker on the scale. Below it there are varying degrees of temperature, which the editor must gauge and adapt to the appetite of his public. It is his business to reach for the stars but he must never fail to grab the topmost apple on the tree.

In the world of magazines, the world where I have passed forty pleasant meandering years, a goal of such excellence as I have attempted to describe seems folderol: it isn't. The same ideals are there as in the world of books and the same hopes. The scale is smaller, the achievements less; but the pace is livelier, years are compressed into months, and the months dash by on the gallop. Only occasionally does the editor find really significant the lines so familiar to his youth: —

> Will there never come a season
> Which shall rid us from the curse
> Of a prose which knows no reason
> And an unmelodious verse:
> When the world shall cease to wonder
> At the genius of an Ass,
> And a boy's eccentric blunder
> Shall not bring success to pass:
>
> When mankind shall be delivered
> From the clash of magazines,
> And the inkstand shall be shivered
> Into countless smithereens:
> When there stands a muzzled stripling,
> Mute, beside a muzzled bore:
> When the Rudyards cease from kipling
> And the Haggards ride no more.

It would be a pale world if all its interest were in the written word. Books and magazines are but reflections, and watery

A Hero, a Heroine, and People in Between

ones at that, even when they do absorb the attention. It is the search for personalities that gives zest to an editor's life. William James's advice to recognize a man when you see one I have never forgotten, and to follow it has been a main current in my life. It is strange how far asunder are the places where you find individuality. I have met it in the cab of a locomotive, I have recognized it on a Montana sheep range where a Scotch shepherd leant motionless upon his crook while his six thousand sheep cropped steadily to the westward. A book was in his hands, a good book I knew, for he never raised his head as I rode up to him. On the backstrap of that volume the title ran *The Essays of Francis Bacon*. Countless other surprising instances spring to mind. Often the sudden overwhelming impression of individuality comes from a letter, even from a chance sentence.

Here is an example. Picking up a stray copy of the London *Times* which had found its way into the parlor of a New England inn, I ran my eye along the inner columns and lighted upon a paragraph about a popular and prosperous nonconformist church in the environs of London. The preacher, a Mr. Edward Lewis, it seems, was eloquent and adored, the pews crowded and — ultimate tribute to success in a Protestant Church! — chairs cluttered up the aisles. To his complacent congregation the word of the preacher had come like a thunderbolt. He announced his immediate resignation. In future, he said, he would support himself preaching from wayside pulpits, in the fields, at the gates of factories. He felt he was living too softly. He was too comfortable, too certain of his future, too unmindful that the Master would provide for those who serve Him. The paragraph concluded with these surprising words: "Before taking up this new work, Mr. Lewis will take a short rest at Assisi."

Assisi! A disciple of John Wesley seeking help and comfort

The Happy Profession

at the shrine of Saint Francis! *There* was a story — and a man! That evening I wrote telling him what a response awaited him from *Atlantic* readers if he would share with them his tremendous spiritual experience. I addressed the letter "Poste Restante, Assisi, Italy," and waited.

A month later came the reply. My letter was, the writer said, in literal truth, an answer to prayer. His resignation had alienated his friends. He had almost no money. Beneath what seemed to him the necessity of his soul's salvation there remained the body's need for food and shelter. He had striven to believe. He had prayed for certain faith. Now that faith was justified. Here was an offer from a complete stranger of instant work promising immediate pay. Could miracle be more palpable?

The correspondence thus begun was long continued. After posting his manuscript to the *Atlantic*, the preacher had begun his mission, sleeping in a cottage of English peasants, paying for board and bed by daily work in the fields. But certain of the old obsessions still remained, ineluctable barriers to his peace of mind. It was the height of the First World War. His son had been sacrificed in the holocaust, and hatred of the Germans had taken fierce possession of him. At every sweep of his scythe he would fancy to himself that the files of grain were serried ranks of Germans. Each time he drew the long curved blade toward him at the end of his stroke he would mutter, "Kill, kill, kill," like a *tricoteuse* counting "One, two, three" as the heads fell into the basket. The bitterness of Hell was entering into his soul and killing it. To renounce comfort, ambition, security, was not enough. He must root out hate. Otherwise in the teeth of physical defeat the Germans would conquer in their war against the Christ.

What could avail him! Fervently he prayed and thought and then — at first it has a comic sound — he hired a piano.

A Hero, a Heroine, and People in Between

Every evening, coming in from the fields, tired and distraught, he would wash away the sweat, slip into a clean shirt, and then, sitting down before the keys call upon the blessed Germans of the race to exorcise the devils of their breed, and play to himself Bach and Beethoven, Handel and Liszt. The ferocious struggle was stilled. The brute beast of hate died within him.

Embarked on adventures like this, an editor makes friends and friendships make a life. My Fidus Achates was MacGregor Jenkins, who scattered the salutary dust of business over my enthusiasm. I love to see him in his happy years, a pencil poised in one hand, "the book" on the desk in front of him. That book had a special sanctity. It recorded the financial history of every month, and from it Mac drew off figures appropriate for the stimulation of the advertising department, reserving the "net" of each transaction for his eyes and mine alone. And life then could not have been the same without Miss Fitzpatrick living subscription lists by day and dreaming them by night. Her little bonnet still bobs merrily through the hall, but my portrait of her dates from Saturday mornings in 1908 when I could detect the telltale sheen of riding boots twinkling under her petticoats, businesslike as was the face just four feet nine inches above them.

In those earliest days our ardors were perpetually boiling over. Oh that first day when subscription receipts actually topped five hundred dollars! Into the secret drawer went the sacred book and out rushed Mac Jenkins to bring back a full five-pound box of sugar plums to be distributed in an impromptu celebration. Always the joy of life is in making something. Mousetrap or magazine, when it is made, it just takes its natural place in the staid old world.

I am cynical enough to believe that there comes a time when a man has his fill of friends. In the final decade enough

The Happy Profession

is enough. There is no time left for degustation and digestion. When I speak of friends I speak not of course of those intimately loved, to whom, as Bacon says, "You may impart griefs, joys, fears, hopes, suspicions, counsels, and whatever lyeth upon the heart to oppress it, in a kind of civil shrift or confession," but rather of pleasant natural associations of months, of years, of a lifetime, with people in whom one detects both sympathy and confidence. At the time for making friendships let them share your opinions or not as they will, but always expect them to be kind to your prejudices and — this is essential — to give a like weight to things which are in your conviction perdurable.

I think of such a friend as this. She was by chance a woman who became famous long after I had known her well. (That is the better way, for fame is no proper lure for friendship.) Just after the war which was to end all wars, I came on a little essay by Mary Webb, not remarkable perhaps but completely individual, expressing a confidence in the healing power of Nature such as human nature is little prone to feel. We exchanged letters, and presently I had an invitation from her to go to a dinner of the P.E.N. Club, an English gateway to professional literary life, of which she very recently had become a member. Shy though she was and burdened with self-consciousness, we were old friends on the instant. Something about her compelled a sympathy that went deeper than awareness of her once-turned gown and her mended gloves, each with a tiny hole inside the thumb. These spoke her poverty and not her will. But in herself there was something of just pride, of distrust of the world's opinion, of confidence in her own purposes; symbols of a gallant spirit going down before great odds. The simple dinner, I knew, represented for her an orgy of extravagance. She asked if I would have a glass of wine. I lied amicably, saying I seldom drank, and we fell

A Hero, a Heroine, and People in Between

to talking fully and freely of what good writing is and whether in general it should conform to the manner of ordinary speech with just a little tilt as it were toward imagination. She went on to talk of the dumbness of criticism and of that inert resistance which the crowd feels toward the quiet reflection of small things. She refused to look on literature as the herbaceous border of life's garden. I could see that she felt her own way barred before her.

The next year I saw Mary Webb again. She was living in Hampstead in oh such a tiny house, the corner of a house rather: a toy parlor jutting over the edge of the hill, a dining table for two as the center of it, and beyond a bedroom. The bedroom door was ajar and drawn across it a cot, for from where I sat I could see a pair of blanketed legs lying at length. And presently she told me that her husband, long delicate (phthisis was at work), lay there much of the time. "Such a dear, dear person," she whispered to me in a voice below her husband's hearing, "so thoughtful, so loving, so good." But very few others knew his worth, and he had no gift for pushing his fortune. "He will never ask for more," she said, "and last year they only paid him one hundred and forty pounds for teaching school." This season he could not work. She was the breadwinner, and found it hard to trade words for bread. She spread the tea things, and sixpence worth of scones, but the crumbs stuck in my throat and the tea was too hot to drink. Again we talked of true success and what it might mean and she spoke of the inspiration of places, of Wenlock Edge and the dear delights of Shropshire. London was a desert to her, and as she talked, there slipped into my mind the thought of that other luckless exile in the waste of London, "Poor Susan," whose vision tells her story.

> Bright volumes of vapor through Lothbury glide
> And a river flows on through the vale of Cheapside.

The Happy Profession

I regret to say that, until my course is decided, I am an undesirably irresolute person. As I latched the door on the outside, I felt that something must be done, but how to do it! A few paces down the street I leaned against a wall and thought. Suddenly I remembered that Admiral's House, the home of John Galsworthy, was also in Hampstead. I walked there and told my story to the most sympathetic of listeners. Of Mary Webb, Galsworthy at that time had never heard, but he took my word for her talent. The very next day I looked up Arnold Bennett and told him that if literature had a duty, encouragement for Mary Webb provided it. Blessings on Arnold's memory! He had the voice of a cockney, the fastidiousness of Flaubert, and a heart twenty-two carats pure. I had reason to think that my petition was not in vain.

That year, the day before my steamer sailed westward, Mary Webb left a packet of a dozen stories at my hotel with a message: would I read them on the voyage and tell her whether the American market offered hope? I read them. I reread them. Each had its delicate individuality, but not one brought hope. How is an American to breathe naturally the air of a Shropshire morning, or listen to the wise talk of peasants in an alien dialect, or even to take pleasure in the contemplation of scenes so foreign to Yankeeland? Yet there was virtue here. That I knew, and it was with a sense of complete frustration that, conscious of the perception and complete fidelity which underlay each page of the manuscript, I wrote sadly to Mary Webb that not through excellence alone can words be minted into dollars.

In those days Mary Webb was forty-two. A novel of hers might sell a thousand copies, and though she had some other flimsy financial resource, she fell into deep depression. "I have this week," she wrote, "existed on bread and scrape and tea."

A Hero, a Heroine, and People in Between

And then occurred one of those sardonic incidents which illustrate in what separate orbits excellence and success revolve in this Best Possible of Worlds. The story goes that, as the Prime Minister was about to step into a railway carriage, he remarked to his secretary, "I have no book to read." The secretary stepped to a bookstand. "Here's something worth your time," he said, and handed the Premier a copy of *Precious Bane*.

It was not long before this letter, written by hand, was delivered at Hampstead: —

10 DOWNING STREET,
WHITEHALL
January the 14th

DEAR MRS. WEBB,

I hope you will not think it an impertinence on my part if I tell you with what delight I have read *Precious Bane*. My people lived in Shropshire for centuries before they migrated to Worcestershire, and I spent my earliest years in Bewdley, which is on the border. In your book I seem to hear again the speech and turns of phrase which surrounded me in the nursery. I think it is a really first-class piece of work and I have not enjoyed a book so much for years. It was given to me by one of my secretaries and I read it at Christmas within sight of the Clee Hills, at home. Thank you a thousand times for it.

Believe me to remain,
Sincerely yours,
STANLEY BALDWIN.

In the autumn of that year, Mary Webb died.

Stanley Baldwin has not earned the gratitude of his country, but the Recording Angel, impervious as he is to such appeals, should set down this note eternally to his credit. Politics were

The Happy Profession

Baldwin's bane, but truth and beauty had meaning for him. It was not by idle accident that he had Rudyard Kipling for a cousin and, for an uncle, Edward Burne-Jones.

Does Luck, I wonder, play a fortuitous part in the world, or will some future Keynes chart in cosmic curves the giant cycles of its influence? I remember once speculating humorously about possible ways of life more lucrative than editing and, noting the aura of affluence which pervades a "successful" modern religion, I modestly proposed to found one. My plan was to raise an altar to the Goddess of Fortune. Consider the idea in its commercial aspect. As a deity for America, Chance or Luck or whatever name you give to happy accident is a natural. I foresaw riches flowing to the shrine of the first feminine deity since the death of Juno. And was ever object more fit for adoration in a feminized community like these United States? My plan was to sound a clarion call to the followers of dog race and horse track, to summon bridge players to prayer and Wall Street to the altar. Devotees of craps and seven-up might serve as minor acolytes. This "Revival" should be all-inclusive and keyed to the American temperament. Full of confidence, I wrote Bertrand Russell and invited that prodigy of celestial mathematics to contribute canticles and a liturgy. He gave his promise, but my hopes died — a-borning. Lady Luck turned the other way.

CHAPTER XV

Faraway Women

LITERATURE with a big "L" loomed large in those early *Atlantic* days — so large it was almost oppressive. Of its nature, Literature is aristocratic, a little deferential to its long line of ancestors, a little lacking in (shall we say?) coziness, and to anyone desirous of building a magazine subscription list, a certain easy geniality of approach is very useful. I could see that a fringe of informality would be of great advantage to the magazine. In spite of its reputation the *Atlantic*, to my generation at least, was hardly a Pantheon on Olympus: its gods were Household Gods, and Penates, once thoroughly domesticated, are friendly deities. I bethought me of the warmest and friendliest among the satellites of Literature and found them in familiar letters. Very soon I began a definite search for them. What I wanted was an unpremeditated record of interesting happenings by an interesting person. Grammar could be overlooked, spelling could come to heel, punctuation could be peppered and salted at will. If only interest were there, and personality, I could stake out an original *Atlantic* claim in the pleasantest of all the outlying territories of Literature.

How warm is the friendship engendered by correspondence! Distance does not always estrange. It blunts the prickles of human contacts. Angularities lose their rough edges when

The Happy Profession

writers are at a safe distance, and how refreshing to office existence are the fresh breezes blowing from brave and faraway acquaintances who seem poised on the very threshold of your friendship.

One such delightful and persistent comradeship I formed with a Woman Homesteader who in the face of every conceivable obstacle had taken up a quarter section in a remote corner of Wyoming. Elinore Rupert was a young woman, vigorous in body and mind, but Destiny seemed determined to test her out before showing her the way. Her husband had been killed in a train wreck and she was left with a two-year-old daughter, Jerrine. She had not a friend, nor was she trained to make a living. In instant need of support, she had turned laundress to a kind mistress, one Mrs. Coney of Denver. This helped her over the blank wall right ahead and a larger future beckoned. She determined to turn homesteader and stake out a claim of her own in the world. After an adventurous year she wrote an account of it to the lady who had befriended her. By happy chance Mrs. Coney was a devotee of the *Atlantic*. She sent the correspondence to me and we were off.

It really mattered very little what life Elinore Rupert had been born into. She could have made a go of anything. She might have become the perfect servant; as a mistress of a great household she would have kept everybody happy, and if the dance of her genes had revolved in high circles, she would have made a very respectable Duchess.

Mrs. Rupert made her start by serving as housekeeper to an old Scotch settler, one Mr. Clyde Stewart. The magnificent export of Scotland is "characters" and Mr. Stewart was a prime sample. It was a "duir gey trip" by stage to his ramshackle lodge but it was lightened by his companionship. Every time the stage struck a root the old Scot would "hoot" until his companion began to hope they would come to a hollow tree "so that he could slip into it with the rest of the owls." But the hooting turned out to be merely a figurative expression of yearning for the "bugpeep" which he had been obliged to leave at home. Once that invigorating instrument was in his hands, his last trouble left him. The instant he came in from his work, out would come the bugpeep, and out of that "the Campbells are Comin', Hurrah! Hurrah!" till it was time to go to bed.

Never a week without its adventure. Every settler had his own story to tell Mrs. Rupert, the tale to be relayed to Mrs. Coney and thence to the *Atlantic*. The Woman Homesteader never tolerated a dull day. She would get lost in the snow, cook a Christmas dinner for pretty much the whole settlement, teach a needed lesson to a horse thief, or induce the likeliest boy in the community to marry the nicest girl. She adored romance, and there was no young bachelor in the vicinity whose safety did not depend on whether Mrs. Rupert could catch sight of an eligible wife.

Everybody else she thought of, but it was all of six weeks before she gave a thought to herself. Then, willy-nilly, she had to. One evening in the ten minutes between supper and the Campbells are Comin' Mr. Stewart asked her to be his wife. In Wyoming, oats are planted early, and there is little of springtime left for the livelier iris to come upon the burnished dove, so the happy pair decided to be married first and do their sparking afterward. The license came by mail and the instant the postman put in his appearance the bridegroom saddled his pony and went to town to inform the Justice of the Peace that he was to serve his papers on "the wooman i' the hoose." When Mr. Justice turned up in person, the bride in a clean white apron had the wedding dinner on the table, and before the pudding was cold, the Stewarts were married folks.

The Happy Profession

Elinore Rupert Stewart, near as I felt her friendship to be, was not the only heroine of my Northwest. There was Hilda Rose, whose arid farm was quite as stumpy as the claim staked by the Stewarts. A new series of domestic adventures came to the magazine through Hilda's letters. Human and dramatic, they long held *Atlantic* readers and the *Atlantic's* editor under a spell of mingled interest, affection, and admiration. It was the Wars of the Roses, new style. Bad winters, dry summers, thin soil, and all the seven plagues the Devil invents for the farmer and his wife drove Hilda Rose and her old husband to the wilds of northwest Canada. There they took up a new claim so remote that during the endless winters the mail, which traveled by dog sled, arrived only once every six weeks. But by that time Hilda Rose's friends were legion and the dog sled which formerly carried a dozen letters as its pack now staggered forward piled high with sweaters, blankets, and comforts of every kind. *Atlantic* subscribers felt as I did about the Stump Farm.

In the field of domestic correspondence it is women who excel. They are less contemptuous of the daily round than men. For them it has more significance and a deal more interest. The little daily decisions which steer a life this way or that fall into a pattern of pragmatic philosophy most men are guiltless of. Two friends of mine, on marrying each other, struck a bargain. When an important decision was to be made, of course the man would make it. But all the little decisions were to be made by the woman. That was many years ago and there has never been any great decision.

It was to women then that my thoughts oftenest turned, and a score of lonely, self-dependent histories were woven into the texture of the *Atlantic*.

Another close friend of the *Atlantic* in later years was Eleanor Risley. In contrast to my ebullient Homesteader, Mrs.

Faraway Women

Risley was an anemic woman with a frail chest and a brave heart beating underneath. The wolf pack which pursued her was led by diabetes. Her doctor, who like most physicians practised in a world of theory, and was more deeply concerned with the disease than with the patient, advised warm southern air and insulin. Insulin is expensive, and the southern sun is often expensive too. Both seemed beyond her grasp, but it was her chance for life and she seized it. She meant to die with her boots on. She and her husband, selling most of their possessions, bought a slender store of insulin, took the train for Mobile, and then set out to walk toward the cracker country of northern Alabama. Then, with what household necessaries still belonged to them piled on a little pushcart, atop of all Mr. Risley's precious violin, they began their journey on foot. Three miles on the first day exhausted the sufferer, but she soon grew strong, swinging along all day, sometimes walking through soft, moonlit nights and sleeping sweetly with a handful of pebbles to support her aching spine.

Everywhere they talked to the people, and Mrs. Risley's pictures of them had a homelike accuracy of detail that pleased the taste of *Atlantic* readers. When, in the evening, they chanced to reach a settlement, out would come Mr. Risley's violin. The mountain folks were austere, hostile to "furriners," and sullenly on the watch for "revenoors"; but music soothed the savage breast and gradually the Risleys were accepted as a pleasant feature of the landscape. But not by all.

"We knew," Mrs. Risley wrote me, "that we were in constant danger. Often men with guns would turn us from our way and quite politely tell us not to look back. Once I slept in a room where there were three other beds. Before I went to sleep, six gaunt mountaineers piled in, laid their guns beside their beds, and presumably slept. So did I. The next morn-

The Happy Profession

ing back of us near the river rose the smoke of a still. The armed guard, quite civilly, accompanied us to the next 'sittlemint.' We grew to love the face of danger. Curiously enough, danger proved a tonic and I thrived on it.

"I doubt if we could have succeeded in winning the friendship of these people without the violin. We lived off the land. The people paid us in fruit, vegetables and eggs for playing at torn-down schoolhouses. Once I attended a musicale where all were lawbreakers. Frequently on Sundays I read to an assembly gathered quickly by grapevine telegraph. Once these reserved people accepted us, there was difficulty in getting away."

Poverty and a fiddle are excellent mixers. Most people came to talk to the wanderers without reserve, and Mrs. Risley kept precise notes of conversations. Her stories were chips from actual life. She set down real names, real places. She had the right to, for she surmised that her friends were not readers of the *Atlantic*.

Her lifeline was insulin. It was in the early days of that beneficent drug and the stuff was difficult to come by. But friends of mine in the Rockefeller Clinic saw that a sufficient dosage was forthcoming, and Mrs. Risley's health steadily improved. On and on the travelers trudged. They saw and felt and understood the problems of an undiscovered country. They talked with chain gangs, they watched a secret snake dance "up Posey Holler," and what they did not learn of rickets and white lightning and the other seven plagues of mountain folk would not have held the attention of a country clinic.

They tell me romance is dead. America is a mechanized society of operatives. Realism reigns. Yet it is my belief you cannot talk with a farmer piling a stone wall, or even sit quiet

Faraway Women

in the corner of a smoking car, without catching one tag end of the silken strain of romance.

Adventures, as Disraeli remarked, are to the adventurous. It is the young who like to share them and, if they are tied at home, at least to share their thrills. But there comes a time when the interest of life shifts from the external. Over the brow of the hill on the further side, one can stop and rest and think. When letters first came to me from Mrs. Ada Cambridge Cross bearing a South African postmark, I was far from such ripe maturity, but sixty had always seemed to me a penultimate date in life and I remembered the striking remark of Dr. Holmes: "At sixty a man comes within range of the rifle pits." Thenceforward the curtain may be rung down without warning and it becomes commendable to take thought of what life means. When the play is over and the theater darkened it is time to reflect on the pleasure and the pain the performance has given us. All up to the imperfect age of fifty-nine, then, should skip the paragraph that follows.

At sixty, adventuring roams through an ampler ether. Mrs. Cross was the widow of an Anglican clergyman who had lived long reflective years. Neither rich nor poor, she was a stranger to the daily risks and excitements of pioneer life. Time was given her to read and think. As a girl she had been devoted to good works and found her satisfactions in the reward of a pious and conventional conscience. As she grew older familiar platitudes of church people ceased to satisfy her. She groped toward her own philosophy of life and at sixty she found it. She knew too well that those who in public yearn for Paradise, oh Paradise, still craved to rest awhile and wait for their felicity where they were, even as they whose deliberate choice it was to stake their claim on this earth. Her

The Happy Profession

ποῦ στο was Here and Now. "The spirit," she wrote, "that had wandered so far and wide like Noah's dove in search of the yet invisible tree, comes back to this quiet chamber of the mind, its ark of origin, with the instinct of the tired wayfarer for his old humble home; here it rests in the vision of its dear past, beautiful because it is past and past so long — the vanished land, the *ain countree*, the old-time ways that are no more; and the big canvases that once were the treasures of the collection hide their diminished charms."

Hers was a woman's experience. There are things a man can more easily say and she preferred to let a man express it. "Confined," wrote J. S. Mill, "by custom to one physical function as their means of living and their source of influence," women have had to adjust themselves to that circumstance, or rather they have been molded by their environment like everything else. The interest of their lives has been to be interesting to men. It is said that women should die at forty, but she rejected that cynical suggestion, and at fifty the bitterness of time had past. Friendships with men become delightful. No longer were you suspected of making love yourself. The doom that confronts you is every year more readily accepted, and to Mrs. Cross the philosophy of a friendly charwoman seemed wise and good: it was not Heaven with its multitude of new duties that she hankered for, but a good square sleep. Lost in the immensity, you have ample room to get out of yourself. The vastness of it dwarfs to nothing the abiding interests of narrowed minds.

At sixty Mrs. Cross felt how unsubstantial had been her old consolations. The Bible she still loved was no longer a holy thing come down from Heaven, but a wonderful old book, historically inferior to certain other books — heathen books at that — of which it was more or less a plagiarism. The endless life! She would cope with that if necessary when the time came. Her business was life as she knew it. The pattern of consolation as it was offered her by the Church became a convention far from reality. When she lay in the hospital at the point of death, the nurse whispered in her ear, "The Doctor of Divinity is here," and she replied, "Don't let him in."

Like many women growing old, Mrs. Cross was dependent upon her children. Dearly she loved them but knew she must be superfluous in a young household. The child who brings a mother home is inevitably married, and though both partners in the firms were dear and good to her, she could never forget that on one of them she had no claim whatever. "I am not *her* mother; *he* is not my son," became a stabbing thought. But all this was part of inevitable circumstance, and her abiding place was the perpetual journey of her mind. That was home and she loved it.

Another decade passed. Threescore years and ten, and from that to fourscore years, were labor and sorrow. She bethought herself that some benefactor of the race should for the sake of decayed gentlewomen establish an almshouse *without alms*. Old people need old people for companionship, and the young are best without them. The World War had created a new army of virgin martyrs, women who would never marry, who never could marry. It was their lives she thought it most precious to enrich. Yet if her daydream came true, and in her imaginary colony the most charming of tiny houses were allotted to her, the price of leaving her family would be too heavy to pay. It would break her heart. No, there is no substitute for the here and now. Here she would live, and now would she enjoy living. She would hold fast to the most comforting of creeds. She would have her wayside happiness and not forget that "we are worth our places in the world up to the last moment even if nobody knows it but ourselves."

Abiding in her mind, I think, was the final remark made by

The Happy Profession

Renan with his habitual courtesy: "I have had so much pleasure from life that I am really not justified in claiming a compensation beyond the grave."

Precious in this world is the light of a penny candle if it be your own.

An esoteric English journal had come my way and I was struck by the originality and vigor of one of its contributions, standing out of a web of involuted ideas from which my mind seemed wholly insulated. Speculations in religion have always had their fascination for me. I had touched on Yoga and knew all that an editor is supposed to know about it — and precious little more. I had skirted the furthest edges of Buddhism and Shinto and derived comfort from the rational teachings of Zoroaster concerning the confused duality which directs our Universe. This article showed knowledge and, I thought, power, and I wrote to the author, L. Adams Beck. For years we corresponded and my mentor fired my enthusiasm by telling the story of a wonderful pilgrimage to Amarnath, a shrine hidden high in the Himalayas. One letter followed another discussing the faith and lore of ancient China and India and, turning to Persia, discoursed of the immortal struggle between Ormazd and Ahriman. The Founder of the Wisdom of the Magi had long held empire over my imagination (who would not be attracted by the philosopher who laughed on the day he was born?), and as I watched the struggles of the world, the magic phrase "Here Ormazd; There Ahriman" always reminded me that under the banner either of king or of rebel, man must fight. Yet through all the intimacies of years of correspondence, never did it occur to me I was not writing to a man and a manly man at that. Not since the days of Lady Macbeth was sex more impenetrably hid.

Faraway Women

Then one day came a disclosing letter and a photograph. The photograph told the story as plainly as the letter. Taken from a portrait which had once been exhibited in the Paris Salon, it depicted the figure of a woman. The countenance yielded nothing to my scrutiny, but, attached by ribands to the waist were three masks, such as Greek actors wore for their contrasted parts. Patently they symbolized the tripartite character of an enigmatic woman.

L. Adams Beck had been born Lily Moresby. She came of a naval race, daughter and granddaughter of admirals. One great-grandfather, a Barrington, had fought under Nelson. Long since she had discarded her family. Her only human tie seemed to be a stray husband, one Colonel Beck. He had been tucked away in the retirement of Victoria, British Columbia, left to his golf and bridge, and apparently played a very incidental part in her strange history. The East was forever calling and she had traveled far. From her earliest years there were within Lily Moresby three incarnations of complete and invigorating diversity. "L. Moresby" thought and wrote, with cynicism and dislike, of very ordinary people. "E. Barrington" was full of the romance of her ancestors. Nelson she loved — and Lady Byron! "L. Adams Beck" was a pilgrim to eternity. She sat beneath her everlasting Bo tree contemplating the infinities where the parallel lines of life join and perspective ceases to be. Each personality in turn seemed called into being, materialized by some impulse deep and half understood. Let Barrington write for money. Let Moresby write for fame or for revenge. It was for Beck to study and to learn the Impassible Way. This undivided sisterhood in their several selves contributed to the *Atlantic*. I came to know each of them well. Moresby was to me a little vulgar. Barrington was sentimental and immensely popular. Beck was a priestess at her own altar. Her I respected, and was deeply interested.

The Happy Profession

It was only at her life's close that I met L. Adams Beck in the flesh. Spending some months in Japan in the spring of 1930, I had a note from her, bidding me come to see her at Kyoto. She wished to take me to a Zen monastery and to show me a little of what meant everything to her. Of Buddhism I had as I have said but a surmise. I had read a book or two. I had talked often with Dr. Sturgis Bigelow of Boston, who through a long and studious life had trimmed the lamp kindled for him in his youth within the walls of a Buddhist monastery. Near Nara I had spent a long afternoon with a sacred scholar whose mind had seemed to me subtler and more complex than any I had met with in the West. I had asked him whether the Dealer of the cards of life did not contrive through infinite ages to give to each of us hands of the same value; whether it was true that a peculiar trial once endured could never be repeated; whether as in duplicate whist chance was eliminated and perfect justice done to every player; and he had smiled a slow, grave smile and said that it was true. This truth, if it be a truth, had seemed to me to roll away a great central obstacle of Christian faith. For it is not just that we should all prepare for the Great Assize by different training, sometimes light and pleasant, sometimes hardly to be borne. The picture of the Wheel of Life and the weights that balance it had been much in my mind; but the vision of the Perfect One had come to me most naturally in a certain little monkish garden, apparently deserted, but lovingly kept in its exquisite decay. I had the habit of going there at dawn, walking lightly along paths too beautiful in their geometric rakings to be trod upon, and sitting beneath a willow I had gazed at the waving shadows in the pool and wondered in my half-vacant mind about the thoughts of worshipers who have sat there for at least five hundred years.

Faraway Women

It was still early one morning when I waited on Mrs. Beck. She proposed that I share her breakfast, but as her morning diet followed the squirrel's pattern and consisted mainly of nuts, I said I preferred to have my porridge later. She was a lady small in size, but with a strained formality about her which kept mundane conversation at a distance. Over her features the skin was drawn tight and the bony structure below bore a faint suggestion of a mummified eternity. Of small talk she had absolutely none, and somehow or other eight o'clock in the morning seems hardly the moment to dive into the profundities. We chatted then to little purpose, but when she proposed that on the following day I should drive her to the monastery where she was conducting her studies, I assented gladly.

The next day was an experience to me; not that it taught me much I could repeat in words, but it fused my vague and rambling thoughts into pictured memories. A long dusky study hall adjoined the Refectory, lined with shelves whereon reposed row on row of manuscript and ancient books. Mrs. Beck sank on a low stool or couch and lost herself in meditation. But it was the faces of the monks that I still see before me — sweet placid countenances, reminding one of the earliest Italian frescoes or of the philosophers who decorate Chinese jars with their thin beards and earnest faces. Their eyes were lowered to the *suttas* each held in his lap or on some low table, but their thoughts were afar off. One old man who spoke some words of difficult English was detailed to give me enlightenment. He spoke of the Noble Truths which I have seen set down in the Encyclopedias; how the Middle Way has been won through this knowledge. The first is the Noble Truth of pain. "Birth is pain, old age is pain, sickness is pain, death is pain." The second is the cause of pain. The

The Happy Profession

third is the cessation of pain, "the remainderless cessation of craving, its abandonment and rejection." The fourth Truth is the Noble Eightfold Path: "right views, right intentions, right speech, right action, right livelihood, right effort, right mindfulness, right concentration." Ah, that right concentration, the most difficult gate of all!

I was lost in an ocean of vague, unquiet thought and felt that for Buddhist or Christian the road is steep and thorny. As the halting explanation went on, my mind winged back to Christian toiling through the Slough of Despond and over the Hill Difficulty. How divergent the road, what worlds between the goals! My feet had been set on the alien path of the West and that road I must follow. But had the choice been offered me, I wondered whether it was not the light of Asia toward which I should have set my steps.

My meditation was interrupted by the call of the Refectory. Then I wondered whether the Pilgrim could have drawn sustenance for his western Progress on a diet of thinnest lentil soup.

On the long drive back to Kyoto I could talk more freely, but my companion was hardly companionable. Our Western way is to try to break down the barriers between man and man. Contemplation had only hardened the walls of Mrs. Beck's reserve. Is there a single way to salvation, or must each traveler be guided by the fitful light of his own immutable personality?

Oh for an anthropometrist who will measure the diversities of the daughters of Eve! I think of scores of ladies far away, but in those intemperate and discomfortable storms when black night descends upon the kitchen, when the cook leaves and the other maids give notice, then like the needle to the pole, my thoughts turn to Juanita.

Faraway Women

The Black Pearl among the servants of this earth is Juanita Harrison. Born in Mississippi, she enjoyed a few months' schooling before the age of ten. Then began an endless round of cooking, washing, ironing, in an overburdened household. Those sordid and unsparing years steeled in her the determination to escape and see the great, wide, beautiful world — the world she lived to write of in the *Atlantic*.

Juanita began her travels at sixteen, moving from one city to another as she found profitable employment. All day she trained herself assiduously to be a lady's maid; in the evening she attended night classes at the Y.W.C.A. and picked up enough French, Italian, and even Spanish to make her simple wants readily understood. At Los Angeles her extraordinary competence endeared her to her employers. She remained four years in their service, and graduated with the perfected knowledge of the art of arts — how to make people comfortable. She could cook, wait, valet, and keep house. Under the kind guidance of her master, her savings were wisely invested and by 1927 her income yielded her some two hundred dollars a year. With this slender security she started on a tour which took her — I have seen her passports — to twenty-two countries, from India to Brazil. When her funds were low she would take remunerative service. To any household in chaos she would bring the great gift of order. For a retired colonel long since robbed of his batman, she would become the perfect valet. To any traveling countess — and she specialized in countesses — she would be lady's maid and courier in one. Employers who realized that Heaven was about them would implore her never to leave, but if there was money in her pocket for a ticket to the next capital, she would bid them the friendliest of good-byes.

Spelling has no terrors for Juanita. She recognizes no rules of grammar. Her writing is artless and vivid like that of some

The Happy Profession

happy pilgrim of Dan Chaucer. She has a faculty for making friends. She knows people will like her and they do. For her exists no barrier of class or color, and when men brown or white find her too attractive, she is superlatively competent to look after herself. Frequently on her travels she adopts the garb of the country which she is visiting. Her slight form, fresh olive complexion, her long hair braided about her head, make her appear younger than her years. And never does her appetite for a good meal fail her.

One beautiful spring morning she set off for London, with two suitcases, two blue dresses, two white dresses and one black, aprons, caps, and references, not to speak of two jars of sour cucumber pickles which are so useful in keeping sea-sickness away. "I always like an upper berth," she wrote. "I don't want anyone making it down on me. I went to the 1st and 2nd class. Their towels looked more linen, so I took 2. The soap smelled sweeter so I took 2. I went up to the writing-room and the paper was the kind you love to touch, so I took much, and tuked it away in my bunk." Tourist-third suited her nicely and so did the Y.W.C.A. in London. Her first English room was pleasant "but on the wall hung two pictures of pretty women weeping at a grave. And when I turn out the light I cannot go to sleep. So I take them down at night and put them in the closet and hang them back in the morning."

It took two days for Juanita to get a job with a lady from Bolivia. La Señora was lonely and cried. "The apt. was nicely furnished but I am disgusted because every time I want a bath I must make a fire in a little choked up heater. The boys go to the Public Bath Houses. La Señora go without. I am bathing in a zink bucket." She looks in casually on Stratford and enjoys Edinburgh. Then she is off for Paris and quickly finds work and excellent wages. And Paris is cheap. "I know French," she wrote, "in a Jewish way and can always jew

[212]

them down," which, when one remembers the talents of a French *patronne*, speaks volumes.

But in Paris one difficulty becomes acute. "The men, like the Spanish men, are great love makers. Lucky for me the 3 French teachers I had, 2 old maids and the other married, didn't teach me one word of how to flirt. Anyway I know how to get rid of them. I said something to them and did not know the meaning of it, but it served well."

In a woman's world the eternal masculine is a persistent dilemma. In London Juanita had learned to avoid boarding-house halls when dusk is falling, but in Paris where the color of a face is not felt — or perhaps felt too deeply — she was in constant need of her woman's wit. The problem was complicated because men were so useful. How else could you go to fine restaurants and enjoy five courses instead of three, to say nothing of fruit and coffee; and to pastry shops where patisserie is in its glory? Then there is the agreeable half hour of somnolent repletion and only after that comes the question of how to get rid of the lover. Juanita reflected that after all the game was sport. Every day she amused herself keeping count of the number of cavaliers who made love to her. The galleries of the Louvre gave her unending opportunity. One morning there the number of competitors was so great she felt called on to shoo them all away, all, except a very nice colored one, "a captain or something in the Army. I saw so many high up officers speak to him, I thought this must be some person. He was so nice and kind, and tried so hard I did not have the heart to tell him to walk away and beside I wanted to see how he would act. I had five o'clock tea with him and I can never get enough of the French pastrys." Then she began to plan. She asked leave to run into a hotel for a minute to spruce up before dinner and, while the gallant waited in the entresol, slipped out of a postern door. I only wish she had given us the picture of the Captain of Moroccans stroking his fierce mustache after he had cooled his heels for an hour or so.

It was heaven for the girl who had so long starved for it. Those were the most "Gelorious" days of her life. She remembered the folly of a lecture in Carnegie Hall when the Professor had spoken of *Paradise Lost*. "It's not lost," she whispered to herself. "It's right here on earth and I have seen so much of it."

Still much more of it there was. There was Monte Carlo, and there was Rome. She saw the theaters and the galleries and when she beheld the "Crucifixion" of Guido Reni, it made the cold chills run up her spine and she thought she saw the lips move. From Rome to Switzerland. From Switzerland to Belgrade and Constantinople, and thence on to India. Earth holds little that she missed. It was at Buenos Aires that my letters caught up with her. Then she needed my help, for her precious bankbook was on deposit in Boston and the South American Branch was not aware of its existence. A few Vice-Presidents set that right and Juanita moved on to Honolulu.

Hawaii satisfied her deepest longings. There was the Mississippi sun, but its rays only warmed your bones, never burned them to a crisp. There were plenty of fine ladies to tempt her with high wages, and on her holidays, which meant five days out of the seven, she could live in a tent and eat in luxury for forty cents a day. It chanced that on a journey to the East I stopped off at Honolulu, Juanita very far from my thoughts. While I was lunching at a friend's table, a newspaper called me up and asked for an interview. When I had given it over the telephone, the reporter inquired, "Is this Mr. Sedgwick, the friend of Juanita Harrison?" I admitted the impeachment and at once the editor was put on the line. "Your names," said he, "are always coupled together. We must have a photograph of the reunion at Waikiki."

That afternoon a procession of eight cars sought out the beach where Juanita dwelt. As I approached her tent, there was a mighty commotion within. "Sakes alive!" I heard in a syrupy gurgle. "I ain't got a mortal thing on me."

But things were found, the tent flap parted, and out came Juanita, her teeth shining under a carmine bandana, her big eyes bright as blobs of Mississippi molasses. "Gord's sake," she cried, "did ever nigger see the likes of this!" and she bent double under the weight of her laughter. So I see her now.

We shall not meet again. Juanita was born to bring contentment to other husbands, and to make the wives of other husbands rejoice and be exceeding glad.

CHAPTER XVI

Men of the Species

THIS IS, or soon will be, a woman's world. These fifty years past, it has not taken a philosopher to learn that, but I have never surrendered my personal loyalty to the sex I was born to represent. It has never occurred to me to change the colophon of the Atlantic to a distaff, and I have taken conscious pains that a preponderance of its contributors should be masculine. My friend Bok pointed out that I was sinning against the light of the cashbox, but I took comfort in the monthly comment of the historian, William Roscoe Thayer, who invariably commented: "I see the men are still ahead in this month's *Atlantic*."

Thus it happened that while it was to women I was forever writing letters of affectionate solicitude, my familiar company has been with men. With a single exception they have never betrayed me, and my heart goes out to them. It is amusing to think what the *Atlantic* would be like had it been turned into a salon, but I prefer the idea of a club.

The members of my club have been of all sorts. I will speak only of a few special cronies.

The lilies of the field had their masculine counterpart in A. Edward Newton. It is true that most of the time he was the most industrious of workers, for it takes millions to build

Men of the Species

a library like his, but it was in holiday time I knew him and then he was all glorious without, not a care on his mind, and on his back a coat of black and white checks fresh from Sackville Street which gave the sun back its brilliance. Straight out of Dickens he came, with his perpendicular collar, his red bow tie, and the ruddy smile which outdid the Cheeryble Brothers both. He looked pure benevolence, benevolence with just a pinch of something tart that gave it character and shrewdness.

Newton had made a fortune from his A.B.C. electric circuit. Not that he was an electrical wizard. He never could find out, he said, just what the difference was between a volt and an ampere, but whatever his electric circuit, he certainly knew the A.B.C. of selling it. Selling is human; that he understood.

Newton was pure Yankee. His intelligent father had never gone very far in the world. In the old man's living room there was but a single shelf of books, but those books held a world. Three of these precious volumes constituted the *Life of Samuel Johnson, LL.D.*, and by the time Eddie was fifteen he knew that Life forward and back. Public libraries widened his knowledge of the Great Cham, and before his apprentice days the boy was reborn into the eighteenth century and knew he was living for a single object.

Success came early; Newton's capacity saw to that. But money was made only to be transmuted into books, and the best of books dealt with Doctor Johnson's circle. Newton's prejudices were strong as his predilections; indeed it was prejudice which gave predilection its intensity. For him America was one vast wilderness. What had wheat fields and steel mills to do with the Great Century? Not until old and sick and in vain search for health did he ever so much as cross

The Happy Profession

the Appalachians. He preferred civilization. In America civilization had all but disappeared. England still had traces of the past. As his fortunes grew and the possibility of vacations grew with them, Newton followed a precise formula. Punctually each year he would make his journey to New York with a single purpose — to take ship for England. On the first morning in London he would enjoy his bacon and eggs with Quaritch, browse for hours among priceless volumes, buy like the Prince he was, take the train for Lichfield, and for a fortnight follow the footsteps of Doctor Johnson. Then home to the Electric Circuit, more sales, more profits, for eleven months. Then again the heavenly twelfth, London and Lichfield, Quaritch and the British Museum, E. V. Lucas and Burbeck Hill.

The first time I ever saw Newton's library at Oak Knoll, Golconda lay before me. Subsequent impressions merely deepened my amazement. The eighteenth century was there in miniature. As the years went on earlier centuries crowded in at the edges, but the eighteenth was always the center. The spirits of Fanny Burney and Mrs. Thrale, of Charles and Mary Lamb, of Boswell and Sir Joshua, hovered about the portrait over the mantel. It was *the* portrait, which Reynolds mentions as most like the Doctor and which had won the plaudits of the entire Club.

Newton married early the daughter of a cultivated Jewish gentleman who once controlled the Bellevue-Stratford Hotel. That marriage was made in Heaven, and for Newton Heaven could not have existed without her patient understanding of the crotchets and unreasonablenesses, the passionate devotions and the shrewd appraisals, which made up his existence.

A hundred pictures of Eddie Newton flit before me. I like best one "snap" of him in my own house at Beverly. Alarmed

Men of the Species

at the size of the automobile at the front door, obviously a portent of strangers, my little daughter gave one shriek of alarm and hid herself in the coat closet. In came Newton in his burly overcoat and, peeling it off, stood there in his checkerboard, which made one long for bishops and rooks and knights to skip about on it. He looked inquiry as to the disposition of his ulster. I pointed to the closet and I cannot forget the double bursts of laughter when my child hid her tousled hair against the squares of his waistcoat.

Next to books it was talk that Newton loved — talk with a sense in it of leisure and of spacious backgrounds. His conversation was full of stories, but these he habitually copyrighted and preserved in his delightful essays. One which he has stowed away, I cannot remember in which volume, I first heard on the scene of the disaster, which gave it point. His household had been living for a fortnight under the shadow of a huge dinner party at Oak Knoll. As the hour approached the tension grew, and on the very day before the great event, the parlormaid could stand the strain no longer and left on the instant. In her perturbation, Mrs. Newton telephoned to her husband news of the catastrophe and he, being a man of infinite resource, turned to his friend, the superintendent of dining-car service of the Pennsylvania Railroad. A Negro waiter of immense experience was furnished, and nothing could have exceeded the orderly magnificence of the dining table when the darkey had given it the final touches. The guests arrived, the sherry circulated, and the little hush which always marks the arrival of *the* moment went round the company. The double doors were thrown open and the waiter, immaculate and thrilled with new authority, fairly shouted the message which he had lived with for twenty years: —

"Last call for dinner in the dining car!"

Edward Newton and Mrs. Newton, halves of one inimitable whole, without precedent and without imitators, the debt I owe you is unpayable.

I turn to a very different partnership: James Norman Hall and Charles Nordhoff, companions of my youth, friends of my old age. I had always supposed that Damon and Pythias, Orestes and Pylades, were like each to each as peas in a pod, but within and without, Hall and Nordhoff are in acute contrast. Hall, son of an Iowa farmer, has all the countryman's gentleness, all of his ruminant philosophy. His fires are banked till they blaze forth hot in pursuit of some cause or quest. Nordhoff, on the other hand, is aloof, and until assured of his company, always a little impatient of the possibilities. Before that ultimate excellence became a scoffing in the mouths of "liberals," I should have termed him a natural aristocrat, and suspect that in a very slight disguise he might play the part of Coriolanus with competence. There was journalism in his blood — journalism of a high order. His grandfather was a correspondent during Civil War days and his father, I think, represented James Gordon Bennett's *New York Herald* in Europe. At any rate, Nordy spent his babyhood in London and Paris and would have been French up to the eyebrows instead of merely to the heart line had not his grandfather died, leaving to his family the responsibility of an enormous tract of wild land in Lower California. So the Nordhoffs exchanged France for Mexico, swapping as it were Voltaire for Rousseau, and during most of his youth until he was translated to Harvard College young Charles grew up after the manner of one of Chateaubriand's heroes in an almost undiscovered wilderness, with peons for company and the Pearl Lagoon he has so beautifully described as the lonely playground of his youth.

Those isolated years made him what he is. They stiffened

his remoteness and matured his fastidious attitude toward civilization. Critical and indisposed to compromise, warm in his friendships, impassioned in his judgment, I saw him then as I see him now. In a long list of friends he has a place apart.

From all this Hall dwells a thousand miles. He is, as the phrase goes, social-minded, and when first I came to know him about 1912, he was working for the Boston Society for the Prevention of Cruelty to Children. It is my secret conviction that "settlements" and all that is akin to them have grown so preoccupied with the Second that they forget the First and Great Commandment. Humanitarianism is a modern religion, and like all modern religions it confounds reform with virtue. But then, Friend and Reader, this is pure prejudice.

Whatever the articles of his creed, Norman Hall has practised a lifelong and universal charity. I have never heard him speak evil of mortal man (Herr Hitler excepted and perhaps a President or two), but I am conscious that tight within his breast is locked a most rigid discrimination of the relative worth of man and man.

In the alchemy of human nature I can think of no real parallel to those friends. Nordhoff and Hall, acid and alkaloid coalesced and for twenty years their combined work was indistinguishable. Somewhere in my bookcase is the story of the *Bounty*, each chapter identified by the author's name. Despite all my intimacy with the two authors, I should have been powerless to distinguish between their contributions; and I feel rather than know that certain qualities held in common wove the filaments which so long bound them together: intense patriotism, never blind to the weaknesses of the civilization they fight for; adoration for France, meaning for both of them light, logic, and the inheritance of Greece; and a prismatic passion for romance.

Theirs is a wonderful story, but that I have told elsewhere.

The Happy Profession

I will only add that for thirty years they have made the Southern Seas stuff of my dreams. There live my own vicarious adventures; there are the sweet odors I long to savor, the colors I long to see. There, when peace descends, dreams will still hold sway. Should it befall me to end my days as an opulent distiller of perfume, I shall not advertise my essential essence as "Ecstasy," "Temptation," or even as "Delirium," but shall simply stamp upon each vial the rational, the persuasive, the convincing label, "Nordhoff and Hall."

I turn from friendship to compelling sympathy. One remarkable young man I followed with eagerness and hope throughout a brief and unhappy career. It happened that I published in the *Atlantic* one of those challenging articles indicting the younger generation much as nations are indicted in spite of Burke's warning, but with a bill of particulars that draw immediate fire. Professor Woodbridge read it aloud to his class at Columbia and, putting them on their mettle, asked for rebuttals. One he selected and offered to the *Atlantic*. When it was published the battle was joined. The student writer taught me little I did not know about the new generation but he opened to me a new and bitter world: a world where men and women are condemned to carry some disproportionate monstrous burden. How grossly are the fundamentals of justice violated when the handicapped are born or made. They will be Humanity's exhibits at the Great Assize and, if only the Promethean argument could be pleaded before a jury of our fellows and not before The Judge alone, they would have a profound effect upon the verdict. Randolph Bourne was born in a sardonic hour. His mind was a beautiful instrument. Education had taught him to control it by the laws of irony. His body was hideous and misshapen. One felt that within it were all the agues and agonies of

Men of the Species

Caliban. His father had, I am told, seen better days but was in no position to help his son on in the world either physically or intellectually. That was his person and his background. Where the boy's talents came from I could not surmise.

My first meeting with Randolph Bourne was a physical shock. The Negro doorman at the Club announced "A man to see you, sir," which in a world of gentlemanly convention was arresting. That was my only preparation. The caller was ushered into the little room dedicated to visitors whose names are not entered in the book. He was a dwarf in stature, without a redeeming feature. His shoulders were twisted and hunched, his face was a mouldy brown, and the skin drawn too tightly over the jaw made his teeth stand out like fangs. In my comfortable world seemliness is part and parcel of manners, and so violent a discord between the inner man whom I had known from his letters and the external produced on me something like a revulsion. Bourne was conscious I know of that instantaneous dismay. Often before he had been subjected to that sort of thing and bitterly was I ashamed of myself. As we talked my control grew. We spoke of personal philosophies, of the Greek virtues, of intellect created to control the world, and he smiled as he mentioned his own strong defense of irony. But in spite of my interest and my contrition, I could not bring myself to ask him to stay for lunch. That the Creator will hold against me. It is not the burly sins that will incense Him but the small meannesses. I make my confession now, but absolution I do not deserve and shall not receive.

In the years that followed I tried to help Bourne; to disarm his cantankerousness and to stimulate his aspiring mind. I was able to assist him to a self-supporting position, but in my little book of human knowledge I set it down that his employers, men dedicated to a journalism designed to help and furnish

The Happy Profession

intellectual leadership for the masses, constantly high-hatted him and the iron was never withdrawn from his soul. Randolph Bourne fought, suffered, and died. He is remembered only occasionally, but there still live a few who felt his promise and his power. Had he been born a Valentine instead of an Orson, the milk within him would not have curdled. He would not have died a rebel. He might have lived to be a reactionary.

I turn to a pleasant picture. Walter Edmonds had not left college but his ambition to write was definite and sharp. An uncle of his had been among my dearest college friends, and he turned to the *Atlantic* for advice. This was a dozen years before the Drums rolled along the Mohawk and Walter had little between him and his first self-supporting meal but a Harvard education and the two stories which he held, neatly typed, in his hand.

Could he write to live? I explained to him that writing and living obeyed two widely separated orbits, that if he lived he might write, and that if he wrote, it was altogether possible he might not live. But something in his manner gave me confidence and editors know a certain look about an unread manuscript which can inspire hope. I asked how old he was, and knowing that a year or two of starvation often improves the youthful figure, I told him that if he really cared, he might put off his clerkship for a couple of years and try out the gift he was sure he had. But of course I added that celibacy is part of such an experiment, celibacy and bread without the butter.

It was spring and vernal impulses were upon him. Walter started visibly. "Oh," he said charmingly, "but I want to be married. I have the girl." That was a poser, but by that time I had larger reasons to hope, for Walter not only wanted to write but had something to write about. He had been brought

Men of the Species

up in Oneida County, New York. His was the country of the Canal, and its history, its bargemen, its locks, its narrow shining reaches, he knew like the palm of either hand. Nothing that had happened there these hundred years was unknown to him or alien to his imagination. It is not in continents but in localities that talent takes root, and Erie country is unique. It belongs to itself, but given a chronicler I felt confident the world would give it heed. I felt little stirrings of expectation when I thought of Erie, and reckoned its possibilities of supporting not three meals a day but six.

I asked Walter to leave his stories with me and to come again in three days' time. Now I had no more effect on that young man's life than a moment's shadow has on a sunbeam, but at least the shadow passed when I read the stories. There was talent there, talent unmistakable as bright flecks in the quartz, and when Walter came back, our talk was full of a shared enthusiasm. "Take a chance," I said, or something like it. "When they try out the three-year-olds, I'll back you for the money."

So they were married, Walter and his girl. And the art of telling stories for a livelihood lived happy ever after.

When a power beyond his fellows is given a man, my belief is that circumstances may retard but cannot intimidate it. Out it comes in spite of everything. Not poverty nor neglect can kill it. Material success is often a matter of chance, but the talent that deserves it will emerge regardless of the reward or lack of it. It may be luckier for the artist to be bred in a garret rather than in a palace, but his performance, whether he "arrives" late or early, is much more independent than we think of the conscientious search of society for promise in young men. Certainly never in history has more painstaking exploration been made for the beginnings of talent, from base-

The Happy Profession

ball to poetry, than are made today. Scholarship scouts for the university go scurrying through lumberyards and coal mines. Children's aesthetic triumphs from the age of five are placed on exhibition. Everything is examined — except the obvious. Like Poe's *Purloined Letter*, talent may hang in plain view on the wall — and be completely overlooked.

A pleasant visit the other day from James Hilton brings this truth back to me. It was twelve years ago that I saw him first. For a full decade before that, ever since he left the university, he had been writing industriously for a living. Several of the most imaginative novels of a generation bore his name on the title page, but they cumbered the bookstores for the most part unbought. *Lost Horizon* had for a year been in evidence — but not for the public to see — and *Without Armour*, admirable as it is, the critics had boggled at.

It was delightful, that first meeting, for by a masterpiece of luck I had in my pocket the key to Hilton's fortune. I held the contract for *Mr. Chips*. That small fragment of perfection had been written under circumstances that deserve retelling. Hilton had met little but discouragement. During ten years of really desperate devotion to his art he told me that not more than four hundred pounds had come from the most rewarding of them. His finances were precarious, and it was for him a stroke of great good fortune when he was sent for by the editor of an evangelical family paper, the *British Weekly*. Behold the way Providence contrives. The Christmas issue of the *Weekly*, full of bright pictures of the triumph of virtue, would not come quite together. There was a gap of four or five many-columned pages. The editor asked Hilton to fill it and to fill it within a very few days. The case was urgent for the deadline was at hand and the reward would be proportionate — fifty pounds. Now fifty pounds was a windfall without parallel in Hilton's career. He thought

Men of the Species

intently, and then and there, as he thought, there rose before him the picture of a beloved schoolmaster. It was like a revelation.

Hilton took the assignment, wrote night and day and finished a story of precisely the required length. Now the next miracle in this necklace of circumstance was that the printers' rule had measured the precise number of inches that Art required. Obviously the manuscript was short for a volume of conventional size, but *Mr. Chips* furnished a case apart, and from the moment I first read the story for the *Atlantic*, I knew it was born for permanence.

But let me go on for a moment to relate the admirable workings of Providence. Providence is usually casual enough in her method, but when once embarked upon well-doing she takes the bit in her teeth and is unwilling to allow the most improbable coincidence to go unused. It had happened that a member of an evangelical publishing house in New York, who had in my youth befriended me, had been gathered to his fathers. I wrote to his partner a line of natural sympathy. This it was which lodged me in that partner's mind, and when in London, happening to be in the office of the *British Weekly*, he came upon the tale of *Mr. Chips* in galleys, he had the great kindness to cable me that here was a story I should like. It had nothing to do with my intelligence that *Mr. Chips* and I were brought together; but at least I had the wisdom to recognize gold without the guinea stamp on it.

This then was the key I had in my pocket when James Hilton came to lunch with me at the Athenaeum Club in London. Well do I remember that pleasant hour. Modesty is a charm that authors forget, but Hilton possessed it. He believed in the merit of his work as an artist must, but was very diffident about the outcome. Had not he given his best to the

The Happy Profession

public and had not the public shown its complete indifference?

When I learned of all the unread novels — were there five of them or more at the time? — I showed my surprise, but my conviction was absolutely unshaken. There was not only a fortune here, but a fortune well earned. I spoke with absolute assurance. I was an oldish man and he a young one. I had the right to advise but my advice filled him with an amused amazement. I bade him once for all keep away from Fleet Street. Let hackwork go to the hacks. Hilton's business was to take the prettiest of little apartments — Mayfair would do very well; to see no publishers; accept no assignments; simply once a year to send me the manuscript of a novel and to live without a care on his mind.

Hilton I think had a latent notion that I was spoofing, but the dream was pleasant and he dreamed it. We parted confident friends.

On my voyage home I had all the Hilton novels in my gripsack. Everything delighted but nothing surprised me. When *Mr. Chips* was published and its editions shot skyward, then and then only his other novels, notably *Lost Horizon*, caught fire and the Hilton bonfire was the blaze of the year. That fire has not died down.

CHAPTER XVII

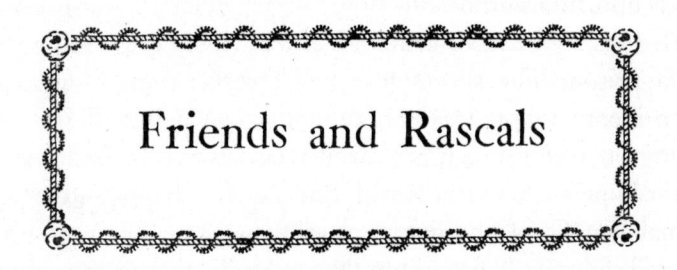

Friends and Rascals

LONG AS I have known the *Atlantic* the magazine has deeply concerned itself with the bitter problem of crime and punishment. With that most baffling of social ills, American preoccupation goes back almost to the founding of the Republic. In the early days of the nineteenth century when the doctrine that every man is his brother's keeper spread through the land, zeal for prison reform crystallized into concrete experiment, and to philanthropic observers everywhere it seemed that we were outstripping Europe both in the fervor of our endeavors and in their success. After a hundred years Sing Sing strikes us as a colossal failure, and we are making up our minds to pull it down, but in the 1830's the idea of a cellular system of confinement wherein the lonely sinner ponders his sins, repents and reforms, seemed to the wise and good an incalculable advance upon those festering congregations of vice and shame which disgraced the old penal system. The new approach marked a revolution in man's thinking. No longer was it sufficient to protect society by walling-in malefactors or transporting them to a secure distance. They were human beings like ourselves and we had no right to rid ourselves of responsibility for them whatever their trespasses against us. Certainly this was a triumph of Christian thinking, and the rising walls of Sing Sing, laid

The Happy Profession

brick by brick by the unfortunates who were to be its inmates, dramatized the event. On both sides of the water men read with uplifting enthusiasm how the imaginative warden marshaled his regiment of criminals and set them to building their own prison. The spectacle of malefactors compassing their own incarceration was unique, and when it became proudly known that not a man ran away from his task, wonder and a great hope arose in the world. But, as often happens, the most signal benefit of the great experiment came from an unexpected quarter. It was ostensibly to study the marvel of Sing Sing that de Tocqueville made his memorable visit and wrote the book which of all books has helped Americans to know themselves.

Since then the blasts of theory have beaten upon Sing Sing and all it has stood for. From the day Cain killed Abel men had thought it a man's fault when he did injury to another. But new winds of doctrine have blown us about. The Old Testament has lost its compelling force. Often it seems the blame is not the malefactor's but, for the most part, society must bear it. Reformers are apt to hold crime a mysterious illness born of maladjustment, poverty, and inequality; the fellow we pack off to prison is merely a scapegoat for the rest of us, and then there has entered the Court of Public Opinion evidence as to the culpability of the pituitary gland, the hidden dangers to society of hormones, the responsibility of adrenalin for rousing fear. Guilt, the old criterion of human weakness, tends to evaporate into a hundred obscure and unpunishable causes. Physiology on the loose is the real criminal. These windy theories have left the *Atlantic* if not untouched at least unshaken, but obviously something is very wrong with the expiation of crime and we tackled the problem repeatedly and hard. Often we got a hearing and twice, as I remember, newspapers gave us such vigorous support that real reforms

Friends and Rascals

were forced upon state legislatures. Here again was the indirect driving power of the *Atlantic*. We persuaded the persuaders. Preachers, publicists, and writers read the *Atlantic* and went to work for us.

The Editor took great interest in these efforts to give men driven from society at least a hope of ultimate reacceptance, and it was a corresponding satisfaction to have the *Atlantic's* influence recognized. This was brought home to me by the man from whom of all Americans of his day I liked best to hear it. Al Smith was running for the Presidency. While it ebbed elsewhere, his campaign was at flood in Massachusetts. The day that marked his Boston visit roused this old anemic town to a pitch of tumultuous excitement without parallel, I imagine, since the mob in Boston streets attempted to snatch a fugitive slave from the clutches of a wicked law. Even during the Police Strike, tense as emotions were, there was no such visible ebullition of popular feeling. That morning I got up early and struggled to my office through a crowd rapidly growing impenetrable. By ten o'clock all approaches to the Hotel Statler, where the candidate lodged, were blocked almost beyond breathing. When I neared my desk my telephone rang. Governor Smith would like me to come over for a talk. Looking out over Arlington Street I saw fifty thousand people packed between me and the hotel, and replied it was impossible to budge. In that case, came the answer, would I try after the evening speech.

That night at the Arena the scene was like a convulsion of Nature. It was an Irish crowd, and lodged within every Irishman is a mechanism capable of developing more steam than a respectable turbine. When you get ten thousand of them together, universal lunacy seems to close about you. I had seen it in Dublin and recognized it in our own Irish capital. At 10.30 P.M. I was a wrung towel, but I kept my date. On

The Happy Profession

the eleventh floor of the Hotel Statler I was led to the Governor's suite. There sat Al in the coat of his pajamas evidently in for a rest before the midnight train. His wise quizzical face lighted up and he greeted me with the warmth that taps a man's affections. "I came," said I, "for just one moment to shake your hand. I'm not going to be that ultimate straw." "Oh no!" he replied. "Have a cigar and stop awhile. I want to talk to you about those poor fellows I couldn't pardon. You were interested in them." We sat on the sofa. The cries and shouts outside were still at full blast — the sort of uproar Carlyle used to style "sibilation of world catcall or wild Tartarian trumpet." Such an ovation could not but stir a man to his marrow. But the Governor's quiet was complete. It was as if Al had raised his hand and at a twist turned off the electric current. His talk was a thousand miles from politics. He spoke of why boys and girls go wrong, and how under layers and layers of evil his religion had taught him never to forget the human bond that links man to men. He talked not emotionally but wisely and analytically. If Al Smith knew as much as any living man of the art of democratic government, it was because he understood intuitively and comprehensively the problems which beset the individual. Humanitarians are apt to build on sentiment; the Governor was too sagacious, too honest with himself for that. Doubtless when my time comes I shall accept the judgment of the Recording Angel, but if at my trial the Spirit of Al Smith presides, I shall be well content.

Among the most intelligent and imaginative of prison reformers of those days was Thomas Mott Osborne. His was a strange character with elements of the fantastic, but he loved men and often understood them. While he was in control of Sing Sing his experiments were of extreme interest, and when after a tragic persecution he removed to the prison at Ports-

Friends and Rascals

mouth, New Hampshire, he continued them with unabated zeal. Of course people called him a sentimentalist and talked of his coddling prisoners, but they were of those who look on prison as punishment alone. Talks with Osborne had much influence upon me, and when prisoners' letters came to the office, as they often did, I would invariably reply. There is something about writing to a *number* in care of the Warden at San Quentin or Atlanta which gives one a terrifying sense of what a man becomes, stripped of his personality, robbed of his name, metamorphosed to a series of digits in a cell block.

As my correspondence grew I would often receive a "gift" from some inmate — usually a cane which the writer invariably declared was made from old copies of the *Atlantic Monthly* molded into the marbleized coating of a steel core. At this moment my umbrella stand is full of them. Without accepting the authenticity of the source of the material, the thing was genuine, and one could always send a five-dollar bill and an encouraging note in exchange. During the high tide of this correspondence I was intent one morning on a very different problem when, at precisely eleven o'clock, my secretary stood in the doorway. "Somebody to see you, sir." Who was somebody? "Well, a man with a message from Mr. Osborne." "Show him in," I said, and asked the visitor to sit down. About the stranger's face I noticed a peculiar pallor as if he had recently emerged from a cellar. Those were the days when Lombroso's philosophy was in the ascendant, and with sudden intuition I scrutinized the man's ears. I felt certain now; the lobes were tightly joined to the cheek. About the eyes there was a look of furtive indirection, and I noted that the man was left-handed. My visitor seemed uncomfortable and sat silent. I brought him to life. "You've been in trouble, my friend?" I remarked, looking straight at him. He became all animation.

The Happy Profession

"Trouble," he replied. "Trouble! No trouble at all. I am the lucky one I am."

"Yes," said I. "But you've been in stir."

Apparently my visitor thought it wise to make a clean breast of it. With a cheerful grin he owned up. "I've done my time, five years of it," he replied. "But I'm free now. I'm free and I've got my job. It's in a machine shop, 246 Franklin Street. Oh I'm the lucky boy!"

"Well, if you're so well off," I inquired, "why do you come to me?"

"Come to you?" he replied. "I come because you're a friend of the boys. Again and again Mr. Osborne, he says to me, 'Mr. Sedgwick has the kindest heart in Boston.' That's what you have."

A compliment from Tom Osborne was praise from Sir Hubert. I could not help showing my pleasure.

"But you don't need a friend," said I. "You've got a job and you're all set."

"Well," said he in a burst of good fellowship, "sure I'm lucky and I've got my job, but there's this here to think of. It's Thursday and I'm to report on Monday morning. But so help me," and here his look proved his sincerity, "I haven't a red in my pants and there ought to be a few meals coming between me and Monday morning. It isn't dough I want. If you'll just hand me a loan of ten dollars to tide me over, I'll be up here Saturday week to pay you back."

We looked at each other. The white drawn face was very persuasive. I handed him a ten-dollar bill. "Good luck to you!" said I. "This isn't a loan, it's a gift, but let me see you again." He left the office looking as if he had pocketed salvation.

That day I went home with the consciousness of a good deed done. It was certainly kind of Mr. Osborne to keep me in mind. There's nothing, I reflected, to set a man up like an unsolicited tribute to virtues he fears are hidden.

Next morning was Friday. My desk was piled high and I went tearing at the mass of letters. When eleven o'clock struck I was lost in a hundred details. The *Atlantic* office was on Park Street then and the clock on Brimstone corner pealed the hour. Just as the last bell went, my secretary came in. "I don't want to be bothered!" I ejaculated, but she stood her ground. Now, at the outset of one's acquaintance, a secretary is the most sensitive and delicate of intruders, but years of association harden her and the training of an employer becomes a habit and a duty.

"Mr. Sedgwick, you'd better see him. He says it's of real importance and that he has a message for you."

I capitulated as usual and in came a new stranger. The former had been tall and lean. This gentleman was short and squat but his face too wore a singular pallor. He seemed a whiter white even than my friend of yesterday. It must have been a subcellar this man came up from.

At my invitation the visitor sat down. Lombroso simply obliged me to examine his ears. The lobes, there was no doubt of it, were joined fast to the cheek. His eyes had a deep-set look as though they did not often come out in the open. He was left-handed. He sat but said nothing.

"You're in trouble, my friend," I remarked kindly.

The man sprang to attention as though I had pricked him.

"Trouble!" he cried. "No trouble at all. I am the lucky one I am."

"You've been in stir." I made the assertion confidently.

"Yes," he admitted without a tremor, "but I've done my time, five years of it, and I'm free now. I'm free and I've got my job. It's in a machine shop at 246 Franklin Street. Oh I'm the lucky boy!"

The Happy Profession

A little coolness crept into my manner as I asked my next question. "If you're so well fixed, why do you come to me?"

My visitor's tongue was fairly unloosed. "Come to you! I've come because you're a friend of the boys. Again and again Mr. Osborne he says to me, 'Mr. Sedgwick has the kindest heart in Boston.' That's what you have, he says."

My pleasure of yesterday was somewhat dimmed. This additional tribute seemed to lay the praise on with a trowel. My voice was less cordial than usual. "But you don't need a friend, you have a job."

"Ah!" he said, and settled down to his work. "Sure I'm lucky and I've got my job, but there's this here to think of. It's Friday and I'm to report on Monday morning, but so help me I haven't a red in my pants and there ought to be a few meals coming between me and Monday morning. It isn't dough I want. If you'll just hand me the loan of ten dollars to tide me over, I'll be up here Saturday week to pay you back."

In the entire speech there was literally one single word altered. *Friday* had been substituted for Thursday. Otherwise even the intonation was exactly the same.

The scene was too comic for anger but it seemed dignified to express my indignation. "You rascal," I cried. "You liar! Only yesterday sitting in that chair another man told me that same story word for word."

If I had run a needle into his trouser leg, my vis-à-vis could not have been more flabbergasted. He started from his chair. "The snide," he cried, "the G——d d——d snide! He was a pal of mine at Sing Sing. We got out together with a suit of clothes and ten dollars apiece, but we thought our faces might give us away so we've been sitting out on a bench on the Common together to pick up a little tan and to think as how we could pan a few dollars without going in for a break. I thought up the plan for myself and I rehearsed it to him just so I could talk it off natural. And what did that s.o.b. do? With nary a word to me he sneaked up here first."

The tale had the ring of truth about it. My education in criminology had taken a step up.

I don't quite understand it, but among crooks and panhandlers I have a marked popularity. There must be some sort of unobtrusive honey in my calyx which my friends do not always find there but which is swooped down upon by these busy bees, with an infallible instinct. Just as I know a red-faced cabby when I see one or a bowlegged salt, they recognize me on sight.

Late one evening I was sitting before the fire deep as usual in manuscript, when the maid entered to say that a relative of mine wished to see me downstairs. "Relative," I ruminated, and wondered what a ten-o'clock-in-the-evening relationship might be. In the hall I was still more mystified. The caller was comfortably stoutish with delightful Celtic features and a brogue richer, I supposed, than any cousin's cousin of mine was blessed with.

"Thanks be to God," said he, "to meet a man of my own blood in this lonely place!"

I looked my surprise. "Why," he continued, "isn't your name Sedgwick?" I admitted the charge. "Well," said he, "what's mine, but 'Patrick Sedgwick Moriarty' I've been thinking it is," and he handed me his card. There, plain as print could make it, was "Mr. Patrick Sedgwick Moriarty."

"Where do you come from?" I inquired.

"Kilcoole, Wicklow County," he replied, "and faith 'tis full of Sedgwicks as an egg is of meat, and before I left the ould sod they told me there was morre of them still in Boston."

The Happy Profession

My genealogy was taking a new twist. So far as I knew the Sedgwicks hailed from Woburn, Bedfordshire, in England. But there was no time for reflection. Mr. Sedgwick Moriarty held out his hand in a gesture of cousinly confidence, and I took it.

"And how do you find yourself in Boston?" I asked.

" 'Twill be hence a full month," he replied, "before I get acclimated. 'Tis a cold place, Boston is."

"Ah, that's all on the outside," I exclaimed. "Boston is homey enough when you get used to it. But what can I do for you?"

"Bless God and His Saints for that worrd of comfort," he said, and his whole face was irradiated by a charming smile. " 'Tis like a Sedgwick that you talk. Well, Father Gildea taught me to speak up when I'm in throuble and tell nothing but the trruth. The trip from New Yorrk cost me forrty shillin's more than the bhoys had told me and it's a ten-dollar loan I'm after from a man of my own blood."

Now that I could hardly be expected to swallow. I knew he was lying and he knew that I knew. But I knew also that he was amusing me quite as much as if I were at the movies and that too he knew well. He pressed his advantage.

"Blood's a lot thicker than water," I remarked, "and there's nothing thin about Sedgwick blood. Here's your tenner. And now just as we've come to know each other, I'm afraid I shall see no more of you."

My cousin's face beamed. Parting is such sweet sorrow. "Thanks be to God," he repeated, "for a friend in throuble! They'll hear me tell it in Kilcoole."

Next morning I was walking down the Hill when I met my friend Judge Frederick Cabot. Judge Cabot dealt with panhandlers professionally, I merely as an amateur.

Friends and Rascals

"Did you know, Ellery," he said, "that Cabot is an Irish name? I was always told we came from the Channel Islands, but it seems we have a Celtic strain in us too."

"How did you pick up that information?" I asked.

"Why," said he, "last night I had a delightful call from an Irish cousin, Patrick Cabot Moriarty. When I saw his card I could hardly believe it. But he knew all about the family. It seems there is a peck of Cabots in Kilcoole."

"Did all this reach you free of charge?" I asked.

"No," replied the Judge, "I let him have ten dollars which he needed. But he's all right. He is perfectly charming."

Then I told him how I, too, was susceptible to charm.

Even a reasonable credulity is attended by some expense, but how much sounder is a heart of mush than a heart of stone! In spite of the Psalmist, the Sons of the Righteous sometimes beg their bread, and I for one had rather be fooled twice, than once, in the presence of real misfortune, to be tragically wrong. After all, when not too depraved, rascals are an amusing lot, and good talk from them is worth the price of a theater ticket. If they enrich you with a pleasant memory, enter "value received" as a sound item on your credit balance; and if you are too proud to risk being fooled, remember that, when a man is in dire need, to pass by on the other side makes in your books an indelible entry in red ink.

Thinking of these things reminds me of an incident which took place many years ago in New York. It was dusk on a mild evening and I was passing through Madison Square. My overcoat was unbuttoned and I was startled when a man leaning forward from one of the benches seized the flap and in a quiet voice declared: —

"I want that coat."

The Happy Profession

It was an unusual opening to a conversation and I fell in with its humor. "I am wearing it," I replied. "It is a new coat. I paid for it. That is a strong claim. What is yours?"

His voice was very deep and very low: "I am cold," he said, "and I *need* it."

The directness and simplicity of the argument struck me. Here was a concrete instance: "from every man according to his ability, to every man according to his need." Saint Martin's reply had been to strip his off but I was not Saint Martin. Yet the claim was not without validity. I took a middle course. I looked at the speaker carefully. He had a firm, lined face, and was decently though thinly dressed.

"I am afraid," said I, "I cannot give you the coat. It cost eighty dollars and I can't afford another. But if you will wait here for half an hour I'll bring you my old one."

He said, "That's nice of you," and then amused me by adding, "Would you believe it? I asked a decent-looking cove that same question not half an hour ago and what did he do but pull loose and walk off without so much as a word in answer to a civil question. What sort of a gazebo do you think he was?"

I walked on to Twenty-second Street where I was living and found my father sitting before the fire in an armchair. "Ell," he said, "manners are changing. As I came through the Square just now a man seized hold of my coat and quietly asked me to give it to him."

I burst out laughing. "Well, I've just come home," I said, "to give your friend a coat myself."

My father was a more charitable man than I but he was of his generation and I of mine.

A year or two later I was again passing through Madison Square. A young man respectably dressed but with a most woebegone expression stepped up to me.

"I beg your pardon, sir," he said politely, "but do you happen to be going out this evening?"

I expressed my intention of staying at home.

"That's lucky," my interlocutor went on, as if the last obstacle from his path had been removed. "Then perhaps you will be so kind as to lend me your dress suit, just overnight?"

"I should suppose," I returned genially, "that would be about the last article on earth you would need."

"No," said he, "I am all right so far as daylight goes, but if I could lay hold of a dress suit, I could earn ten dollars tonight by giving a song and dance at the Manhattan Club."

I explained to him that sound business practice requires full particulars before granting a loan. Then he told me his story.

He was, it seemed, the son of an Evangelical clergyman in Pennsylvania and, as clergymen's sons will, developed a passion for the stage. His father was unalterably and not improperly opposed. So the boy had run away from home, taken up with a stock company, met with some success, and then had been overtaken by disaster. At Fond du Lac, Wisconsin, his company had come its final cropper and disbanded. "It wasn't so bad for the men," said my friend, "but it was tough on the women. I sold my clothes, my dress suit with them, to help out. Now if I can get home, that's all I want."

That was the story. Whether to believe it was the question. There was truth, I was sure of it, in his manner and the directness of his glance. If he had really stripped the coat off his back to help a woman he was worth a risk, not perhaps of my very best but of my second-best suit. There is propriety in all things.

"I'll tell you what I'll do," I said. "We'll go together to a telegraph office and I will pay for a message to your father. Then we'll share a dish of ham and eggs and I'll lend you my extra dress clothes."

The Happy Profession

The sequel proved that he had spoken the exact truth. He did his turn at the Club, received his ten dollars, returned my suit at one o'clock in the morning, and two days later, his father's remittance in his pocket, came to bid me good-bye with the warmth of an old and obliged friend.

It was an entry on the right side of my ledger.

CHAPTER XVIII

Pure Prejudice

IT IS AN editor's duty to have prejudices — and to keep them to himself. Indeed, although schoolteachers do not know it, the inculcation of prejudice is a vital part of education. Wrongful and stupid prejudice, of course, abounds, but prejudices at once wise and discriminating not only make for virtue, for friendship, for loyalty, they can be exquisitely adapted to individuality, most priceless of human possessions, which the fashion and manners of the modern world are doing their best to stamp out.

Prejudices stem from ideas, but it is not ideas which mould the modern world. It is words, and against the misuse of words every editorial prejudice should be fixed in concrete. The blind confidence of most Americans in the validity of words is a direct inheritance of the Declaration of Independence. We forget it was not God Almighty but Thomas Jefferson who declared all men born equal and free in spite of very considerable evidence to the contrary. Ever since that startling manifesto, politicians have attuned their long ears to the sound of words. Straight words, honest words, words that call up an accurate picture of any cause they advocate they consistently eschew, but instead twist to some alien meaning sweet and pleasant words which have hitherto borne an utterly different connotation. Their favorites are words which people have always associated with well-loved causes. In our politi-

The Happy Profession

cal vocabulary these are the weasel words against which Theodore Roosevelt used to launch his choicest invectives. Call them rather jackal words, for they know no decency and hunt in packs.

Take the most threadbare of them all, "liberal," once a noble word. "Originally," says the dictionary, "the epithet for those arts which were worthy of a free man," it came naturally to signify an attitude favorable toward change in the direction of all the people. But it was slow and prudent change that the "liberal" favored. If it were swift and utter transformation the politician desired to express, a word stood by capable of its accurate expression. It is an honest word but "radical" has about it a certain sense of disruption, a complete break with the past. So the politician eschews it, and in its place slips the soothing syllables of "liberal." Any revolutionary change today is in the *liberal* direction. The closed shop is a *liberal* policy, sit-down strikes are expressions of *liberal* tolerance. And it goes without saying that all in opposition are classed as Tories, Tories such as fought against the American Revolution and have been at it ever since. Note for example any speech of Harry Bridges. Mr. Bridges merely desires to overthrow the Government of the United States, but never, never would he do it otherwise than by the advocacy of strictly *liberal* principles. And did you ever hear Mr. Hillman confessing to the prosecution of a *radical* design? Meanwhile Americans with some understanding of the past and reasonable hope for the future go on using *liberal* in its time-honored meaning, thus making it every day a more valuable prize for radicals to steal.

I have said these jackal words are used to hunt in packs. It is a poor stick of an orator who from CIO platform will not couple "liberal" with "democracy," tub thumping that chameleon word, employing it as an argument in itself. Once

Pure Prejudice

you get men to think a program part and parcel of the agglomeration now masquerading as democracy and you will be spared the painful effort of pleading your case on its merits. And it is observable that when an argument is shaky, then as if the Lord were speaking from Sinai, the name of Thomas Jefferson is invoked. And how many in the audience do you suppose realize that Jeffersonian Democracy is as much like the democracy of today as Paul Revere's copper mill is like the Anaconda Company? A third beloved word is "fair" — such a pleasant-spoken word it is that the more one-sided a proposal, the more necessary to use it. To some future lexicographer I leave the study of degeneration of words. What I want to mention here is simply that once you style a thing *liberal* or *fair* or *democratic* and keep reiterating it till in men's minds word and thing are synonymous, then the word has become the thing. How is it possible to contravene anything *liberal, fair,* and *democratic?* This is a jackal victory. The editor runs with the pack and the pack wins. So much for the unprejudiced editor.

Business too does not despise the jackal word. Take "service" — in my youth perhaps the most consecrated word in the language. Now every department store dedicates itself to *service*. From the pride with which it is used, you would suppose service synonymous with profits. But strip it to its kernel and you will get the real commercial significance of the word. It is simply the last charge against sales resistance. Can it be that the world has become more cynical? Oldsters are apt to think so. I can see myself in corduroys, making new resolutions which sound mawkish to a boy today: —

> For the cause that lacks assistance,
> For the wrong that needs resistance,
> For the future in the distance,
> And the good that I can do.

The Happy Profession

Prejudice has a bad name, yet what is it but suspended judgment? It is a brake on hasty action. Though it narrows the opinion it does not close the mind. When an untried idea is presented, it makes a man sniff — and perhaps the nose is a sounder guide than people think. When, in the agony of the First World War, our Secretary of State was outraged by the thought of Americans actually *fighting* for a cause, the British Ambassador said to me, "Your Mr. Bryan is an evil smell." Much as I esteemed the Great Commoner, I felt that the undiplomatic metaphor was correct.

My advice to beginning editors then is not to neglect prejudice but not to bear down upon it in too many directions at once. However strongly you feel, the important thing is never to *seem* to be intemperate. When your hopes are dim and your spirits dark, do not give vent to your own feelings but let some contributor speak his full mind for yours. Let him, if he can, paint the world blacker than it is. Let him take up the cudgels in behalf of your prejudices and exaggerate them to his heart's content. Remember that troops of readers whose bias runs counter to your own are always longing to have a go at you. Let the contributor draw their fire. Make him the editor's buckler and his stout shield. Once when my spirits drooped and the world seemed to be reaching an all-time low, the temptation came over me to break my own rules and be for once my own Jeremiah. Then it was, the Lord raised up a ram in the thicket and delivered me.

The letter which lay on my desk one morning was postmarked from the Belgian Congo, and had been months in coming. It was from a total stranger, elicited by some favorite prejudice appearing in the *Atlantic*, I forget which, but certainly the voicing of some doubt as to the upward and onward development of the human race. Anyway, the letter expressed vehement disagreement with the course of PROGRESS in the

Pure Prejudice

writer's native Europe, as in all the world besides. I suppose my correspondent was extremely illiberal but he had been educated to believe that in the individual lies the hope of the race. Of the wisdom of rule by the people he had grave doubts and saw proofs of his theories in a universal degeneracy of manners. The strength and definiteness of his views struck me (an editor is or ought to be objective). But it was much later that I came to understand how inevitably they were the product of the writer's life and education. Count Hans Coudenhove had been born rich, now he was poor. He had enjoyed large estates. Now he was landless. He had grown up in the alluring precincts of the Court of Schönbrunn, the most formal, reactionary, and aristocratic in Europe. The Emperor, unwilling to lower the barriers separating him from his inferiors, habitually sat solitary at his meals, but at Court receptions and balls he dispensed imperial hospitality, offering the favored few unequaled opportunities to learn manners in their exquisite perfection. A trumpery service in the modern world! you will say, but to me it seems that perfection or something near it is worth keeping, whether it be in dancing or in the social services. At any rate, this was the school in which Count Coudenhove was trained, and education thus acquired is in constant and peculiar need of cash to support it. Through the tumultuous years his estate brought smaller and still smaller a return. There could no longer be a thought of marriage for at court it is notorious that two people live at the price of four. But in order that a famous name might be preserved for posterity it was agreed between him and his nephew, Count Coudenhove-Kalergi, that two slender patrimonies should be united, that the younger man should marry and furnish descendants while the elder, unwilling to compromise and live a dependent where he had been brought up to command, should shake from his feet the gilded dust of Europe and, shifting his common denominator from gentleman to savage, go to live in the heart of Africa.

It is written in the code of aristocrats that their letters should not speak of money; neither should they make a fuss over misfortune. From sources other than my correspondent's letters I compile the details of this account.

Hans Coudenhove — he had dropped the "Count" and signed himself as a commoner — gave as the reason of his change of scene his growing distrust of the modern world and the black shadow which even then hung over what he had once thought of as civilization. He had found means of permanent support by serving as the agent for a rich Belgian who owned huge territories along the Congo, but whether his duties as factor were light or onerous I could never discover. At any rate, he had found time to discover the natives, to classify them into races and tribes, to understand their folkways, and to make friends with every bird and beast that ranged about his solitary camp. He lived quite alone without even a boy to cook for him, but friendly talks with the natives were never unwelcome, and from frequent meetings he had assembled a mass of multifarious and unusual information concerning the tribes and subtribes about him. A tiny hut, thatched from ridgepole to eaves and below largely open to wind and weather, a cot, a stool, ink, paper, and a book or two: his world had shrunk to this. Of Europeans his distrust grew steadily stronger with time and distance. Each morning, he wrote me, he would climb to a favored station high up in the branches of a tree, and there with his telescope sweep the horizon. If all was still, all was well. But if a wisp of smoke betrayed the distant advent of some traveler or trader, that day he would determine to move. I recall his phrase "My love of my kind varies inversely as the square of the distance which

Pure Prejudice

separates us." The further his kind retreated, the better he loved them.

Yet he was not lonely. Whenever he came upon a new tribe of savages with variation in the pattern of their customs, he was intensely interested, and every evening he had visitors — not one but scores. His cabin was in the center of a circular clearing, and precisely as the sun dropped into the forest, the chatter of monkeys would be heard. Scampering, scurrying, swinging through the underbrush, they would come to the very edge of the clearing and sit there in one great, comic, grinning circle, chattering their heads off, gabbling today's news and tomorrow's plans, patting their foreheads and their bellies, in unending hope their host would fill their stomachs and their minds as a Great White God ought to do. And while the hullabaloo of monkey talk filled the air, down would flutter a flock of inky ravens lighting on the ridgepole of his hut and fluttering their wings in apparent rhythm with the bedlam below.

Such was the life of my fastidious correspondent. I felt its fascination and happily he too was interested in the idea of writing a book. As our letters passed I looked forward every two months to a packet of his manuscript telling me some new strange history of a Negro tribe. I encouraged him to work systematically, promising to put the chapters together in a volume. I can see his odd manuscript before me as I write — the old-fashioned foolscap, inches longer than the present style, with the writing always on the right half of the page, leaving the left clear for notations or titles. In that way he had written his compositions in school fifty years before.

The day the first Coudenhove chapter was published in the *Atlantic*, a limousine drew up at my office door. The chauffeur had a note for me from Mrs. Jack Gardner. It read in sub-

The Happy Profession

stance that she had not supposed any American beside herself knew Hans Coudenhove. It appeared they had been great friends in Vienna, and more than once he had traveled in her company through Europe studying the galleries and ransacking the dealers' shops, appraising and buying pictures. This was personal news which I knew would be interesting to Hans Coudenhove. It was, and a common friendship with the most remarkable woman in the American scene lent a certain familiarity to our exchange of letters.

This correspondence of ours lasted nearly three years. The book was almost ready. Coudenhove wrote that his health was not of the best and hoped that the book might be brought out promptly. Then there was silence. I wrote and wrote again, but finally there made its appearance a fat letter bearing stamps from the Belgian Congo but addressed in an intricate foreign hand very different from Coudenhove's bold and vigorous characters. It was with premonition I opened it. Yes, he was gone, but the Dutch missionary who wrote the news added a chapter without which the story of Hans Coudenhove could not have been complete.

A fortnight before the end, the missionary, who knew him well and never irked him, had run across Coudenhove, who was on one of his extensive circuits of compulsory travel. His face was drawn and about his features played that unearthly look which so often tells the story of what soon must come. Coudenhove had chatted of his book. He had spoken of me. He had seemed quite serene, and when the missionary bade him be sure to send a runner should he ever be in need, Coudenhove dutifully promised. But when the forest trail closed behind him, the padre was uncomfortable. For one week he waited with impatience. Another, and a sense of Fate came over him, and on the twentieth day he could hesitate no longer. He made the long day's tramp to the little lonely

Pure Prejudice

camp. Toward evening he reached his journey's end. The sun was sinking into the endless forest and as it touched the tree-tops there arose an almost intolerable chatter. About the limits of the clearing, gibbering and grimacing in an unbroken circle, sat the row of monkeys, fearful of coming into the open and clinging to the very edge of their forest. And there too in a dense black line strung along the ridgepole of the cabin was a funereal row of ravens, croaking in harsh and solemn chorus. "Caw! Caw! Caw!" they cried in unison with the howls of the monkeys, the recurrent raucous rhythm rising and falling like the cacophonies of a Black Mass in a witch's cavern. The Dutchman bore within him a strong Calvinistic soul. He feared not the Devil nor his works. To his friend he had looked up as to a superior being. He mourned for him and in his ears this inarticulate hymn of grief was the canticle of Nature for her dead. So moving was the requiem of bird and beast, so fitting and so primal, that he felt himself an intruder in some sacred precinct held from the first inviolate to man. Here the human race was strange and alien, yet he well knew the scene before him was a consummation of everything his friend had desired. All that the dead man had really cared for drew close about him now. The fever of life was past. Again he was one with Nature.

For minutes the good priest stood half irresolute, half under the spell of that wild liturgy. Then he walked slowly to the hut. On the cot within lay the body of Hans Coudenhove hardly cold.

CHAPTER XIX

An Opalescent Chapter

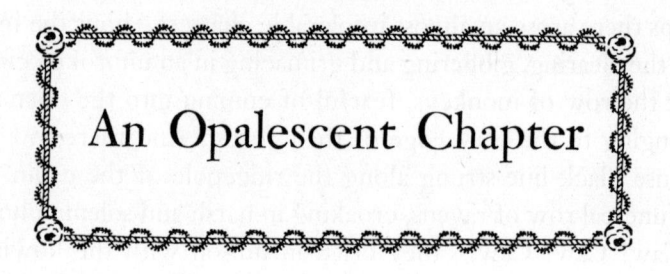

IF AUTHOR and editor have their work cut out for them, the reader has his duties too. True he is coaxed and coddled, but if he would be paid for his time, he must join in the common effort. To read means a change of mood, and the reader must give way to it. Not for nothing has he been appealed to as the Gentle Reader. He must put away all cantankerousness and suffer himself to be led like a dutiful medium when the "Professor" waves his hands. Good teachers lay stress on the position of a child learning to read. A reader must be at ease. He must be comfortable. As a woman knits to have something to keep her mind on while she talks, so a reader must have ease to keep his mind off everything but what he reads. A good book deserves a good chair, deep and satisfying, and I suspect that inside the chair the rightness of the disposition a reader makes of his back and legs, arms and elbows, has a great deal to do with his appreciation. When the story grows exciting, his chair must have an edge to it so he can draw forward and give his backbone full play for the shivers. Timing too is important. We all know the effect upon a ghost story when the great clock on the stairs strikes twelve for midnight. The ghost in the first act of *Hamlet* is not real at nine o'clock in the morning. Again, for a love story, I recommend to ladies a huddled position with the elbow pressed against the heart,

An Opalescent Chapter

and, of course, there are arrangements of body and mind to harmonize with the entire range of emotions. Indeed I have been credibly informed that there is but one way in the world for a lonely reader to cope with the Tales of Poe. Draw up a table and place it across the extreme corner of the room. Plant your lamp squarely upon it, then tuck your chair behind your breastwork so that your shoulders rest solidly where the walls meet, and you feel their steady, comforting support. Nothing now can crawl behind you. The House of Usher cannot fall upon you there and you are armored against the cutting edge of the Pendulum as it swings noiseless over the black pit dug in the very center of the library rug. As for the *Turn of the Screw*, black coffee and moist towels are a help, though they hardly suffice, and my advice is to slam that book tight shut, turn off the lights, and go to bed.

An open mind, says Chesterton, is like an open mouth, swallowing all that comes its way. But Chestertonian truth must be taken in a Pickwickian sense. To an editor open-mindedness is of the first importance. There is a point just below credulity and very far above skepticism where his mind should stick and open not one jot further. The so-called hard-boiled editor has none of the juices of life in him after the boiling is done. His role is to judge all that may be by what has been and to trim the possibilities of boundless experience to the metes of his own conventional mind. On the other hand there is the editor whose antennae are always a-quiver. This is an excellent characteristic for saints but not for editors. What the editor needs is imagination with tentacles on the fringe of it, in kind though not in degree such as faith has and science requires. If he meets a strange experience totally foreign to the probable, he should put on the brakes gently but let the motor run.

Twenty-five years ago I had reason to reflect on these things.

The Happy Profession

For those whom Nature loves, the Story of Opal is an open book. They need no introduction to the journal of this Understanding Heart. But the world, which veils the spirit and callouses the instincts, makes curiosity for most people the criterion of interest. They demand facts and backgrounds, theories and explanations, and for them it seems worth while to set forth something of the child's story undisclosed by the diary, and to attempt to weave together some impressions of its author. I quote from my record made at the time.[1]

Late on an afternoon in September, Opal Whiteley came into the *Atlantic's* office, with a book which she had had printed in Los Angeles. It was not a promising errand, though it had brought her all the way from the Western Coast, hoping to have published in regular fashion this volume, half fact, half fancy, of *The Fairyland Around Us*, the fairyland of beasts and blossoms, butterflies and birds. The book was quaintly embellished with colored pictures, pasted in by hand, and bore a hundred marks of special loving care. Yet about it there seemed little to tempt a publisher. Indeed, she had offered her wares in vain to more than one publishing house; and as her dollars were growing very few, the disappointment was severe. But about Opal Whiteley herself there was something to attract the attention even of a man of business — something very young and eager and fluttering, like a bird in a thicket.

The talk went as follows: —

"I am afraid we can't do anything with the book. But you must have had an interesting life. You have lived much in the woods?"

"Yes, in lots of lumber camps."

"How many?"

---

[1] I am indebted to G. P. Putnam's Sons for permission to quote from my Preface to *The Story of Opal*.

An Opalescent Chapter

"Nineteen. At least, we moved nineteen times."

It was hard not to be interested now. One close question followed another regarding the surroundings of her girlhood. The answers were so detailed, so sharply remembered, that the next question was natural.

"If you remember like that, you must have kept a diary."

Her eyes opened wide. "Yes, always. I do still."

"Then it is not this book I want, but the diary."

She caught her breath. "It's destroyed. It's all torn up." Tears were in her eyes.

"You loved it?"

"Yes; I told it everything."

"Then you kept the pieces."

The guess was easy (what child whose doll is rent asunder throws away the sawdust?), but she looked amazed.

"Yes, I have kept everything. The pieces are all stored in Los Angeles."

We telegraphed for them, and they came, crammed in a hatbox, hundreds, thousands, one might say half a million of them. Some few were large as a half-sheet of notepaper; more, scarce big enough to hold a letter of the alphabet. The paper was of all shades, sorts, and sizes: butchers' bags pressed and sliced in two, wrapping paper, the backs of envelopes — anything and everything that could hold writing. The early years of the diary are printed in letters so close that, when the sheets are fitted, not another letter can be squeezed in. In later passages the characters are written with childish clumsiness, and later still one sees the gradually forming adult hand.

The labor of piecing the diary together may fairly be described as enormous. For nine months almost continuously the diarist had labored, piecing it together sheet by sheet, each page a kind of picture-puzzle, lettered, for frugality (the store was precious), on both sides of the paper.

The Happy Profession

The entire diary, of which this volume covers but the two opening years, must comprise a total of a quarter of a million words. Upwards of seventy thousand — all that is contained in this volume — can be ascribed with more than reasonable definiteness to the end of Opal's sixth and to her seventh year. During all these months Opal Whiteley has been a frequent visitor in the *Atlantic's* office. With friendliness came confidence, and little by little, very gradually, an incident here, another there, her story came to be told. She was at first eager only for the future and for the opportunity to write and teach children about the world which she loved best. But as the thread of the diary was unraveled, she felt a growing interest in what her past had been, and in what lay behind her earliest recollections and the opening chapters of her printed record.

Her methods were nothing if not methodical. First, the framework of a sheet would be fitted and the outer edges squared. Here the adornment of borders in childish patterns, and the fortunate fact that the writer had employed a variety of colored crayons, using each color until it was exhausted, lent an unhoped-for aid. Then, odd sheets were fitted together; later, fragments of episodes. Whenever one was completed, it was typed by an assistant on a card, and in this way there came into being a card system that would do credit to a scientific museum of modest proportions. Finally the cards were filed in sequence, the manuscript then typed off and printed just as at first written, with no change whatever other than omissions, the adoption of reasonable rules of capitalization (the manuscript for many years has nothing but capitals), and the addition of punctuation, of which the manuscript is entirely innocent. The spelling — with the exception of occasional characteristic examples of the diarist's individual style — has, in the reader's interest, been widely amended.

An Opalescent Chapter

Opal Whiteley — so her story runs — was born about twenty-two years before I saw her manuscript — where, we have no knowledge. Of her parents, whom she believes she lost before her fifth year, she is sure of nothing except that they loved her, and that she loved them with a tenacity of affection as strong now as at the time of parting. To recall what manner of people they were, no physical proof remains except, perhaps, two precious little copybooks, which held their photographs and wherein her mother and father had set down things which they wished their little daughter to learn, both of the world about her and of that older world of legend and history, with which the diarist shows such capricious and entertaining familiarity. These books, for reasons beyond her knowledge, were taken away from Opal when she was about twelve years of age, and have never been returned, although there is ground for believing that they are still in existence.

Other curious clues to the identity of her father and mother come from the child's frequent use of French expressions, and sometimes of longer passages in French, and from her ready use of scientific terms. It is, perhaps, a fair inference that her father was a naturalist by profession or native taste, and that either he or her mother was French by birth or by education.

After her parents' death, there is an interlude in Opal's recollection which she does not understand, remembering only that for a brief season the sweet tradition of her mother's care was carried on by an older woman, possibly a governess, from whom, within a year, she was taken and, after recovering from a serious illness, given to the wife of an Oregon lumberman, lately parted from her first child — Opal Whiteley — whose place and name, for reasons quite unknown, were given to the present Opal.

From some time in her sixth year to the present, her diary has continued without serious interruption; and from the suc-

The Happy Profession

cessive chapters we shall see that her life, apart from the gay tranquility of her spirit, was not a happy one. Her friends were the animals and everything that flies or swims; her single confidant was her diary, to which she confided every trouble and every satisfaction.

When Opal was over twelve years old, a foster-sister, in a tragic fit of childish temper, unearthed the hiding place of the diary and tore it into a myriad of fragments. The work of years seemed destroyed, but Opal, who had treasured its understanding pages, picked up the pitiful scraps and stored them in a secret box. There they lay undisturbed for many years.

Such in briefest outline is the story Opal told; and month after month, while chapters of the diary were appearing in the *Atlantic*, snatches of the same history, together with descriptions of many unrecorded episodes, came in the editor's mail; and though the weaving is of very different texture, the pattern is unmistakably the pattern of the diary. Dates and names, peregrinations and marriages, births, deaths, and adventures less solemn and less apt to be accurately recollected, occurred just as the diary tells them. The existence of the diary itself was well remembered, though for many years Opal had never spoken of it; a friend recalled the calamitous day when the abundant chronicle of six years was destroyed; and a cloud of witnesses bore testimony to the multitudinous family of pets, and some even to the multicolored names they bore. There were many letters besides, which came not to the *Atlantic* at all, but were part of Opal's own correspondence with people "of understanding," members by instinct of that freemasonry which, as she learned long ago, binds folk of answering hearts and minds. Many of these letters (which rest for safety in the *Atlantic's* treasury) are messages

An Opalescent Chapter

of thanks for copies of that first book of Opal's — engaging letters, very personal most of them, bearing signatures to delight the eyes of collectors of autographs: M. Clemenceau, M. Poincaré, Lord Rayleigh, Lord Curzon, members of the French cabinet, scientists, men of letters, men of achievement. Opal has sought her friends all through the world; but her lantern is bright and she has found them. Her old Oregon teachers also have been quick to bear witness to her talents, and to recall the formal lessons which often she would not remember, and the other more necessary lessons which she could not forget. They would ask too whence came the French which they had never taught her. An attempt to answer that would take us far afield. All we need do here is to recall that first time, when Opal, full of puzzlement over letters that simply would not shape themselves into familiar phrases, turned to her early advisers and was told that they were French.

"But they can't be French! I never studied French."

But French they are, nevertheless.

If the story of Opal were written by another hand than her own, the central theme of it would be faith. No matter how doubtful the enterprise, the issue she always holds as certain, simply because the world is good and God loves His children. Loving herself all created things, from her barrelful of caterpillars, whose evolution she would note and chronicle from day to day, to the dogs and horses, squirrels, raccoons, and bats which peopled the world she lived in, she would thank God daily for them, and very early in her life determined to devote the rest of it to spreading knowledge of them and of their kind far and wide among little children.

To accomplish this needed education, and an education she would have. Those about her showed no interest; but by picking berries, washing, and work of all rough sorts, Opal

The Happy Profession

paid for the books which the high school required. But she must do more than this. She must go to college. To the State University she went, counting it nothing that she should live in a room without furniture other than a two-dollar cot, and two coats for blankets. Family conditions, however, made college impossible for her. After the illness and death of Mrs. Whiteley, whom Opal regards as her foster mother, Opal borrowed a little money from friends in Cottage Grove, Oregon, and started alone for Los Angeles, determined to seek her livelihood by giving nature lessons to classes of children.

The privations and disappointments of the next two years would make an heroic tale; but she persevered, and her classes became successful. The next step was her nature book, for which, by personal canvass for subscriptions, she raised not less than the prodigious sum of $9400. But the printers, with a girl for a client, demanded more and still more money, and, when the final $600 necessary to make the booty mount to $10,000 was not forthcoming, with a brutality that would do credit to a Thénardier, first threatened, and then destroyed the plates.

Although I have seen the book, of these details of its manufacture I have no knowledge other than Opal's own testimony. To many other separate episodes of her story, I have secured abundant corroboration.

A struggle for mere existence followed, but gradually Opal triumphed, when she was overtaken by a serious illness and taken to the hospital. New and merciful friends, such as are always conjured up by such a life as Opal's, came to her assistance, and after her recovery she soon started eastward, to find a publisher for her ill-fated volume. The rest we know.

Yet, after all, our theme should not be Opal, but Opal's book. She is the child of curious and interesting circumstance, but of circumstance her journal is altogether independent.

An Opalescent Chapter

The authorship does not matter, nor the life from which it came. There the book is. Nothing else is like it, nor apt to be. If there is alchemy in Nature, it is in children's hearts the unspoiled treasure lies, and for that room of the treasure house, the Story of Opal offers a tiny golden key.

No hieroglyph with the Rosetta Stone for its alphabet involved more puzzlement than the reconstruction of Opal's story. And for Opal herself provision had to be made. My mother-in-law, whose children had long since fled the nest, lived alone in a huge Brookline house, and under her protection we installed Opal. Leading from Opal's bedchamber was a large sitting room. All furniture was swept away, and on the floor inch by inch she pieced and patched the scraps of diary. Month after month she labored, toiling her eight hours and then roaming the fields and woods making close friends of every bird and creature that flew or scampered within a mile of her abode.

The wonder grew. Opal's talk was full of the tags of French phrases. Invariably she spoke of *"mon père"* and *"ma mère"* who had made her earliest years so bright, but of the mystery of her birth she made no claim to solution. Only as the diary came into completer being did little references tumble out of it which seemed to point to great people and greater places in a land beyond the sea. But even in the first chapter, printed in the big capitals of a four- or five-year-old, there were allusions not often gossiped of in an Oregon lumber camp. Lars Porsena of Clusium, Aphrodite, Jupiter Zeus, Chantilly, Iona, and Saint Columba, the Pensée Girl, Aristotle, Grand'mère, and a hundred more. As the successive installments of the story appeared in the *Atlantic* interest rose to a high pitch. Many readers were utterly incredulous, but in the large circle who knew Opal and watched her at work, there was no doubt whatsoever that, whether or not Opal was the daughter of a casual laborer in a logging camp, she believed with all her heart and soul and mind that she was born to a very different destiny. Letters poured in, many from people bearing well-known names, captivated by the simplicity and imagination of her journal. One of these came from Sir Edward Grey, who chanced to be in this country. Charmed by Opal's intimacy with bird life, he arranged a visit, and during the thirty years I guided the *Atlantic* I have never watched two more delighted and understanding friends than the statesman and the child of the woods talking back and forth of wrens and pewits, of orioles and cuckoos. The following year it was Sir Edward who wrote the preface to the English edition of Opal's story.

Opal ran the gamut of scientists and doctors. She was a somnambulist and there were other symptoms of abnormality about her. But what little we could glean of her past apart from the diary came from scores of letters from persons, many half illiterate, who had known her in the rough Northwest. Tantalizing clues kept turning up, but none led to a straight path. One of the most perplexing came to me from Ontario in the form of a parcel of handsome portrait photographs in the aristocratic old-style manner of the '70s and '80s bearing the French name of a Paris studio. They pictured handsome bearded men with pointed mustachios, and scribbled on the backs in pencil were briefest words of identification: "Opal's father," "Opal's uncle," and so on. Of course it was entirely possible that some confederate or chance reader, amused to add to our obfuscation, had dispatched them and decamped from the Calgary Hotel whence they came. There by telegraph I had prompt but vain investigation made, but the Oregon constable who wrote to inquire whether we had heard of elaborate pieces of silverware in the possession of Mr. Whiteley, Opal's reported father, complicated the conun-

An Opalescent Chapter

drum. There were a hundred other shadowy clues hardly less baffling, but to tell the full story of Opal Whiteley would require a documented volume, illustrated by photographs, of the masses of material still in the *Atlantic's* possession, and to complete it, strange adventures of my own should be added, tales of espionage, flights, and pilgrimages, still difficult to understand, to say nothing of people of note who slipped in and out of the story.

A quarter of a century has passed, but still letters come in, one this very week, asking questions it would take a block of foolscap to answer. A thousand people have put it to me straight, "Do you believe Opal's story?" I will make one final answer now.

What Opal may have come to believe, grubbing in libraries, poring over out-of-the-way biographies, patching little phrases from her diary against the history of Henry of Bourbon, scientist, hunter, Orléanist heir to a monarchy long since swept into the dustbin of empires — that is a very different matter from the question of the veracity of the journal of this child of fancy. Of the rightness and honesty of the manuscript as the *Atlantic* printed it, I am utterly convinced; more certain am I than of the authorship of many another famous diary, for I have watched the original copy reborn and subjected it to the closest scrutiny. We all know what happens to people who brood upon a single idea, who sleep and wake with it and come thereby to feel themselves singular and apart. Who can say that here or here runs the boundary line of sanity and verity? But such questionings belong to later years. The child who wrote Opal's diary believed in it. She knew it for her own.

How can one account for remembrances so natural yet with so strong an admixture of something strange, foreign, and beyond the horizon of normality? To this I would answer

The Happy Profession

that I have no knowledge but I have a theory and hold to it. Among an infinitude of letters came one written by an American of French parentage, whose father, so he told me, was a sergeant in the Franco-Prussian War of 1870. Of this sergeant's regiment, the colonel or perhaps the general of his division was Prince Henry of Bourbon, and toward the close of his life the prince, traveling across America, stopped in Oregon to have a chat with his old soldier. Whether or not this is fact I cannot say, but my correspondent had no doubt of it since, chief among his childhood memories, was the arrival of the prince at the cottage door of his father. "I sat on his knee," he told me, and I believed him.

Now, according to my theory, the visit of a prince of the blood to an Oregon hamlet was an event. The truth and the legend of it spread through the lumber camps, and what is more likely than that such a tale captivated the mind of a lonely and imaginative child and that her daydreams centered about it. At the heart of every little girl Cinderella sits enthroned, and with Opal the legend grew to be true, and the truth magnified with the years, and finally permeated her entire mind, her fancy, and her life.

Such is my theory of Opal's childhood, but in after years the story becomes an attested record of fact and yet, to my thinking, loses nothing of its wonder thereby. Opal, who had come to know many notable people in New York and Washington, and who had been petted and patronized by them, grew sick of it all. She went to England, always making friends, took up the faith of her "father," and established herself in a Catholic community at Oxford. Then one day I had startling news of her. A friend of my youth, Mrs. Rosina Emmet Sherwood, mother of a playwright long since grown famous, wrote me asking whether it was possible to believe a correspondent of hers who stated that with her own eyes she

An Opalescent Chapter

had seen Opal sitting like the princess in the story in an open barouche driving in state down the streets of Allahabad, royal outriders clearing the way for H.R.H. Mlle. Françoise de Bourbon! The story was credible for it was true. I verified it beyond conjecture. First I wrote to Opal, who sent me a collection of photographs of her Indian tour. There she was perched in a howdah on an elephant's back, ready for a tiger hunt (Henri de Bourbon, be it noted, was famous for his bag of thirty-six tigers, and I laughed as I recalled Opal chanting French verses in honor of his victory), and there she stood the center of many another turbaned group. Photographs, as I have remarked frequently in the narrative, can be liars and many of them stem from Hollywood which hardly contradicts the term. I was not satisfied, and since Opal's narrative identified two of the greatest Maharajahs who had been her hosts, I wrote to both their courts. In due time two letters returned, emblazoned with regal crests, each informing me the writer's royal master bade the secretary reply that it had been his high privilege to entertain H.R.H. Mlle. Françoise de Bourbon, and that a series of fêtes had been given to do her honor. And the wonder of all this had not subsided when an unsolicited letter arrived from a lieutenant colonel of His Majesty's forces occupied at the moment with maneuvers at Aldershot, informing the editor with some asperity that the colonel himself had been honored by an order to attend Her Royal Highness at an official garden party given for her entertainment, and further he begged to ask who it was that had questioned the authenticity of the lady who had graced the occasion.

I close this account on a melancholy note. In the journal which Opal sent to accompany her photographs, no vestige remained of the contagious fascination of an earlier day. She described things as they are. The dew of the morning had vanished. The hard sunlight of middle age beat down upon a world that everybody sees only too clearly. The fairy kingdom was now the playground of other children. Its gates were closed, and Opal stood without. But while she was still the Opal of the *Journal of an Understanding Heart,* she had had her vision, and that vision was true. There is no truth more certain than that which makes bright the heart of childhood.

CHAPTER XX

The Borderland of Genius

READERS who like to believe what they believed before the evidence was heard, and those who pride themselves on the intelligence of their skepticism, may be relieved when I turn to a story of documented fact. But many there are like me who will feel that the tale of Mary Antin is no whit less marvelous than Opal's story for all that it follows the beaten path of history. For at thirty, Miss Antin had lived at the very least through seven centuries. Prester John could do no more than that.

When Mary Antin was born, her little congested world in Polotsk, Russia, had a fence about it, the very same Pale which had stood for hundreds of years, shutting the Jews in but never the Gentiles out, when a pogrom was afoot, or police tried to make trouble, or there was money to be wrung out of Jewry by some Christian brigand lining his own pockets and gaining grace from the Lord Jesus by revenging His murder on the Tree. In Polotsk everybody was afraid and lived fearfully as long as great-great-great-grandfathers could remember. The only sense of security which ever came to the little girl growing up there was when, with shutters closed and door bolted, the house was made clean, shining, and holy "even in the corners where nobody ever looked," and she in her best dress sat down at the feast, culmination of Passover Week. Then she was free to ask the Four Questions about "unleavened bread and bitter herbs and other things," and the family, reading from their books, could answer her in peace. Of course there was no more real security then than on Monday when she trudged to school, a prey to every Russian child who cared to spit at her, but the presence of God made it seem so. And, to be sure, there was also the protection of a large colored print of the bad Czar hung in the parlor which gave an excellent impression to the police.

Mary came from a well-to-do family. The father was a scholar, a *rav*, and what *rav* wants bread, bread and respect, within the Ghetto? But her mother, daughter of Raphael "the Russian" (on account of his peddling journeys among the Gentiles), brought a desirable dowry which stood the family in good stead when they were allowed to emigrate to the Promised Land. She it was who taught the children the undiluted joy of the penny saved by the seller and lost by the buyer, but it was from Raphael who traveled in Russia, even as far as Kherson and Odessa, who brought to his family the sense of the shackling of old ways and the urge for what we call progress but which a philosopher might regard as the barter of conviction for experiment.

What was wonderful fortune in Mary's life was that the family hegira took place when she was old enough to absorb the meaning of ancient customs and to digest as it were an immemorial life. Well did she understand this herself. "All the processes of uprooting, transporting, replanting, acclimatizing and development" took place in her own soul. "I felt the pang, the fear, the wonder, and the joy of it. I can never forget for I bear the scars. But I want to forget — sometimes I long to forget. I think I have thoroughly assimilated my past. I have done its bidding. I want now to be of today. It

The Borderland of Genius

is painful to be consciously of two worlds. The Wandering Jew in me seeks forgetfulness. I take the hint from the Ancient Mariner who told his tale — in order to be rid of it. I too will tell my tale for once and never hark back again any more. I will write a bold 'Finis' at the end and shut the book with a bang."

The same thought was in her mind when she closed the schoolgirl chapter of her life in the Promised Land. She had come back from a field day on the ocean shore with the Natural History Club, and then — on the steps of her university, the Public Library, "I parted from my friends. My heart was full of a stirring wonder. I was hardly conscious of the place where I stood or of the day or of the hour. I was in a dreamland and the familiar world about me was transfigured. My hair was damp with sea spray. The roar of the tide was still in my ears. Mighty thoughts surged through my dreams and I trembled with understanding."

She stood on the isthmus between two worlds. She had come from an illimitable past. She looked forward to an endless future. She had been a child of the Ghetto. She was an American.

The wonderful chapters of her autobiography brought to the *Atlantic* abundant life from a new quarter. But when Mary Antin shut her book with a bang, she did not know that, while years of satisfaction lay ahead, her real work was done. Of the changes and chances that followed she says, "A combination of shock and reverence drove me into the bypath of public life." But one observer thinks differently. America has many voices, but the loudest in those days was Theodore Roosevelt's. Like everybody else he felt the significance as well as the fascination of her story and, like every Roosevelt, thought no career too valuable to be twisted from its orbit to do him service. President Roosevelt called to Mary

Antin and no warnings could dissuade her from following his chariot. She took the stump for him. Her weak voice and frail presence made a shallower impression than the deep-voiced eloquence of her book. The indiscriminate applause surrounding her platform, whether the talk was political or touched on deeper issues, altered her true sense of values. More and more she became Mary Antin, author of *The Promised Land,* less and less the expression of the genius of an ancient race, and gradually her voice was stilled altogether.

How sane are any of us? Often I think asylum walls make the wrong divisions. At any rate, there are comfortable little conspiracies among those of us who have more or less the same distorted idea of the universe to regard our conception as beyond all doubt the Creator's view of things. "All the world is queer save thee and me, Martha, and even thee is a little queer." There is a passage, I forget where, in Ben Franklin (and if he is not a test of sanity, where, I wonder, can one be found?) describing the competitive certainties of religious beliefs. Poor Richard avers that certainty about the truth reminds him of a huge crowd on a murky day. As you look about, you see all the groups which make it up so enveloped in rain and cloud you wonder how they can see at all, but right round you things are so much more distinct. You can see whole yards ahead. Poor blind folk: clear-sighted me! There is always the similar danger of an editor's taking a self-centered view in which he is judge and jury in all things and, if he wants a specific against this poisonous form of sanity, my advice is to have a chat with a first-rate crank. About a crank there is an aura of something wholesome, something outside himself, something that self-righteous sanity can always profit by.

I remember myself caught in the toils; marveling on the

The Borderland of Genius

uniform stupidity of others. Then in came a little lady with bright eyes, pink cheeks, and a charming air of uncertainty about her. "What can I do for you, Madam?" I asked. And she with sweetness replied, "That's not it. It is what I can do for you. I've brought you something wonderful, something perfectly wonderful. I have brought you the most beautiful idea in the whole world." "And what is that?" — "Oh," she replied, and her blue eyes took on a most laughable shrewdness, "you must tell me first what you'll pay me for it." "How can I tell its worth till you tell me what it is?" "Oh, but if you know my secret it isn't mine any longer, it's yours, and then of course you will have no reason to pay." And as she went away she kept murmuring, "Oh, it's all my own and it's beautiful, it's so beautiful!" I thought to myself, "There may go the secret of happiness and I shall never know it."

For several years my personal bulwark against traces of egregious sanity was one Cloudesley Johns. What a distinguished name! Were I writing an aristocratic novel, it should belong to my hero! But what puzzled me was to see that blue-blooded signature on such inappropriate stationery. The letters which came every week, sometimes oftener, were written on the backs of envelopes, scraps of yellow paper, and the like. The addresses given were all different, but invariably bore the stamp of a post office in a remote section. The letters themselves were of such a philosophical cast that I became interested. Johns's favorite philosophers were Greeks, and amongst them Epictetus had the foremost place. Indeed certain Epictetan maxims seemed to form the basis of his personal creed. Apart from the will, Johns maintained, "there is nothing good or bad, and it is our business not to anticipate or direct events but to accept them with intelligence." Admirable doctrine, I agreed, in this eminently compulsive world; but

The Happy Profession

all the time I kept wondering what profession supported my correspondent during his researches.

One day I learned the answer. The date was long ago. I was working late in my little New York office, struggling to bring an impossible magazine fractionally nearer the blessed possibilities of solvency. The door opened and our diminutive office boy announced, "A man to see you, sir." Since in the office vocabulary a man is always "a gentleman," I was less surprised than I should have been by the outward appearance of my visitor. He was a ruddy, pleasant-faced fellow in a bright red shirt, no cravat, and trousers imperfectly supported on one side only. What was it Epictetus used to say? It came grotesquely to my mind: "Every thing hath two handles, the one to be held by, the other not." A physical illustration of the master's doctrine, I thought to myself as I welcomed Mr. Johns to a seat. For an hour he held forth and I was vastly entertained by his adventures. All doubts of his profession were removed. He was Homo Vagrans, a tramp, in the vernacular a Hobo. Halfway through a law course in California he had vamoosed, his wanderlust become too much for him, and for two years he had hoofed it this way and that, not with the purpose of arriving anywhere but simply to keep on the move. Evidently Einstein's doctrine of the Fourth Dimension wrung from motion had laid hold on him before the promulgation of that surprising law. In his wanderings Johns had picked up a fraternity of hoboes. One amongst them, an ardent, engaging chap, was very stimulating to his philosophy, and with him he made many journeys, the two of them living like crows off the land, while they planned the reorganization of society and disposed of Heaven and Hell. The young man's name was Jack London.

Johns told his tale at length. After he had crisscrossed California and Oregon, far-flung thoughts came to him of seeing

The Borderland of Genius

all America. He had agreed with Jack that it would not be long now before the land would be restored to the people, so this seemed an opportune time to look the estate over. Three-hundred-mile walks he had found pleasant strolling, but with a three-thousand-mile trail ahead, he compromised on a Hobo-Pullman. At Fresno he had swung on the brake beam, making use of a technique well known to brothers of the road. On the under side of every freight car, paralleling its length, run several lines of steel rods connecting, I suppose, with the brakes. Upon the outermost of these, lying transversely, the Pullman passenger rests his neck. Beneath the small of his back runs a second, while the tendon Achilles of each heel hooks over a third. On an unoiled track the dust is considerable and the springs have a certain rigidity. But after all, the trip is "on the railroad" and petty discomforts can be borne. The real "out" in this method of travel only becomes apparent when the engine stops for water. Then along the line of freights walk trackmen with long hammers which they swing vigorously under the cars to dislodge ticketless passengers. On such occasions Johns always made a point of strolling a little way along the tracks. Being young and supple he made the journey not too disagreeably, yet his mind was not at rest. In the Fresno library he had been deep in his Epictetus. He had learned that as a member of his community he was also a member of the Infinite City of Gods and Men of which the City Political is but a copy in miniature. But try as he would, he could not recall the next step in the famous argument. So, at the last stop before Chicago, Johns swung out of his berth. The next three days he spent from nine till closing time in the Newberry Library, and not until the book was well digested did he resume his journey.

The next extended stop was Baltimore, and the B. & O. freight yards, Johns told me, are anathema to every honest wayfarer. The cops there are unscrupulous and rampant, and the whole train of Johns's thought was dislocated as he dashed under one car and over another with a pair of cops at his heels. It was undignified and disagreeable — damnable, Johns called it and the word was not too strong. Anyhow he made his New York connection and here he was.

So he talked and I listened till the street lights came on and it seemed dark enough to risk my budding reputation walking with a man at whom at every corner policemen looked askance. I led the way to a snug little restaurant on Avenue B, and there we finished our evening of philosophy and adventure. We were shaking hands on a pleasant dinner when Johns suddenly asked, "Where are you putting me up for the night?" That was a poser. My salary was precisely thirty-six dollars a week, but the thought of sharing my boardinghouse bed with a tramp was more painful still. So I stripped off one third of my roll and, handing him twelve dollars, bade him go to a certain hostelry on the Bowery which I thought adequate to his purpose.

When my friend entered my office next morning he was in an irritable humor. "That is a hell of a place you sent me to, Sedgwick," he said crossly. "It's buggy." I told him for shame! Never would Epictetus have allowed himself to be distracted by such company. But Johns was not satisfied. The whole week he spent with me, after long and companionable discourse, he would upbraid me for my stinginess in not sharing my all with a comrade. Much that he told me opened a new world. Always beside his books ran running brooks, and his sermons in stone were the tiny cairns which well-disposed hoboes erect at turnings of the road to make sure that friends following them shall not go astray. Place the stones this way and you build a warning that the next farmhouse is disgraced by a ferocious dog. But lift the position of this

The Borderland of Genius

little conical rock and the meaning is that the woman who lives down the lane has a kind heart and a full larder. Then there are special monograms and initials to be wrought in tiny wayside rock piles which tell who it is that passed that way. It was in such hieroglyphs that Johns had read Jack London's signature at a crossroad and found him on the morrow.

The communion of friends hath an end. When the time came to say good-bye, Johns was still dissatisfied with his host. "Think," he said, "of the good time I have given you!" "Think of how full your belly is!" I retorted, and then continued forcibly: "Think too how full it has been for a week at my expense! It is you who owe me something. You, Cloudesley, have the experience and I the need of profiting by it. Tell me, for a philosopher like you ought to know, just what is the happiest moment in human existence?" He became quite grave and thought awhile. Then he ruminated slowly, "The happiest moment? Why, it is strolling along a meadow path to the westward under a row of willows alongside the river and the sun about to set in the red ball which foretells a good tomorrow. Comfortable within, your dinner just completing its digestion — and without the slightest idea where your supper is to come from." "But, Johns," said I, "wouldn't it put the button on Fortune's cap if you had just an inkling as to where your next meal is to come from?" Johns scowled. "That's like you, Sedgwick. You're a simon-pure materialist. You think as brute beasts do. To a man," and here he touched his forehead, "such questionings serve to keep the soul awake and the mind alert. To a philosopher a shadow of doubt is the very light of happiness."

Often and often I have thought of those words. There is more than a grain of truth in them.

CHAPTER XXI

Home without the Bacon

OF ALL the recognized orders of cranks, the choicest for a man given to reflection are the Baconians. How well you learn to recognize the breed. When they slip into your office they walk delicately like undertakers, their furtive air reminiscent of the Pirates of Penzance. They ask whether "we may not be quite alone for ten minutes," and almost always they carry black cases bulging with papers. The name "Baconian" descends not directly from the great Francis but more immediately from an American lady, Miss Delia Bacon — a spinster wedded to a theory. If you seek a delightful account of her, look up John Fiske's essay upon his Delia in the *Atlantic*. It cannot be gainsaid, however, that Miss Bacon was a scholar and a clever one, full of Rosicrucian learning and with a sharp eye for a cipher embedded in the printed page, so sharp perhaps that where never cipher was, she could see it clear as crystal. Delia's disciples were many, the most famous of them Ignatius Donnelly, politician, scholar, and visionary whose diverting life has never been satisfactorily written. From countless lecture platforms, from pamphlets, books, and magazines he sowed the infectious Baconian seed. In his employ were two maiden ladies, "the works" of his factory, the Miss Gallops, whose agreeable duty it was with intricate outlines of ciphers stamped on their intelligent minds,

Home without the Bacon

to apply one or another to all the greater works of the Baconian period, and thus disentangle countless dramas enmeshed in the poems and plays of a dozen ostensible poets. Through the centuries it seems these poetic names have served as dominoes concealing the transcendent genius of Francis Bacon, true author of all the works which have made his age supreme in letters since time began. Sidney, Peele, Nash, Greene, Florio, and the rest were, as I understand it, privy to the plot, conspiring together in order to protect the temporal reputation of Francis Bacon, a sober scholar dedicated to Science uncontaminated by the folderol of fantasy and make-believe, and permitted to preen themselves forever in his immortal feathers. Quite a theory to support you say, Incredulous Reader. But in fact this is the facile and persuasive side of the argument. The really difficult half of it is the monstrous addition the theory puts upon the author's labors; the infinite complexity of the mathematical combinations whereby the cipher in its strict and formal mosaic of consecutive letters is patterned cunningly beneath every lyric outburst, every marvel of character and description throughout the most glorious flowering of all time.

A Baconian cannot be unless he is gifted with perpetual enthusiasm. For him the trail is always hot. Perhaps this is what makes him so stimulating a companion. A member of the ardent race who bore the honorable but unrelated name of William H. Prescott handed me one day in his library a facsimile of Sidney's *Arcadia*. I turned to the title page and a ludicrous light broke over me. Two fluted columns decorated the title. Each bore a girdle about its middle of six dangling masks. Too easy a cryptogram, I thought. Those are the twelve vizards of the twelve poets who hide from view the lineaments of the supreme artifex. Then I looked further. The colophon at the bottom of the page was in the likeness of a blooming rosebush and sniffing it, his snout fairly sucking the sweetness from the petals, stood a porker. For one second there was puzzlement. Then I almost shouted. I have it! Francis Bacon smelling the Tudor Rose! Francis, as every Baconian knows, being the illegitimate son of the Virgin Queen. "Yes, of course. That's the signature plain enough," said my friend, "but the important cryptogram is in the text. When I deciphered that, I felt as if I were really entering history. There it is plain as print, as my cipher shows — the last will and testament of William Shakespeare giving the whole case away. I followed the trail through England and was within inches of getting to the end of it when a most unlucky accident overtook me." Then he told as extraordinary a saga of adventure as I have heard. But this tale of the pick which rang against the iron chest, deep buried at the confluence of the Severn and the Wye, the chest that holds the testament of William Shakespeare — that is his story and not mine.

A year or two afterwards, however, my own story turned up. This, too, ought not to be mine. It belongs of right to the *Arabian Nights' Entertainments,* but since Scheherazade did not live to tell it, I will. The reader will please remember that what follows is not romance but a literal record of facts indelibly remembered.

After some preliminary correspondence I received a formal call from Colonel F. — I won't give his name for I liked him well and he rode so colossal a theory that it might be thought I was making fun of him. Anyway, he was an impressive gentleman, broad of beam, forcible of speech. There was no nonsense about him; facts were facts. He told me simply that he had the proofs. They would convince any fool. (Fool was evidently his euphemism for editor.) The only difficulty in

Home without the Bacon

the way of exposing the whole conspiracy was the enormous vested interest involved.

"Vested interest?" I muttered.

"Yes," said he, pounding the arm of his chair so forcibly I feared it might dislocate the supporting spindles. "Every chair of English in every college is at stake. Every department of English in every school. You cannot count the jobs that would be swept out on the dungheap if these preposterous theories about William Shakespeare were swept away. That dummy of Avon who couldn't even spell his own name! Oh, it would be ridiculous if it weren't so tragically wrong."

I saw it was not a propitious moment for argument so I merely looked my interest.

"Come to Chicago and I'll show you," he said, and to Chicago I went.

A few days later the Colonel (in his big limousine) called for me at my Chicago hotel and we swung south along the famous Shore Drive. For two hours we drove exchanging merely casual talk. Suddenly we passed a huge pile of the carcasses of automobiles — wheels, chassis, steering gear, hoods, formed a mighty pyramid. "Gracious!" I murmured. "What an accident!" "Accident?" said the Colonel. "Why, it's a little venture of mine. I make a business of accidents. I have arranged with the police whenever there is a crack-up that my agent should be notified instantly. He buys the wrecks for spot cash. You see, there is quite a discount. Then we reassemble the machines when we have a chance and make 500 per cent profit."

Before such business acumen I felt humble, but I could not help thinking of Crassus and his private fire brigade, bargaining on the spot for the blazing houses of rich Romans. We drove on. Of a sudden from the woods on our right came a yelp, then a whole series of wild barks. I knew that sound though it was years since I had heard it one night on a Colorado plateau when I had kept piling up the fire as a protection against the howling coyotes. "Wolves," I remarked tersely, although central Illinois is not their natural habitat. "Yes," he replied indifferently, "I keep a pack in my park." It grew obvious that my companion was no common fellow, but the sense of his individuality was intensified when he threw open his wide front door and went in search of his wife. I looked about the spacious living room. It was full of deep-seated chairs. Sofas and tables were scattered about and yet the whole apartment was pervaded by a sense of quiet emptiness. I could not tell why but I felt instantly that I had never seen a room like it before. I took a second look and the oddity was half explained. There was not a leg on any piece of furniture. Nothing touched the ground. A midget might have skated over the whole surface of the floor. Beneath all the pieces was a clear expanse of polished parquetry. Still it was a further instant before I perceived that no law of nature had been broken. The furniture — chairs, tables, stools, sofas — all hung straight from the ceiling. The upper reaches of the apartment had the appearance of a rather intricate gymnasium, but below it had a pleasant vacancy. In a moment my host returned. I asked no questions. "Now you will want to wash your hands," he said, and led me to a spacious bedchamber. A huge four-poster occupied the center of it, the posts all wound with garlands to the very ceiling. "There at last is something solid," I remarked, but in rebuttal the Colonel gave the side of the great bed a gentle kick. Up it swung high like a trapeze. "Such a convenience!" murmured the Colonel. "Dressing for dinner the essential stud slips from your fingers, rolls right under the center of the bed. Here there's no catastrophe. You just kick the bed and retrieve the stud." "How is it," I gasped,

Home without the Bacon

"that no one ever thought of this before!" I slipped into the bathroom. There was the marble basin, there the supersized cocks, but there were no handles. Here at least I understood from varied hospital experience. I pressed my foot on a lever on the floor and the water gushed forth.

We returned to the drawing room. The Colonel's lady welcomed me very graciously. She was wont to play the organ before dinner. Did I care for music? I dropped into an immense easy chair and swung gently to and fro, charmed back to childhood by the easy motion. The Colonel walked round the room, threw open the windows. "It gives a charm to music," he remarked, "if it comes from a distance." It was true. As my hostess pressed the stops the sweet strains floated *in* from every window. "You see," interjected the Colonel, "I have the music piped to the garden. It comes back through the windows."

"This is Circe's Isle," I thought, and a new strange sense of distance came over me as I looked through a window straight down the garden path. "There is Fuji!" I exclaimed, and there Fuji was, its delicate cone rising a hundred yards away, white-capped and perfect as a Hiroshige – looking for all the world like a vision a hundred miles away.

One final surprise I had before dinner. I had returned for a moment to my room. The dusk had fallen and I could see indistinctly that the long narrow hall had a sharp turn. Just as I rounded it something like a shriek rose from my lips. I felt on my shoulder a convulsive clutch and was sensible of a preternaturally hairy arm. A hand armed with claws held me with the grip of a bird of prey. Then and there I should have succumbed had I not heard the cheery voice of the Colonel calling from below. "Don't mind him. He's only my baboon!" The grinning ape slipped back his arm through the bars of his cage and I went downstairs curious what would turn up for dinner. But dinner held no surprise. The conversation was a tribute to sanity, solid as our roast beef. The Colonel and his wife were normal people in a normal world. Had they stood on their heads it would have been no surprise to me but I confess their complete normality was.

When the last excellent piece of pudding was eaten and we gentlemen had lighted our cigars, the Colonel said jovially, "And now how about a gammon of Bacon?" The cryptograms it seems were stored in a little frame house on the Colonel's estate. A field separated it from the mansion. Round the field ran a high fence, but when I made to scale it, my companion remarked: "I wouldn't do that. There's an Andalusian bull inside." I readily acceded to the suggestion we should walk round. Five minutes brought us to the house wherein once for all it should be settled whether Shakespeare was a liar. The Colonel knocked. The door opened and I found myself in the presence of two frail old ladies both dressed in gray and both bearing perhaps a misleading but to me delicate and sure suggestion of New England spinsterhood. Encouraged by the Colonel, they told their story. Before my eyes stood the two Miss Gallops, twin caryatids of the Baconian theory. It was to Mr. Donnelly they owed their professional reputation for to them he had imparted his secrets and since his death now several years past, they had been guests of the kind Colonel. Already their collection of plays was enormous — as I remember it numbered two hundred fifty-four — if the old or what might be termed *matrix* plays were combined with those newly smelted from the ancient beds of ore. Doubtless many more were still undiscovered, but at their rate of progress, the collection could be made absolutely complete and definitive. The method was complex. Skill, knowledge, and experience were required although the modesty of the ancient ladies admitted it very prettily. Of

Home without the Bacon

course, there was at their disposal a great number of Elizabethan texts, all in facsimile, and from Mr. Donnelly they had inherited I cannot recall how many separate ciphers. Perhaps they might give me a clearer idea if they explained the simplest of all the ciphers, the one they called the Pearl Necklace.

It was an excellent name I soon saw, for it was perfectly descriptive. Figuratively you throw a string of beads around the text of a printed page, threading as it were the letters next the margin. A code of rules permits you to skip so many consonants, so many vowels to make allowance for faulty letters, and to enjoy a certain latitude carefully limited by your scholarship and, as I conjectured, by your sense of the fitness of things. Anyway the results were astonishing for, as one of the Miss Gallops interpreted a page, the blank verse ran smoothly and dexterously. I strained my ear for a faulty accent but certainly the rhythm had the sound of authentic poetry. The other methods were a little elaborate to comprehend in a first lesson and I will let them pass. "Wouldn't you like to hear," they asked, "an act or two of one of the *newer* plays?" "Most certainly," I assured them. Almost every scene of what used to be called Shakespearean history was recorded on their shelves. Perhaps I would suggest an episode. "There must," I said, "be a drama culminating at Fotheringhay." For of course the death of Mary Queen of Scots so movingly described in the Fugger Letters could never have been portrayed upon an Elizabethan stage while Elizabeth was on the throne. But to preserve that scene of scenes for posterity would have been a marvelous lure to the poet's genius. The two ladies smiled in unison. "Yes, of course. One of us will read you the *Tragedy of Essex.*"

I ought at that moment to have stepped straight through the Looking-Glass. It was a situation Alice would have understood far better than I. What I did was to listen with intentness. I have always found it hard to test the merit of poetry when it is rather rapidly read aloud, but I felt sure that this ten-syllable blank verse had no technical flaws. On and on they ran rhythmically, smoothly. The characters imperishably connected with the most romantic story of all time were there at Fotheringhay. Three Marys stood about the fourth, and through my mind the old rhyme coursed.

> Yestreen the Queen had four Maries,
>   The night she'll hae but three;
> There was Mary Seaton, and Mary Beaton,
>   And Mary Carmichael, and me.

But through this verse there was no such poignance. There was no wild beating of the wings of poetry. All was correct. I had no criticism to make, no proof that the whole performance was a travesty of genius. It was only that the words gave forth that hollow sound which invariably accompanies the sayings of great men when from beyond the grave the medium trumpets them back to earth. Yet the experience was to me of enormous interest.

The next morning I went back for more instruction from the Miss Gallops. There they were working indefatigably on their daily task, a scene a day, an act a week, a play God knows how often!

Then I felt the time had come to face the Colonel. "What do you think?" he asked. "Think?" said I. "I think furiously. What do you want me to do?" "I have brought you to Chicago," he replied with a certain asperity, "for a single purpose. I want you to destroy the whole vast ignorant ridiculous monument to Shakespeare. I want you to be the first publisher in the world of Bacon's plays." "In two hundred fifty-four volumes?" I asked very quietly. "I don't know in how many damn volumes. What I do know is that you're

Home without the Bacon

afraid. You haven't the guts." "No," said I, "I haven't the guts because I haven't the faith. I haven't the instinctive belief nor have I the scholarship to controvert this extraordinary experiment." "If you're not one, how can I get a scholar?" "I'll get you one," I replied, and then and there I called up Professor Manly of Chicago University — Manly, spirited Pollux to Kittredge's Castor, blazing the Shakespearean trail across America.

What I told Manly in the privacy of a telephone booth was this — here was a mare's-nest without a peer in the scholarly world, and puzzles enough for an academy of Professors, mazes that Daedalus could never have threaded. "If you come out here you will not regret it, for I promise you the time of your life."

I left in disgrace but Manly came. He stayed, I think, nearly a week, but when he went, he left no hope behind. He wrote me that all I had said was true, that never had he more extravagantly enjoyed himself, and eventually he sent me his report. The gist of it was that the ciphers permitted of so many exceptions, that the printing of Elizabethan books contained so many chance faces of type, so many broken or inverted letters (which in the codes can be counted or omitted at will), that there was no volume of the period from which a poem or play could not be sucked. So much for the system and the two hundred and fifty-four dramas of Francis Bacon. But for the human ingenuity, the patience, the faith, the whole comedy of manners he had witnessed, he had nothing but astonishment and admiration.

And so it is that you still see on the backstrap of the plays *The Works of William Shakespeare*.

CHAPTER XXII

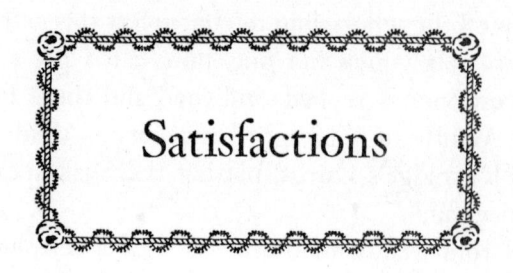

Satisfactions

WHEN THE Good Time comes and men are paid in strict proportion to the agreeableness of the tasks society calls on them to perform, it will cost editors a good deal to pay for their positions. Theirs is the happy profession. They can lay down the law flatly as any preacher, and far more effectively than he, can they control the criticism leveled in return. For they can answer it as they please and no woman can snatch the last word from them. They travel when they like, see whom they like, do what they like, and, when the editor entertains his clients, although the sensible fellow in the cashier's cage may roll up his eyes, he always honors the lunch check. But these favors of Fortune and the distinguished consideration of his commercial partners are mere by-products of his contented days. Other men are forced to work against the grain, to follow, as the classic phrase is, where duty calls, but the editor is bade to stick like a leech to what interests and diverts him most. The business of his life, the pleasantest business in the whole world, is to make friends, to keep them — then to exploit them for the profit and fame of his magazine. He is a sort of glorified Tom Sawyer getting the other fellow to paint his fence. But if the editor is wise, when the fence is bright as paint can make it, he will never steal the credit but turn it handsomely over to the chap who has earned it.

That trait of course is about the least common and the most useful in the range of human intercourse. I used to ask Colonel House, after one of his extraordinary adventures in political persuasion, just how he did it. With the slightest twinkle in his steely blue eye, he would reply, "Bringing the man to our view, that is cash in my pocket. I give him the credit *always*." But then there is only one Colonel House in every century or so.

The editor is bade to make friends and given money to make them stick, but when was a friend ever bought in the "open market"? To make men friends and make them stick needs much more than money. It needs an editor's ideas; it needs his sagacious counsel, it needs his enthusiasm, it needs a store of human qualities such as authors are short of. Once an editor is an expert at his trade, he comes to understand how every man has a story locked inside him, and the puzzle is to pick the lock. The truth about this world is there are no absolutely uninteresting people in it. There are only people who seem depressingly uninteresting. Almost everybody has his little private "godown" where his treasure lies buried. Once you adopt this view of the universe, it makes a worth-while place of the planet. True it is that digging out the gold that lies in most of us is a hard and costly job. What was Emerson's message to young women who distrust their powers? "Oh discontented girl, take what you will, but pay the price." On the shop counters of the world goods are desirable but prices are high.

Often have I tested the theory, to everyone his story. Generalizations are always wrong, but in this I am certain there is a large element of truth. Start talking with your seat-mate on a lengthening journey, and it is ten to one that even in a dreary mind you strike a slumbering spark. The very fact that you two have no tie and will never see each other again frees you both from the sin of self-consciousness. Priests have told me that the confessional is usually a dull hour but in these cases, I suspect, the suppliant for pardon is apt to confess little overt acts of petulance and naughtiness, but to suppress the real story — the slow dynamic growth of the cardinal sins, and it is big faults, not little ones, that are interesting to hear about. They are the real expression of human nature. They are the stuff of drama. Had I a friend of sociable disposition, handsome income, and a passion for dipping into the minds of others, I should advise him to rent an attractive house in Aden on the shores of the Red Sea and give nightly dinners there to wayfarers. It is at Aden that P. & O. liners and ships voyaging from the vast of the Indian Ocean put in for an overnight stop. Ladies bored with bridge and ship talk, gentlemen off on new careers, their reputations well behind them, all wholly conscious that at dinner tonight some sympathetic stranger will listen to their histories with fascination and tomorrow never hold against them that whispered confidence. A situation of such sort will make conversation very human and sociable. The pair who last night were bosom friends will never meet again.

There are simpler ways of drawing out confidences. Traveling across Iowa on the most tedious of journeys I noticed out of a dusty window a drab little station. A rickety Ford drew up and out jumped a farmer's wife dressed in her city best. The prettiness of her youth had not quite left her, her figure was still trim, but what I noticed was that, as she picked up her suitcase, she walked straight to the train with never a backward glance at her husband. But he, as he sat in the car, followed her with his eyes to the very second the conductor

Satisfactions

waved his arm and the train started. The woman came to my seat and flopped down beside me. Then half under her breath I heard her mutter, "Thank God that's over — Never! Never! Never!" — and her words trailed off into silence. "Never is a long time," I remarked, looking into space. She started as though I had stuck her with a pin. Then, just as if we had been brought up together from childhood, she went running on. "He is impossible, perfectly impossible. I've tried and tried and tried." "How sensibly have you tried?" I asked in the tone of an old, old friend. "Why he even made a fuss about my going when it's my own egg money I'm going on." I asked whether he was mean or just stupid, and she replied that stupidity was the worst. "All evening he just sits and reads the paper. He won't even listen in on a party line." So she talked and as I did not bury my face in my own paper, she seemed satisfied with my attention. Finally she summed it all up. "And what do *you* think I ought to do?" "I think," said I, taking on a look of the wisdom of the ages, "I think you ought to go back and have a baby." She opened her mouth in a round O. "That's an idea!" she said.

That is the tiniest wisp of a story. Yes, but it has in it the entire plot of a novel about folks on Main Street. This novel ended as no self-respecting novelist would permit his story to end today. It has too much of the simplicities of life in it. From a look she gave me as she left the station at Dubuque, I am confident that my little lady followed my advice.

An editor should believe in his magazine. The trouble is many of them don't. You see all sorts of balderdash in the appeals they make to their readers. "Our readers edit our magazine. It is they who tell us what to put in." That is the sort of thing politicians say to their constituents. It is worse than nonsense. It is a lie. Every editor of quality gathers about his magazine readers who are in one way or another all of a kidney like his own. As I write I think with sorrow of the death only the other day of my accomplished friend Albert J. Nock. He put together a magazine admirably written, diverting, original, and full of unpredictable quirks, but for its support it needed readers with minds faintly adumbrating his own. Think of collecting thousands of readers whose ways of thought followed Nock's ways! Nock was unique. That was why I loved him, but as an editor through the years he could only have performed in the void. It is tragic not to see Albert Nock again with his Montaigne in one pocket balanced by Artemus Ward in the other, asking his Socratic questions and disagreeing as to the answers with all other dwellers on the planet. He was the ideal anarchist, a special creation of the Potter fashioned after an intricate design never to be classed as "open stock."

Take, on the other hand, the impressive case of Edward Bok. Edward Bok, Edward W. Bok as his sponsors in baptism named him, was an original if ever there was one. Assuming as was natural that the world was big enough but for a single Bok, he threw off the encumbering initials. He was his own hero, and habitually wrote of himself in the third person: "Bok" — just that. Of the engrossing affairs of women's lives, he was a scientific student. I have the impression he was annoyed when a woman laid claim to individuality and entered the unfeminine world of ideas. Women in the mass are never unwomanly, and he understood them with uncanny precision. In a streetcar though he might carry a *Philadelphia Bulletin* to hide his face and disguise his interest, he never read but ever listened to soprano voices about him. Ninety-nine times out of a hundred it was styles they talked of, and when it wasn't bonnets, it was stockings. I liked to watch his shrewd blue eye as he stroked that lean jaw of his and discoursed of the sex which had made him rich and famous.

Satisfactions

"Why didn't the Lord make you a woman?" I would ask him, and he would reply: "Because a man understands them better."

Like many men who have shouldered their own way through the world, Bok was an egotist of size and intensity. This annoyed some people; to me it merely added to a diverting personality. During the First World War we traveled abroad together. It happened that a good friend of mine, Sir Geoffrey Butler, M.P. for the University of Cambridge, had the idea of bringing England closer to America by importing a party of editors and journalists to make personal contacts with English newspapers and magazines. I told Butler it would be a great card if Bok were to join us. Bok did; and a party of a dozen of us spent several rewarding weeks in London. To me personally the mission was of enduring consequence, for during those tense days I formed friendships with Englishmen important in public life, friendships which lasted through decades to come.

One morning towards the close of our visit we received official summons from the King to spend the day with the Royal Family at Sandringham. It was a vastly amusing visit, worth recording, but in telling of it Bok quite forgot that others besides himself were of the party. In his reminiscences, he devoted a chapter to his audience (it was really an all-day affair of the utmost informality) and duly described the invitation which had come personally to Bok to wait upon Their Majesties. It was merely an accolade bestowed on the first of American editors.

We went down to Sandringham in state. The great house had been the gift of the nation to the Royal Family to express its rejoicing at the recovery of the Prince from a serious illness of his youth. All the luxury of royalty was about us — the private train, the silken chairs in the waiting room of the

The Happy Profession

private station. In a reception line in the big and ugly hall of Sandringham House stood the King, the Queen, the Queen Mother, the Princess Mary, and a row of pretty countesses. I noticed myself that Queen Mary was a little unhappy and probably intensely bored, but it was Bok who had an eye for feminine perturbation. I wish I had his account before me, but it ran much as follows.

When Bok entered the reception room the King shook his hand warmly and entered at once into familiar conversation, but Bok's eyes turned toward the Queen. She was obviously embarrassed and kept running her long, light-gray glove through the palm of her left hand. Though she was a fine figure in her modish gray gown, she seemed to have difficulty in framing the familiar phrases of welcome. Then Bok's description of the scene ended in a sentence graven in my recollection, for it is certainly unique in the literature of the Republic: —

"It remained for Bok to put Queen Mary at her ease."

You will look in vain for this passage in the famous Autobiography and the reason is this. Mr. Scribner put his foot down and insisted it should come out. Bok was an autocrat, and no critic, however friendly, could tamper with a manuscript of his. But Mr. Charles Scribner — I mean of course the admirable Mr. Scribner of my day — had once employed Bok as his secretary. That was in the days when Frank Doubleday was packing books in the basement of the same establishment and the two young men held their employer in lifetime respect. The tale is authentic, for with many a guffaw, Mr. Scribner told it to me himself. I respected his prejudice but I think the publisher was mistaken in his insistence on the proprieties. No man should eradicate from literature a sentence like that.

It is of the inimitable Bok I am writing, but I cannot refrain

Satisfactions

from relating a little episode of that day which belongs to my own story. When the formalities were over, the party broke up in groups and the talk was as familiar as at any *conversazione*. I had been chatting with the Queen at length, and since the convention is that any turn in the conversation must be led by Royalty, I was rather desirous of turning to an attractive Lady-in-Waiting, who stood at the Queen's elbow; but the Queen herself gave me my directive. "I want you," she said, "to talk with the Queen Mother. Queen Alexandra is totally deaf. She cannot hear one word, but she will speak to you and you must be ready with an answer. And mind," she added, "never let the conversation flag. She is sensitive on that point. Keep at it steadily."

Queen Alexandra stood there like a noble ruin. The beautiful face which had once been the toast of all England was coated with brittle and crinkling enamel, but she was very gracious and animated. She told me of her various needlework charities and bade me not fail to visit them before I left London. On and on she ran, chatting of matters of no conceivable interest to me. Then suddenly she paused. It was my turn. I made an effort to express my enthusiasm for embroidery and lace-making, but well I knew that my helplessness was stamping itself on my features. I remembered my orders to be lively and felt uncomfortable. We were standing apart. No one could overhear if I were to recite in a low voice. It gave me an inspiration. In the most exuberant of whispers I chanted the Tennysonian welcome to the bride of long, long ago: —

> Sea-King's daughter from over the sea,
> Alexandra!
> Saxon and Norman and Dane are we,
> But all of us Danes in our welcome of thee,
> Alexandra!

The Happy Profession

Welcome her, thunders of fort and of fleet!
Welcome her, thundering cheer of the street!
Welcome her, all things youthful and sweet.

The ancient lady smiled at my exhilaration, and to tell the truth I felt that my conversation had been worthy of court circles. When I returned to Queen Mary she complimented me. "You have pleased her," she said graciously.

First, last, and all the time Bok was an individualist, but there was very little for which the millions cared that was alien to him, practically nothing, from women's frocks to his Dutch tulips. He became a power in the land, manipulating women inside and out, but devoted as he was to his vast constituency, he always hankered to lay hands on a magazine not too big to be really expressive of one man's personality. He got interested in the *Atlantic* and oddly enough rather envied me my job. We were great friends. One day I told him the exact number of subscribers the *Atlantic* had on Beacon Street. He telephoned his office and found that the *Ladies' Home Journal* had almost precisely the same number in that refined but limited locality. The coincidence amused us both. "But there is a difference," Bok remarked. "You see, Sedgwick, you go in at the front door, and I at the back. I know my place."

Bok did know his place, and his place was not to be sneezed at. He was fully aware of his influence. He was not cynical about the conglomeration of his audience. He enjoyed its vagaries and if he laughed at his readers, it was in a friendly and understanding spirit. That contempt for an audience which makes you what you are and rewards you for your sneers! How often have I seen it elsewhere, and how often I have despised it, trampling underfoot, as good people do, temptation that does not assail me. On the *Atlantic*, the tongue was never tucked into the cheek, but then it was never my

Satisfactions

business to profess an interest in buttonholes or the beauty of wing collars nor yet greens for the Christmas table. Readers, writers, and I had interests in common and new ones once a month. In fact, the continuous editorial pattern in my mind was of a huge dinner table with plenty to eat and more than plenty to talk about. Divergence of opinion stimulates conversation. It must always be encouraged. The business of the head of the table is to direct the talk. Two other duties must be on the host's mind: boredom must be banished and good manners the invariable rule. After all, politeness does not mean emasculation.

A little magazine, as Bacon would say, maketh not a great fortune. But if it be conducted with enterprise and discretion, not as a multifarious catchall but as an intelligent and sympathetic extension of the editor's powers and interests, then shall he have his adequate reward. A corner mansion on the Avenue may not be his but that he would not value if he had it, and his comfortable house on a leafy if unfashionable street will lack no comfort. When I first took over the *Atlantic*, my wife and I expected to live on the modest scale of a professor's family. The magazine (now it can be told) was in 1908, when I acquired it, selling some fifteen thousand copies a month. In the interests of solvency I consulted a friend wise in the devious ways of advertising, but even to him I dared not confess a figure which any self-respecting businessman would feel must be concealed. "Would you," I asked tremulously, "solicit advertising on the basis of a sworn figure, or would you go it blind, extolling the fame of your name and decrying the cheap argument of circulation?"

"If," said my mentor, avoiding my eye, "your sales are twenty-five thousand copies a month, I would boast of them. Otherwise, I would keep d——d quiet."

And d——d quiet I kept. I saw that a steep hill had to be climbed but two comforting thoughts came to mind. First, if the *Atlantic* had more subscribers and was losing less money, then I could not possibly have scraped up dollars enough to buy it. Secondly, I remembered that when Walter Hines Page had sat in my chair ten years earlier, the total circulation of the magazine had not exceeded six thousand copies a month; yet it was a poorly educated American in those days who had not heard of the *Atlantic*.

When in that first year of grace, MacGregor Jenkins and I took over the *Atlantic* and set to work with pencil and eraser, we scratched and scratched until the last drop of red ink disappeared from the books, and when we balanced them at the end of a year, the profit was four thousand dollars. Four thousand dollars! Here was a nest egg such as many a famous businessman has recorded with respect in the first chapter of his autobiography. So these figures are stamped on my commercial soul alongside one other unforgettable digit — the ten dollars which after college my father had given me to take me to my first job, thus marking the historic hiatus between paternal benevolence and the first gatherings of sweat on a man's brow.

The *Atlantic* prospered continuously, in its small way mightily, but the satisfaction of life bears scant relation to cash balances. My correspondence, increasing at compound interest, bore witness to the expanding influence of the magazine. People of notoriety, then of eminence, began to show a disposition to write for the *Atlantic* and through its pages unknown writers began to become very well-known writers indeed. In those days, it was my practice out of eighteen contributors in an issue to include at least eight who were making their first bows to the public. I remember the office jubilation when we were reliably informed that sermons on *Atlantic*

Satisfactions

topics were preached simultaneously in twenty churches. What the congregations suffered therefrom was beyond our caring, and we only rejoiced when, from London, the Dean of St. Paul's, the gloomy Dean himself, wrote that an *Atlantic* paper had been his text for three successive sermons. But not until the politicians began to notice the magazine did we feel certain the *Atlantic* had made a definite impact. Of his own will, President Wilson sent a priceless article — and received in return hundreds instead of the thousands he might have had for the asking from any big magazine. Al Smith, after an infinitude of consultation, decided that the *Atlantic* was the proper sounding-board for an article certain to have a crucial influence upon his career, and in later years Wendell Willkie testified that, though his advisers counseled some magazine of millions, he believed a more intensive influence would, in the long run, prove more effective in promoting his ideas — and after the event assured us he had been proved right. To inoculate the few who influence the many is the *Atlantic's* perpetual formula.

Anonymity, as I say, has been an abiding comfort to me. Like every other man I am not insensible to the occasional praise that comes my way, but compliment has no warmth in it unless from a discriminating source, and sometimes it is the unpremeditated word that warms the heart. A year or two ago, suffering from the thirst of a hot day, I dropped in at a saloon, took my seat on a high stool at the bar, and called for a Bock. The man next me turned. He was a healthy roustabout in a blue flannel shirt open at the neck and undecorated by a cravat. I was conscious that he was studying me, and presently, raising his own glass, he looked me in the eye and spoke: —

"Did you once see Shelley plain, and did you once see Ellery Sedgwick in a *common* saloon?"

The Happy Profession

Who my admirer was I have no remotest idea but his surprise was grateful to me.

One of the editor's duties I have spoken of is to travel — to learn at first hand what it is that men talk of, here there and everywhere, and when the talk interests him to siphon it into his own channel. I used often to visit the universities of the Middle West and pick up in Faculty Clubs ideas of moment. The offices of the better newspapers, too, are sure to be tenanted by interesting people. How well I recall the foursquare figure of old Scott, once a Senator and at that time still the sage executive of the *Portland Oregonian* — the only paper of my time to preach its righteous gospel in ponderous paragraphs such as the Thunderer of London might have envied. In Memphis I used to find the Irish Mooney of the *Appeal* who added honesty and acumen to the witching charm of his race. In St. Louis it was William Marion Reedy — a versatile minor prophet, for in *Reedy's Mirror* you could always see the strange new shapes of things to come, and in Emporia lived the beloved among editors, as authentic a saint as ever wrote American.

It is Virtue's practice to pay in credit, very seldom in cash, but Will White prospered like Job in the first chapter and the last, and unlike Job in all the chapters in between. I like to think of him as the man "rewarded after God's heart" and used to ask how it was that in Emporia, a town no bigger than it had been in his father's day, the *Gazette* could enjoy such affluence. But he would only remark that it was criminal how much he was paid for running a country paper and then add: "The population is the same. It is the bank accounts that have done the swelling." Will lived simply as his remarkable mother before him, running the lawnmower after hours while Mrs. White put up the jams and jellies, but about his house there was an aroma of unadulterated friendliness.

Satisfactions

There are three classes of goodness: good enough, good, and too good. The Lord understands what gulfs divide these three quite as well as we do. The good enough are not worth His attention, nor ours; the too good are too interested in themselves to interest Him or us. It is the simply good who are His anointed. There is no odor of sanctity about them. Intelligence is the deodorizer of that pervasive smell, and that White had in abundance. Mix in just proportions goodness and intelligence, pour it into a Yankee mould, and you have Nature's recipe for Will White. Now the mould is shattered.

> If all the good people were clever,
> And all clever people were good,
> The world would be nicer than ever
> We thought that it possibly could.

Often in those journeys it was chance which brought the reward. I recall a transcontinental trip along the topmost reaches of the Canadian map following the convolutions which those unlovingly remembered pathfinders, Mackenzie and Mann, introduced into the lines of their Canadian Northern to justify the contract of so much a mile wheedled out of their confiding government. Fortunately, it was not such adventurers as these who set the pattern for Canada's great railroads. There was Sir Thomas Shaughnessy, but the superlative exemplar was Sir William Van Horne, whose monument is the Canadian Pacific. In the give-and-take of trade between Canada and the United States there never was a more important business transaction than that accidental bargain whereby the two countries traded a pair of boys, the U. S. A. exporting William Van Horne and importing in his place the young Jim Hill. It was a quirk of fate that changed the histories of two nations.

The Happy Profession

This was a journey with my friend Mark Howe leaving bright memories behind — brightest of all, the day we spent with Van Horne who, in 1915, was old and famous. His mansion in Montreal contained a collection of Spanish and Italian pictures famous through the world. Armed with good letters, I asked permission to call. Where is the man whom Velásquez and Goya cannot carry at their will to an undiscovered country? Yet I will admit that for one excited moment I forgot them altogether — I had caught sight of a bust a little larger than life which stood on a long console table in the hall. I walked over to it and lost myself completely. The artist was great, the subject great as the artist: that and that only I knew at the first glance.

"You like him?" asked Sir William, quizzically. My expression gave him his answer. Then he came alongside and, hopping on the table, threw his arm around the broad shoulder of the bust.

"You like him, too," I said.

"I love him. How can I help loving him! He saved my life. He is Donatello's idea of Niccola Pisano." Many questions I asked and this is the story they called forth.

Years earlier, when Van Horne was fighting his first, fierce battles for doubling the size of freight cars, he had come to New York for a meeting with the bankers. The times were conservative. The Board represented the times, and doubts of victory assailed the enthusiast. This is prehistory. There were no taxis then, and from the Grand Central Van Horne drove south in a hansom. With every block his spirits sank to a new low. Something must be done. At Thirty-sixth Street, he ordered the driver to turn east. For ten minutes he would lose himself in the showroom of a famous art dealer and see something beautiful, something certain to give him courage. He climbed the brownstone steps and there in the

Satisfactions

back parlor was Niccola Pisano waiting to greet him. Infatuation, sudden and complete, laid hold of the railroad builder. "I will take him," he exclaimed. And then the dealer named so hideous a price that as Sir William remarked to me he could see the reproachful eyes of his children and his children's children fall gravely upon him. He gave his head a melancholy shake. "You make a cardinal error," said the dealer. "Anything like that won't stop here for many hours. I shall soon find a purchaser."

The voice of duty prevailed and Van Horne continued on his melancholy way. His spirits grew jet-black. What confidence he had evaporated, and when he faced his bankers he was no man to set up against their serried rank. After a futile interview, he regained his cab. "There is only one cure for me," he said to himself. "I must have him and I will." Back in Thirty-sixth Street, he fairly bounded up the steps. "I will take him," he cried to the dealer, but the dealer's countenance took on the look of Jack Ketch upon "an occasion." "He is sold, sold twenty minutes after you left. Don't say I didn't warn you." "Who bought him?" "That," said the executioner, "is a secret." Then, Van Horne said, the black sack was thrown over his head and he could feel the drawstrings closing about his neck. Back he struggled to Montreal, a beaten man.

At this point in his story Sir William's voice took on a new animation. "I am fortunate in having friends," he said. From them he learned that Pisano had gone to Boston. Of course, my mind jumped to Mrs. Jack Gardner but who the owner really was he would not tell me. What he did was to ask his friends whether Mr. X would consider an offer of the "hideous price" plus 10 per cent, but they had counseled him that such an inquiry would be resented. So he contented himself with issuing blanket instructions to his agent to wait for the next

The Happy Profession

financial tempest and at the moment of crisis the original price should be offered.

Years passed. The crisis came, as crises do. The offer was made and accepted. "But," continued Sir William, "Niccola did not come a moment too soon. I was ill, very ill, so low in spirit that I thought of turning my face quietly to the wall. Then the news came." "Hurry," he telegraphed. The bust arrived. It was unpacked on the instant, trundled into the sickroom, and placed alongside the sick man's pillow.

"And," Sir William ended his story, "I threw my arm around his neck, laid my cheek against his, and slept like a child."

Sir William said he felt unwell and that night he was starting for a rest on his Saskatchewan farm. Wouldn't we come with him for a day or two and compare blooded cattle with works of art. We knew the sick man would be better off alone and that evening we left for a trip over Mount Robson with Prince Rupert as the ultimate goal.

A month later we were traveling homewards. The papers told us that Sir William Van Horne was seriously ill. Daily bulletins were issued and the gravity of the situation was obvious. At Montreal I called again at the mansion house and handing my card to the butler inquired after Sir William's condition. The butler's face took on a smile that marked the devotion of the servant of a lifetime.

"Sir William is *much* better. This morning he had a cable of inquiry from His Majesty."

On the next day Sir William died.

In these meanderings I have not come on the question of taste. Taste underlies judgment. Often it is arbitrary and none the worse for that. In this world, it is quite as important to hate as to love. If you hate insincerity, if vulgarity has an

Satisfactions

instant effect upon the balance of your diaphragm, you won't go far astray. Like every other quality, taste grows from habit and, habitually exercised, it will become part of your fiber and bone. American education is apt to look on taste as an airy grace of life. In teacher-minds it is coupled with fastidiousness and gently laughed at. But I am grossly mistaken if the cultivation of a fastidious taste goes not closer to the root of the matter and accomplishes more in building what we call character than all the instruction in the curriculum and all the athletics of the campus. Once persuade a child to identify *bad* with *ugly* and you have made its instinct your strong ally. The homely motto on the wall has gone the way of the lambrequin and the antimacassar but it once taught a vigorous lesson. A threadbare distich, worked in worsted, hung over the piano.

> Vice is a monster of so frightful mien,
> As to be hated needs but to be seen

became a part of visual memory forever, in time of crisis to be thrown up large upon the screen. I remember a Scotch sailor telling me how, after a long voyage, he had taken his first shore leave at Vigo, thirty-five dollars in his pocket. His companions knew where they were going but he was daydreaming until he found himself in the parlor of a brothel. In one flash of lightning there came before his eyes the little oblong frame which for two generations had hung in the nursery of his home. In the crude reds and blues of the original he saw the words: —

> My God hath sent his angel, and hath shut the lions' mouths, that they have not hurt me: forasmuch as before him innocency was found in me.

That monition had fascinated his childish mind long before he knew what it meant. Now he knew.

The Happy Profession

Of course taste exfoliates into all sorts of ornamental arabesques of character such as most of us think of as belonging to the world of la-di-da. But the essence of it has structure and solidity, and enjoys an enormous advantage over moral lessons taught from without, in that it is instinctive. Taste is born in us. Education merely strengthens or smothers it. Sheep-headed people looking on this world as the Garden of Eden run to weeds since Adam ceased to cultivate it may think of the Ten Commandments as part of man's natural inheritance. But whether they are God-given or man-given, they are certainly practical regulations in a disorderly world. In keeping them, where precept fails, taste is a powerful support.

The great American sin is vulgarity and taste is its antidote. A curious vice this is to attach to a pioneering people but it did not come upon us until the pioneering stage was past, nor did it come flooding in with immigration. The Irish are beautifully immune to it. It is not characteristic of the Italian. Scandinavians are coarse, but not vulgar. But those who love America best feel how omnipresent vulgarity is amongst us. Hollywood is too tiresome an instance to cite, but look at a wedding breakfast on the screen, or the decoration of a room supposed to represent wealth and culture, and before a word is spoken you will see what it means to be vulgar. About vulgarity there is a self-consciousness which is the root of bad manners and bad taste. Compare the advertisements of our current novels with similar announcements in foreign papers. Our emphasis is always carried by notes at the top of the scale. Never the positive, the comparative never, always the superlative. Be blatant *and* be heard, is a rule of the trade. In writing, how rarely in America is realized the power of understatement. "Unique," which occurs once in a lifetime, has become a familiar quality of every novel, and

Satisfactions

"stupendous" is an everyday synonym for "large." How exaggeration defeats itself should be a lesson of earliest youth. I hear again the admonition of my uncle, Professor Child. His daughter had enjoyed an agreeable evening and reported her partner as "a fascinating young man." Professor Child sniffed fastidiously, giving his round nose a look of indescribable squeamishness: "Fascinating! Fascinating!" he repeated. "What you mean, Helen, is that your young man is honest — and possibly clean."

Of course superlatives do have their place. When a thing *is* best it deserves to be called so. Our famous painter, William Morris Hunt, had a word for masterpieces. They were "ultimates," and as his gift for profanity was on a par with his other talents, his "ultimates" became on occasions of appropriate commendation "those God-damned ultimate things."

At a certain famous dinner given by the Tavern Club in honor of Hunt's achievements, the artist was introduced by the Club president, Professor Norton. The exquisite propriety of Norton's speech, its gentle modulation and quiet resonance, had been a community tradition for fifty years. Now his peroration was indeed unique and roused a glorious shout of applause. Norton had been speaking of the testament of Beauty and how wonderfully Beauty was enhanced by its exceeding rarity. Finally he turned to the guest at his right: "And now, gentlemen, I have the pleasure of introducing to you one — of — those — God-damned — *ultimate* — things, William Morris Hunt."

Vulgarity is a total misconception of the values of life. Real values have not a touch of it, and these are the editor's everlasting lure. If he can find them under dramatic circumstances, so much the better, for drama is a very present help in the trouble of turning out an issue. There is no sharper barb to the editor's hook.

CHAPTER XXIII

Adventures by Proxy

"I AM SENDING you a packet of letters written to me by a college mate," a friend told me over the telephone. "If the class of '98 could divide his experiences, there would be plenty for all of us and more." This was an auspicious introduction and I went at the parcel with a will.

The signature on the letters was blacked out, and in its place appeared the initials "H. D. P.," which were, I assumed, a *nom de guerre*. The background, which from stray references to earlier years seemed to have been abysmal, could only be guessed at. What was in sharp relief were present facts with the immediate events which had led up to them. The writer was a young man of thirty-five gifted with imagination, energy, and courage, but often these qualities were drowned in dissipation. Six months before, he had enjoyed an income of more than twenty-five thousand dollars a year from a wholesale commission business in Boston which showed great promise of further gains. H. D. P. had a wife, children, and a position in society. Then the thunderbolt struck him, as, I gathered, it had struck him once before. This time the wreckage was complete. His money had gone, all of it. His wife and children had left him. Drink had become his only solace. His family, who apparently were not inexperienced in crises of this kind, had packed a bag

[306]

Adventures by Proxy

for him, slipped a one-way ticket to Seattle in his slender billfold, and bade him a permanent good-bye. H. D. P. as was natural had recourse to his friend John Barleycorn and the story in his letters opens when he awakes in a freight car in the Seattle yards, his head splitting, his baggage gone, his wallet containing precisely three dollars and fifty cents, and one tin of cigarettes in his trousers pocket. He was up against it.

It takes different atmospheric pressures to make men crumple. The writer of these letters had evidently a hard core and I admired it. He was down but not out. The first step was to clear his head and clean his clothes. He sought out the basement of a cheap tourist hotel, found the Turkish bath and — spent a week there. A Turkish bath has its advantages. It offers heat, bed, and a washtub for clothes. Shirt studs and cuff buttons paid the freight. The second day he ran into an old acquaintance, an ex-hotelkeeper whose once comfortable capital was reduced to four dollars. A companion in misery was a comfort and he made another friend by serving as second to a prizefighter who attended the bath. He rubbed the champion down, flapped a towel in his face between rounds, and felt something more of a man than before. He called at twenty-eight offices, asked for any kind of work, and found none.

After twenty-six consecutive hours without food, he walked up to a stranger, bold as brass, and said, "Give me a dollar." He got it. That, too, made him feel better. He had not borrowed the money.

As any gambler knows, luck does change. The head stevedore of the Grand Trunk Pacific Railroad bade H. D. P. report at midnight to discharge coal on the *S.S. Princess Ena*. What the head stevedore did not tell him was that it was *hot* coal. What followed I quote from the letters.

The Happy Profession

"Ten of us went into the lower hold and started loading the tubs. At two, an hour later, Jones [the ex-hotelkeeper] fell over, and about twenty minutes later two others. Gas from the coal. Three of us stuck it out to the end, 10.30 Friday morning, whereupon I created quite a scene. On calling for our pay, 9½ hours at 35¢ an hour, we were told by the paymaster to call between 3 and 4 in the afternoon. I fainted and fell flat on my face in the snow, my last meal having been on Thursday at noon. The ten cents I had left I gave to Jones when he keeled over. I was pretty dizzy from the fumes. I felt like a damn fool when I got up, and got out of sight as quickly as possible. When I reached our dump I found Jones in bed, but he had saved my ten cents and only used his own. So I had coffee and doughnuts and went to bed. I ached so I didn't sleep much and also I strained my back, but we were at the paymaster's at 3. Jones collected 35¢ and I $3.35. Whereupon we were reckless. We ate $1.10 worth of steak and coffee."

From dawn the next day the friends shadowed the railroad shipping agent but it was afternoon before they persuaded him to speak the words of salvation. "Mac," he called, to a section boss, "can you use these lads?" Mac allowed he could, so, packed into a freight with some seventy-five other hopefuls, they started up the river. Four hours later they reached the camp, pitched at a point where concrete piers for a bridge were going in. Their bellies were full, they had a job, but it was with a guilty feeling that they approached the office. The regulations required blankets and they knew it, but in extenuation they remembered that after settling their bill at Prince Rupert they had between them been one dollar short. Blankets could not be put on the bill, but blankets they must have. After a harrowing interview in which Jones fairly broke down, the storekeeper handed them two cotton blankets and chalked $6.50 against their account.

From that evening, H. D. P. had three meals a day and a bunk to sleep in, but the work was hazardous and hard.

"Rather a nasty accident," he wrote. "The anchor-line on one of the bridge derricks broke and the whole shooting-match pretty nearly went into the river. After dinner two other chaps and myself climbed out on the end, about 40 feet above ground, to pass a line, when the leg fell. Both my companions were killed, one instantly, the other dying in about an hour. As I write, the bodies are lying at my feet covered up with meal sacks. A good horse is worth $500, but a man nothing, in this country. When I felt the timbers going, I jumped outwards and landed in the river, reaching shore some 200 yards downstream in an eddy. All the clothes I have were on my back and I have no credit at the store, I am taking the afternoon off to dry out."

Down but not out! Always he was up for the count. The amiable qualities we so much admire were crowded out of H. D. P.'s character, but they left room for something more uncommon. Not many weeks elapsed before H. D. P. was noticed. It was not his nature to hide his light under a bushel, and he kept the boss regularly and reliably informed as to his capacities. Even a boss has his limits of resistance, and H. D. P. was accepted at about 20 per cent of his own rating. He became timekeeper of the job and was put in charge of stores at Camp 26A. The old standards of comfort began to trickle back into his mind. In odd moments, he hung a screen door on his cabin, shutting out the flies from the kitchen a few feet away, and fitted in a neat window for additional light. At the pumping station he scooped out a circle of mud, hollowed a clay bathtub, and wheedled the engineer into furnishing him with a hot shower. After that, there could be counted on ten blissful minutes at the end of each intolerable day. But always in his heart was a longing for his children. He had, too, a sense of desperate loneliness but even this he assuaged. From a litter of puppies sired by a forest wolf, he picked a devoted companion, with a temperament not dissimilar from his own.

There the letters left him. On the evening of the day a selection of them had been published in the *Atlantic*, I chanced to dine with Mr. Brooks Adams, youngest and not the least astringent of the famous brothers. We were drinking our last glass of champagne when Mr. Adams leaned forward and said in a low tone: —

"That is an unusual man whose letters you printed. There is something in him that ought to come out. I wonder whether a thousand dollars would help him. I would like to stake a chap like that."

The incident impressed me. It was the way I felt myself and Mr. Adams enjoyed a reputation for cynicism which left little room for sentiment. In the weeks that followed, I had reason to know that scores of readers would be glad to make a practical demonstration of their interest.

But H. D. P. had that in him which needed small help from without. It must have been a full year later that I was excited by a call on the telephone. H. D. P. was on the line. He was in Boston. He had made good. He had come East to add to his little capital and take over the construction of a section of the railroad. The sense that his letters had been worth publishing had given him a lift on his way. Would he lunch with me? Of course he would. The next day we spent three hours in uninterrupted talk and the story he had to tell eclipsed all that I had learned of him before.

For H. D. P. was Lester Monks. That name has been for-

Adventures by Proxy

gotten but there was a time when it was discussed at every dinner table and headlined in every newspaper. His face was a study when he began his tale and the overpowering feeling came upon me that Louis Stevenson had died too young. Here was a saga shaped for his telling. If a talk with Sam McClure had brought Jim Pinkerton of *The Wrecker* into existence, what might have come to pass from a chat with Lester Monks!

From earliest boyhood, Monks had made a specialty of excitement. His family was armored by every Bostonian convention, and to the polite social pressures of his environment he had reacted violently. Drink first diverted, then interested, then absorbed him, and I gathered that before he went to Harvard he was a veteran of the bottle. The Dean soon took notice and toward spring of Lester's freshman year his relation with the University terminated with abruptness. But this was not the worst phase of the matter. His nerves were gone, his digestion ruined, and the doctors reported that delirium tremens was not far off. The only possible cure must be immediately applied. For a considerable period the patient must have absolute quiet. His environment must be entirely altered and for a young man normally so active it was desirable that some mild interest be introduced to occupy his mind. Lester had been an enthusiastic and skillful sailor of small boats. Why not send him on a long voyage where he would have nothing to do and where the life about him would be simple and vigorous? The discipline aboard ship, so the doctor thought, could not fail to have an invigorating effect upon his character. Between Deans, doctors, and a distressed and distressing family, life had become rough and Lester welcomed the idea of putting long sea miles between himself and his troubles. His parents, too, stipulated that wherever it led the voyage should at least be long. The barkentine *Herbert Fuller*, bound for Rosario, the Argentine, with a load of lumber, seemed

The Happy Profession

to fill the bill. A bargain was struck with Captain Nash that the passenger have a stateroom to himself. The boat was to sail on July third and on the glorious Fourth the family would be free to toast their wayward son, wishing him a pleasant and an enduring voyage.

Among the friends who came to see him off was his Uncle George. I had long known Dr. Monks, a kindly, warmhearted man, and Lester's references made me sure it was he who best understood what trouble means to a young man. Putting his hand on his nephew's shoulder he told him simply that he still believed in him. The boy had a chance and a good one, but it was now or never. And then he added that there might be a man's work to do before the voyage was over. This was no pleasure cruise and a lumber schooner was not a yacht. "So," he added, "I have brought you this," and drew from his pocket a revolver and a box of cartridges. They saved a life.

How tightly Lester Monks's courage was screwed to the sticking place can only be guessed. At any rate what resolution he had summoned was bolstered by five dozen of beer and two bottles of whiskey stowed in his cabin.

No question regarding the record of any seaman seems to have been made in recruiting for this extraordinary voyage. Nobody knew what sort the next man was. There was pervasive doubt as to whether the first mate's name was Bram, Brom, or Brown, though afterward the correct name was burned into the consciousness of everybody aboard. Another important actor in the ensuing drama was Charley Brown — and it made little difference to his mates that his real name was Justus Leopold Westerburg. Odd uncertainties distinguished the nomenclature of the crew generally. But one remarkable member of the ship's company — a young mulatto steward — was rightly known as Jonathan Spencer. Captain

Adventures by Proxy

Nash had his wife aboard as was his custom. They were part owners of the ship and decent people — about all that was decent on the *Herbert Fuller* excepting a sound deckload of planking, piled to the height of the forward house, and in the sequel seriously interfering with a clear view of the deck.

Tragedy loves to begin slowly. The voyage opened auspiciously. Jonathan Spencer served meals in the cabin shared by the Captain and his wife, the two mates and the passenger. Harvard gave tone to the talk. Monks alluded to yachting experiences and chatted of Clark Russell's *Voyage to the Cape* and Harding Davis's *Three Gringos in Venezuela*, while Mrs. Nash inquired about studies at college. Unfortunately amateur yachting and Harvard College were much to the disgust of both mates, whose only common bond seemed to be a low opinion of such topics.

Monday, July 13, was the day Fate fixed on. The *Fuller* was 750 miles out somewhere between Portugal and our eastern shores. There was little night life aboard ship; diversion grew pale at sundown. Captain Nash was in the chartroom, in one corner of which stood his bunk. The passenger's room led directly off it and just beyond were Mrs. Nash's quarters. The main cabin was empty. A murky lamp swinging above the dining table offered little attraction to a reader. At eight bells the passenger went to bed. A little sea was on. The door rattled. Monks locked it. To enjoy a more luxurious feeling of security he pulled out his sea chest and jammed it between door and washstand. All was snug now and off he went to sleep. Something like a scream waked him. He thought it a woman's. He sat up and listened. Next came a gurgling noise from the chartroom. Monks slipped his hand over Uncle George's pistol lying under his pillow, reached under his bed for the cartridges, loaded the chambers, and listened. The unpleasant sound from the chartroom still continued, but in a lower key. He slipped on his dressing gown, yanked away his chest, turned the door lock, and stepped with caution into the chartroom. The Captain's cot was overturned. Beside it lay the Captain in a bath of blood. Monks cried out, "Captain Nash! Captain Nash!" There was no answer. He touched the man's shoulder. It reeked with sweat. He ran to Mrs. Nash's room and called. Her door was open. She lay in her bunk and the blankets were dripping blood.

What to do in such emergencies is not taught to freshmen. Revolver in hand, Monks started up the aft companionway. Then very sensibly it occurred to him that the murderer, axe in hand, might be waiting above for a third victim, so he turned and went up on deck forward. As his head emerged above the level of the flooring, he saw Mate Bram walking the deck. He pointed his pistol at him and the mate, with every appearance of terror, picked up a plank and threw it at him. Monks was not certain whether the action was hostile. It might come from fright. He cried out, "Come below for God's sake! The Captain has been murdered!" The mate seemed incredulous. He muttered, "No, no, no," but he came.

The time was two o'clock in the morning, the chartroom was not a pleasant place, and the two men soon returned to the deck and seated themselves by the rail, their backs turned to the water. The talk was constrained. The mate remarked, "There is a mutiny," and then, bursting into sobs, he clasped the passenger's knees begging for protection. When he straightened up a sudden nausea seized him. He was violently sick.

"Someone must have drugged my whiskey," he muttered.

The situation was a nightmare. Interminable interviews with the Dean, exacerbating talks with his father, seemed to Monks now to slip into their proper perspective. There he was sitting side by side with a man who might well be a murderer. His

Adventures by Proxy

own pistol pointed toward the crew; they, too, might be murderers. Mate Bram covered the man at the wheel.

Night dragged on and the terror mounted. The intelligent mulatto, Jonathan Spencer, after viewing the Captain's body, noticed that another door leading to the second mate's cabin was ajar. He stepped across the threshold. Murder once more! The mate lay still in his cot, his head gashed wide open. It was not news to calm the passenger's nerves. What would that Boston doctor have recommended in this emergency?

Silence was safer, but on deck there was occasional talk. Suddenly Bram pointed across the ship. "There is the axe that did it," he said. And there, half hidden under the deck lashings, was an axe red with blood. "Shall I throw it overboard?" asked Bram. Then the passenger said a foolish thing. "Yes," he exclaimed, "for fear the crew may use it against us." Spencer yelled, "No!" but already the axe that had murdered three people was flying out to sea.

"You shouldn't have done that," said the steward. Bram's reply was full of stupid cunning.

"We don't find no axe," said he.

"What do you take me for, a G——d d——d fool?" Spencer's words were packed with meaning. "Don't you know a man has seen you with the axe?"

There were now nine living souls on the *Herbert Fuller;* one knew, the others could only guess who the murderer was. Bram and Monks kept the crew covered with their revolvers. In this attitude they waited for dawn.

Bram was now legally captain of the ship, but he avoided privileges; and there was a general consultation. Everybody was against completing the voyage. They must make the nearest port. Bram stated this was Cayenne, but Cayenne was 1500 miles away, not an inviting spot when you got there, and certainly not convenient under the present circumstances.

The Happy Profession

There was Bermuda 400 miles north, but the wind was dead ahead. It was agreed that they should steer for Halifax. Bram was the only navigator on board. Nominally he was in command of the ship. In the mind of the passenger this was an invidious situation. God knows, he thought, whether there is mutiny aboard as well as murder.

It was well to take precautions. The handles of all tools in the carpenter shop were sawed off. The bodies were locked in the cabin.

Late that afternoon suspicion shifted violently to a new quarter. Charley Brown had cast overboard a pair of overalls and one of the sailors confided to the passenger that on the night of the murder Brown had changed his clothes. Bram, Spencer, and the passenger had a huddled talk. Then they seized Charley Brown, clamped irons on him, and dumped him into a sort of well between the piled planking. The sailor made no resistance, merely remarking that he had changed his clothes because he was cold. The days passed miserably, all hands on deck. The nights were cold, the days hot. The bodies were brought on deck and placed in a lifeboat and canvas was nailed tight over the horrors below. The passenger suggested it was fitting to read the Burial Service. The emotional Mr. Bram seconded the proposal and added a touch which brought into relief certain eccentric passages of revivalism later introduced into his record. He suggested that the organ should be carried up from the cabin so that a proper musical selection could be performed. This, thanks to early training, the passenger vetoed, but over those bodies he read the sacred ritual for the dead. It was a strange service. The murderer, whoever he was, standing before the bier of his victims and uttering *Amen* to the prayer that they should rest in peace.

On Saturday in the hot sun the presence of the bodies be-

Adventures by Proxy

came intolerable. The murder boat was swung over the side and towed behind. Sunday came and with it another extraordinary revelation. One of the sailors not out of sympathy with Charley Brown's predicament chatted with the prisoner. Brown confided to him that, shortly before two o'clock on the night of the murder, he was taking his trick at the wheel. A moan came from the chartroom. Looking straight through the window of the after-house he had seen Mate Bram strike at a figure lying on the cot below. Of his figure he could only see the legs, but the mate he could identify absolutely from the hat he was accustomed to wear which had the crown torn off and the brim remaining. Fearful for his own life, Charley Brown had kept his knowledge to himself.

This damning evidence was brought to the passenger and, in consultation with Spencer, it was decided that Bram, too, must be put in irons. Apathy often appears as a sequel to murder. Like Charley Brown, the mate Bram made no resistance. "Don't ill-treat a man. I am innocent," he muttered as they secured him alongside the mainmast. Then Monks's yachting lore stood him in good stead. During the rest of the voyage it was he who navigated the ship — standing at the wheel, his back to the ocean, his loaded pistol on the binnacle, the ship's crew in front of him carrying out his orders.

"There were six days in this hell," I said. "When did you sleep?"

"I didn't sleep," he answered, "unless I nodded at the wheel."

On Tuesday the murder ship made Halifax. A pilot came alongside. "There's murder aboard!" Monks shouted wildly over the side. The pilot came up the ladder and took command. On reaching the dock the police took over and, after an agonizing period of questioning, Monks pitched forward on a jail cot. It was, he said, thirty-six hours before he stirred.

The Happy Profession

The Prodigal had returned. He had been gone not six months but seventeen days. In his account Lester passed over the family welcome, but it must have been a study in domestic relationships. Considering the speculation concerning the identity of the murderer and not unmindful of the impression the young man's personal record might make on the jury, Mr. Monks, Sr., suggested it would be well for Lester to consult the family lawyer. Mr. Bartlett, long counsel for the Monks family, was a sober, judgmatical man. He had already digested some twenty columns of newspaper narrative and speculation when the young man turned up. He motioned Lester to a chair, turned his own swivel seat to his desk, and said kindly, "Now tell me the entire story." His attitude was judicial, but Lester took comfort in remembering those ample lunches when Mr. Bartlett had devoured Sunday roast beef and Yorkshire pudding at his father's table. He plunged into his story. As he went from point to point, Lester, who had the promoter's gifts, felt he was telling his tale effectively. Now he was confident he had a friend. For two hours the tale went on in all its gruesome details. Mr. Bartlett's head was in his hands. He seemed lost in thought. "Is that all?" he asked. "Yes, sir," replied Lester brightly, thinking it quite enough. The old gentleman swiveled his chair about, put his hand on Lester's shoulder, and said, "My boy, tell me why you did it."

With two active candidates for a Grand Jury verdict, the evidence against Lester gradually melted away. Mate Bram was tried and convicted. Unfortunately certain extraneous evidence had been admitted. The Supreme Court ordered a new trial. Again Bram was found guilty but by a dazzling stroke of luck, just before the second trial took place, a new law had been placed on the statute books permitting in federal cases of murder an alternative verdict carrying life imprisonment instead of death. So it was that Thomas Mead

Adventures by Proxy

Chambers Bram, after fifteen years in prison, came to be selling peanuts in Charleston; and in 1919, for his exemplary conduct on parole, was through one of the least known acts of President Wilson, during the Peace Conference in Paris, presented with a full pardon.

But this is not Mate Bram's story. That has been fully told elsewhere.[1] We are following the trail of Lester Monks. Before he and I parted that afternoon it was not difficult to divine that the prescription of the Boston doctor had been at fault after all. The only adequate description of such nerves as Monks's comes from Sairey Gamp. Her concise summary still stands. "Which fiddle-strings is weakness to expredge my nerves this night!" In another case the reaction might have been different, but what nerves like Lester's really needed was not quiet but monstrous and mounting excitement. The drama aboard the *Herbert Fuller* had galvanized him into intense activity. It threw all his faculties into top gear. When he went into the world again he made a fortune, and when he lost it, all the energy of his character seemed to die within him waiting for some further stimulus. Once more it seemed that everything was lost. He was homeless, wifeless, childless, friendless. Then, as on the *Herbert Fuller*, his very desperation saved him. In his pioneering experience the sense of drama buoyed him up once more. It exhilarated him to know that what he was undergoing would spell quietus for another man. Confidence returned, and confidence brought success. He was off to make another fortune.

Lester summarized his history for me. He had accumulated a little capital by his work on the railroad. He had been promoted to boss a gang. Then he had secured a subcontract for a section of the G.T.P. To raise more money he had come

[1] Mr. Edmund Pearson, amongst others, has chronicled it in a capital compilation of memorable murders.

The Happy Profession

east. He had been to Washington, he told me, and was surprised at the number of old friends who had turned up to wish him well — he was successful now — even to chip in on his new enterprise. He began to take his old place in society. One afternoon he dropped in at an "at home" in the house of Mrs. White, wife of the Chief Justice, who had been an old friend of his father's. The hostess welcomed him with cordiality. Her husband, whose mighty back was broad as the blacksmith's under the spreading chestnut tree, was deep in conversation with a lady. Mrs. White touched his shoulder. "Edward," she said, "you will want to shake hands with our old friend, Lester Monks." In the hum of talk the Chief Justice caught only the last words. "Lester Monks!" said he in his reverberant voice. "Yes, I always believed he did it."

Incidents like this, perturbing to ordinary folk, slipped from Lester like water from a duck's back. He went straight ahead, built his section, collected his money, and soon after, I heard of him in the coal business buying barges to ship his anthracite. Right and left he contracted for more. The First World War was in the offing. Ships were trebling in value. His company stock which he had been pushing at $40 a share jumped to $240. The Harrimans noticed his ability as a salesman and took him into partnership in their Hawaiian Line. There were millions in it! Then Fate, who always stood at the elbow of Lester Monks, stepped straight across his path. The Government clamped down. His new ships were taken over. Once more Lester Monks was ruined. He turned again to his oldest friend, drink, and one night something in his feverish brain gave way. He never woke again.

I leave his story to the moralists. For me it is enough to remember there were times when he played a man's part. I am glad I knew him.

CHAPTER XXIV

Pictures in the Night

THERE IS no editorial platitude so stale as "Trying to satisfy everybody satisfies nobody." Readers like you or they don't. They tag you as "lush" or "arid," "liberal" or "conservative," and let it go at that, but an editor is seldom one thing or another. This leads me to a bit of self-analysis. I am not sure whether it is the same with other people accustomed to a moderate degree of self-examination, but throughout my more reflective life, I have been conscious of certain settled differences in outlook between Myself and Me. Myself, so far back as I can remember, has been all for progress, always in favor of tinkering with the world machine, patching its weaknesses, and experimenting with new contraptions designed to increase its efficiency, while the more sophisticated Me keeps asking inconvenient questions as to which way progress, indeed whether progress may not be an illusion after all, and counseling a little salutary delay while we consider the matter. Philosophic friends tell me that in such cases Me is apt to grow a trifle more obstinate with the years. Myself certainly holds that Me does, but as the decades pass, I, the arbiter, incline to believe that progress is not a ladder, not even the spiral of Victorian hopes, but rather a meandering maze leading now up, now down, over difficult and hilly ground. If this be true, a certain quiescence which

The Happy Profession

Myself calls "torpidity" and Me "caution" is scarcely a reprehensible attitude. The most congruous friend I can recall, Barrett Wendell, to whose consistency I have paid repeated tribute, maintained that change was invariably and indubitably bad. It must come, but it must be resisted. With that arbiter I, cannot agree, and yet a bit of procrastination is not a vice.

Though reformers may chant with enthusiasm: —

> Truth forever on the scaffold,
> Wrong forever on the throne,

Truth, Right, and Wrong are rather shadowy characters. A definition with more reality seems to relate to the behavior of Virtue and of Folly. Too often these are inseparable companions, while over against Folly, Sagacity is prone to keep company, not so often with Vice but with a more elusive opposite of Virtue, Self-seeking. These get along swimmingly together and the result is not happy. The truth is, Virtue is much more reliable as an inspiration than as a guiding star. When trouble comes, it is Intelligence, not Virtue, which is most apt to point the reasonable way out. The Good (tell it in Gath) have their limitations. The mere phrase "unco guid" tells a story both of religious and of political reform. Perhaps the most profitable memorial in a democracy would be a gigantic model of a pendulum set up in the market place for all to see. The lesson a pendulum implies it cannot fail to teach.

I am led to these remarks by recalling how greatly my youth was stirred by the appearance of Mr. Bryan on the political scene. Myself and Me, my heart and my head, moved violently in opposite directions. I ought to have asked myself the conundrum, "When is a hero not a hero?" and listened for the answer, "When he is a fool." Some such puzzle I did

Pictures in the Night

ask myself, but time passed before I caught the answer. In the unforgettable campaign of 1896, when Bryan first invaded the "enemy's country," I was a reporter on the *Worcester Gazette*. The Great Commoner was standing on a cart tail drawn up in the principal square. How wholesome, how handsome he was then! How confident of his creed! How certain that the hour of liberty was striking! The campaign had gone far enough already to mark his opponent, William McKinley, as the greatest master of platitude our world had ever seen. When, with a magnificent gesture, McKinley declared that it was better to open the mills than to close the mines, I heard it whispered in bitter satire, "It is better to be in the swim than in the soup," and felt a gentle nausea stealing over my diaphragm. Now here was a man ready to die for the truth that was in him. But hardly had he opened his mouth when the glorious illusion collapsed.

The great propagandists of those days were Coin and his Financial School. All the intricacies of finance, of banking, of currency, Coin told us, were stuff and nonsense. Any child could comprehend them, and his Primer with baby drawings and infantile text told gaping millions how.

Democratic education in America, generations of it, was bearing the fruit which we now so regularly harvest.

It was the Primer of Coin's Financial School which Mr. Bryan held in his hand that day. The scorn with which he referred to bankers who bamboozled honest men into obfuscation and made what was plain as the nose on your face into one of the higher mysteries, was utterly genuine. His exposition of the doctrine of "16 to 1" still strikes me as a classic of nursery nonsense. You cannot be fooled, he told the howling audience. You have all of you seen a good old-fashioned well sweep. Now, drop in the bucket, sixteen ounces of silver, and hang one ounce of gold at the end of

The Happy Profession

the sweep. When the sweep goes down, up comes the bucket; when gold goes down, up comes silver. That's the currency problem in a nutshell. That's the whole of it. And think of the abracadabra bankers throw round it. God never makes important things too difficult for a plain man to understand.

There the problem was posed between Myself and Me. Flapdoodle and Integrity, one and indivisible. I saw it all. I knew it all — and I voted for Mr. Bryan.

That victory of Myself was a vote of conscience, yet Me contends it was a vote against McKinley rather than a vote for Bryan. The choice between the candidates was a relative question. The very day after the election I heard the great Mr. Godkin of the *Evening Post* remark: "We've worked and worked and *worked* to get McKinley in. Now we must work and work and *work* to get him out again." But this, remember, was the McKinley of 1896, not the McKinley of the Buffalo speech.

A number of times after that, I saw Mr. Bryan. I saw him as a hero at Baltimore. I saw him as a fool on the stump, and once at least I saw him as an enigma. It was at a private luncheon given for Mr. Bryan, then Secretary of State, by Colonel House at the Century Club in New York that I found myself intensely interested in a conversation centering about the Federal Reserve Act, the most important fiscal measure of a quarter of a century, the liberator of money from a central tyranny, and the utter negation of Mr. Bryan's fantastic theory. There sat Mr. Bryan, smiling and complacent. I asked across the table, "What is your personal opinion of the Bill, Mr. Secretary?" "I am for it," he replied, "but I have not read it." "Not read it!" I exclaimed, knowing it dealt with issues dearer to him than life. "No," said Mr. Bryan in his resonant voice, "I have the President's word that monopoly is intolerable and indefensible. That is sufficient for me. I have

Pictures in the Night

not read the Bill." The incident is worth recording. It is an index of Mr. Bryan's mentality. But it is more than that. It is a tribute to the complete intellectual domination of President Wilson.

If you live long and have a good seat at the show, there are certain external aspects of it in which one never forgets a lineament or a detail. At night — it is a singularly unprofitable practice — I am apt to gaze on old scenes and see again old faces. Look carefully. Every face carries its own story, some drab and empty enough, some worth remembering. The eye, shifting or steady, is a window disclosing what goes on within. The forehead, dominant or recessive, needs no phrenologist to proclaim its character. The eyebrow, "the actor's feature," may shrug you off, but the nose makes no concealment of the will to do or the apathy to leave undone. The mouth, coarse or fine, is the very index of the degree of culture. A chin may run away with a man's reputation or prognathically assert it. Great people have great faces. Some which I have seen once only, others long familiar, hang in my nightly gallery of portraits. Across more than sixty years I see a face like none other. I was a child in Rome. My parents promised to take me with them to their audience with Leo XIII, the Supreme Pope of modern times. All winter long my French governess perfected me in my address, *"Votre Bénédiction, Saint Père"* — again and again I was taught to say it — but as, clasping my mother's hand, I walked through those stately antechambers, the Swiss guard in Michelangelo's red and yellow at the door, the Guardia Nobile grouped about, gentlemen in black silk smallclothes and long gold chains showing the way, my ten-year-old trepidation shook me in my shoes. I felt I must be approaching the presence of the Eternal. Clearly as I saw him then, I see him now: that

The Happy Profession

erect and stately figure dressed in purest white, the only color the immense violet stone on the middle finger. His face, cut like a cameo under a skin of palest parchment, seemed to shine from within. In my childish mind there rose the picture of an alabaster lamp diffusing its shaded light, for by a curious illusion the classical features seemed translucent. Such a link between earth and heaven I had not seen. My tongue stuck fast. The toil of months was gone. As I kissed the ring I bumbled over my *"Bénédiction,"* and His Holiness, smiling at my mother, gently boxed my ears and blessed her child.

Another face that will not leave my remembrance is that of Rabindranath Tagore. I had talked with him once or twice and corresponded with him much, and one evening Professor Royce took me with him to the house of the Professor of Indic Literature at Harvard, where a group of philosophers gathered to discuss the immortalities. The slow and earnest talk flowed over me. I was fathoms deep beneath immensity, but not for two hours did I take my eyes from the poet's face. It looked the symbol of eternal contrast with the philosophies of the West. The delicate olive of his cheek, the high-bridged, aquiline nose, the sensitive mouth, were purely Oriental. Across my mind fluttered remembrances of Saladin, the glorious Moor, and I remembered that other contrast when the sword of the Lion Heart, which hacked a steel bar in twain, was powerless against the silken pillow, parted at a single stroke of Saladin's scimitar. But the memorable feature of Tagore's face was his eye — the eye of a hawk without its cruelty. The lids were like a bird's. The poet often closed them in meditation and, as the eyes slowly opened, the lids rolled up not in curves but like horizontal curtains. Then his penetrating glance would shoot out, escaping like a beam of imprisoned light. The pupils were dark, the whites a pale gray.

Pictures in the Night

To me, fancifully enough, those eyes seemed not like man's but Nature's. I see them still.

Actors' faces belong not to themselves but to their parts. To me the face of all stage faces was Madame Duse's. It was not its beauty that held me, but its exquisite mobility and the look of the eternal feminine which poets have praised from Lilith to the Blessed Damozel. Duse's voice had not the range and power of Bernhardt's. Hers was not a dynamic art, startling you from your seat, but her charm was infinite. When she smiled, the radiance of it purled and rippled over the footlights. A thousand shared it, but you felt it yours alone. When Bernhardt played *La Dame aux Camélias*, she *was* the heroine of that slightly grubby drama. She was everything that Dumas *fils* wrote into it. Madame Duse lifted the part to another sphere. Melodrama became tragedy. All the suffering of woman was in her face when, turning from her lover, she cried in a voice that pierced to the heart's core: "Armando, Armando!" In the middle of the night I would start from sleep, "Armando, Armando!" sounding in my ears.

When, in Sir Edward Grey's tragic phrase, the lamps went out all over Europe, one beacon light remained. High and steady Cardinal Mercier held it aloft. Its spiritual authority never dimmed. Now the long agony was over, and the great Cardinal had come to America bringing us thanks. An honorary degree was to be given him, and I sat on the Harvard platform immediately behind his chair so that I could rivet my eyes on that incorporeal face silhouetted, as it chanced, directly against the powerful and mundane features of Cardinal O'Connell. The countenances overlapped as if posed by some classical medalist to carve the dual profiles on a Roman coin. Between the two the contrast was wide as the two worlds they represented. I whispered to Dr. Bradford, who sat next to me, "The Church Temporal and the Church

The Happy Profession

Eternal." Newman and Manning, I suppose, offered the same tremendous study of opposites, the two divisive halves of Christianity. "Can Heaven live without the solid support of earth?" I asked myself, for there before my eyes was set forth the twofold picture of the religion of Christ. We cannot live by bread alone, but will the Word that cometh out of the mouth of God support the breath in our bodies? I thought of innumerable statues of Faith, with their stereotyped features and beatitudinous inanity. In the very idea of faith there is a suggestion of doubt. The face of Cardinal Mercier was the image of Certainty. To him the incredible was the natural, the simple, almost the obvious. His gaze never wavered from his Reality.

The next portrait in my gallery is of a very different cast, a face pagan, Praxitelian, shaped before the "pale Galilean" had made the world grow gray at His breath. The hour was hard on lunch. I was signing letters with a will, when my secretary brought in a bearer's note from my friend Lowes Dickinson. Anything from Dickinson meant much to me, and I asked that the stranger be shown in. The visitor startled me. A young man more beautiful than he I had never seen. Tall beyond the common, his loose tweeds accentuated his height and the athletic grace of his walk. His complexion was ruddy as young David's. His auburn hair rippled back from the central parting, careless but perfect. Hermes had stepped from his pedestal. "Rupert Brooke is my name," he said, "Dickinson told me I mustn't miss seeing you." That name was unknown to me at the time. Brooke was halfway between Cambridge and his reputation then, but when he took from his pocket the proof sheets of his "Grantchester" verses and we had read a few stanzas together, I felt I knew much of him. He was on a trip to Hawaii where he wanted to hunt on the mountains — "sticking pigs" he told me in his Byronic way, and then

Pictures in the Night

we plunged into talk of a poet's life in a mechanized world. If poetry was ever made flesh, there it was visible before me. I knew it and was lost in the moment. Unfortunately Brooke was to lunch with Amy Lowell and was off to the West that very evening, but on his return from Honolulu he would surely drop in again.

Man's beauty is much more rare than woman's. I went home under the spell of it and at the foot of the stairs cried aloud to my wife, "I have seen Shelley plain!" Ever since I have known that it was so.

Years later, cruising in the Mediterranean, our yacht put in at Skyros and I went to see Brooke's statue perched on a hilltop, the face turned toward home. The sculptor had attempted to "idealize" an unapproachable reality. To me the marble meant less than nothing, and I turned to his real memorial dimly seen in the distance, the shore where he lay buried,

> . . . some corner of a foreign field
> That is for ever England.

As I glance down my gallery I notice that the portraits on the walls are not usually American. Remarkable men live here as well as in Europe, but I am not sure whether the faces of unusual people on this side are not of a more uniform type. So far as American genius in the administration of great businesses goes, this is natural. If you walk through the corridors of the Vatican, past the impressive busts of the togaed senators of ancient Rome, you will be struck with their close similarity to the countenances of American executives. Those same wide foreheads, deep-set eyes, and heavy jowls you can see any day at noon in the leathern armchairs of the Chicago Club, but newspapers notwithstanding, business and politics do not make up America. Of all the faces I see before me, one

The Happy Profession

seems most amply to sum up the great American tradition.

At Harvard College in the '90s, President Eliot seemed to us undergraduates the visible embodiment of all austerities. He did nothing to promote our good cheer, and when we caught sight of him moving down the central path of the yard, we were apt to hurry up the diagonal. That Mr. Eliot was a human being we had absolutely no conception. To us he was a companion piece of John Harvard, sitting in his bronze chair by Memorial Hall.[1] How different is the picture that sticks in the mind of those who knew the man behind the President. I recall the testimony of a classmate beset during his college years by desperate poverty. This young man pared down his rations till his jacket hung loose about him. Then, like everybody in trouble, he went to Dean Briggs and asked whether some small sum from the charitable endowment known as Price Greenleaf Aid could not be allotted him. The Dean was sympathetic but the matter was beyond his control.

"You must go," he said, "to see Mr. Eliot."

Now, "to see Mr. Eliot" seemed a good deal like calling on Solon in person. All that night and all the next the frightened young man rehearsed a halting speech. Then at the appointed hour he rang the bell of the little house on Quincy Street.

President Eliot would see him. He knocked at the study door and heard a deep voice within: "Come in, Mr. Crandon."

Crandon had his supplication by heart but no argument was necessary. Mr. Eliot was entirely conversant with the case. In half a dozen sentences he outlined the situation and offered the aid. Crandon could hardly believe his good fortune. His one desire was to get away before the vision faded. Mumbling his thanks, he edged toward the door, but just as he was closing it securely behind him, he heard Mr. Eliot's

[1] French's admirable statue now stands in front of University Hall.

Pictures in the Night

measured voice, "One word more, Mr. Crandon." The boy's heart froze, he felt some impossible restriction was to be imposed and stood to attention, awaiting sentence.

"I fear, Mr. Crandon," said the President, "that you do not eat properly." The visitor protested that bread and cheese were nourishing but Mr. Eliot continued, "What I would recommend to you is veal loaf. Veal loaf, Mr. Crandon, is at once the most economical and nutritious of viands. It is compounded in this way," and then, with the utmost precision, the President gave the astonished applicant a detailed recipe for compounding the dish of all dishes most substantial at the price.

The incident paints Mr. Eliot in his habit as he lived, judicious, helpful, and meticulous.

Of such things as these the Class of '94 was ignorant.

But a boy does grow up (perhaps this is the worst of it) and when I returned to Boston to take over the *Atlantic* and was invited to join the Saturday Club where solid men of Boston representing many interests foregather for monthly luncheons, President Eliot was always in the Chair. When I entered the dining room, I could not but notice that on either side of him the seats were empty. Evidently the undergraduate tradition had not evaporated. With the brass polish of New York fresh upon me, I slipped into one of the vacant chairs, and from that moment found a friend.

President Eliot's "durable satisfactions of life" were part of every Harvard man's education. When he turned his grave and sculptured head toward me, there was the slightest smile about the full lips. "What is the good life, Mr. Sedgwick?" he asked. I was ready with the right answer. "Marriage, Mr. Eliot," and we were off on a pleasant journey. Thereafter habitually I took the same seat, and no course in adult education was more valuable to me. His largeness of view, his sanity,

The Happy Profession

his directness, a certain loneliness of judgment unvexed by convention or precedent, an inflexible dedication to the right as he saw it — all found expression in that erect figure born for authority, the oarsman's back, the sober impersonality of his glance, his large and noble features. The sanguine birthmark spreading over one cheek was in maturity no blemish but an emblem of triumph over the handicaps of life. His whole personality was indeed the summary of a great tradition. Like Lincoln he was one of Plutarch's Men.

What have memories like these to do with editing? My answer is that all experience goes to make an editor, and that the eye harvests memories, more accurate perhaps than the brain, and quite as penetrating.

A man lives by what he has been. Mistakes, failures, efforts, successes, aspirations, all make up the sum. He lives by what he has been, and we hope that, when his books are balanced, it will be recorded that he lived by what he might be. For the best part of a man's life is what he means to become. Forty-five years ago, when I was an ardent student of my profession, this was my substance of things hoped for: —

> To be honest. To be fair. To look with leniency on faults beyond one's own temptations. To cherish enthusiasms and to hate cant. To love friends well and books better. To be endlessly interested. To try to believe and to be reasonably credulous. To enjoy life and doubt its all-importance. To accept opportunity with gratitude. To hold good writing as the art above the arts, and to forgive him much who can write like an Angel.
>
> Amen.

Index

Index

ADAMS, BROOKS, 167, 310
Adams, Charles Francis, 22
Adams, Henry, 167
Adams, Sam, 145
Addams, Jane, 184
Agassiz, Ida. *See* Higginson, Mrs. Henry
Aldrich, Thomas Bailey, 174, 177
Alexandra, Queen Mother of England, 292, 293–294
All This and Heaven Too (Rachel Field), 25
American Magazine. See Leslie's Monthly Magazine
Antin, Mary, 267–270; quoted, 268, 269
Appleton, D., and Company, Ellery Sedgwick book editor for, 148–153
Appleton, Daniel, 152
Appleton, Tom, 6
Appleton, William, 152, 153
Arnold, Matthew, influence on Ellery Sedgwick, 67
Assisi, Italy, 189, 190
Atlantic Monthly, 96, 107, 146, 179, 181, 186, 187, 197, 216, 222, 224, 233, 246, 262, 276, 294, 331; Ellery Sedgwick's ambition to run it, 154; early editors, 154–156, 173, 174; staff members under Ellery Sedgwick, 176, 191; early history, 178; publishes Edward Lewis, 190; publishes Elinore Rupert Stewart, 198, 199, 200; publishes Eleanor Risley, 200, 201, 202; publishes L. Adams Beck (E. Barrington), 207; publishes Juanita Harrison, 211; interest in prison reform, 229, 230–231; office on Arlington Street, 231; office on Park Street, 235; publishes Hans Coudenhove, 249; publishes Opal Whiteley, 254, 256, 258, 261, 263; publishes Mary Antin, 269; circulation, 295–296; influence of its articles, 296–297; publishes Lester Monks, 310
Ayer, Mr. N. W., 97, 198

BACHE, JULES, 170
Bacon, Delia, 276
Bacon, Francis, 189; quoted, 192; Baconian theory, 276–278, 283
Baker, Newton, 179
Baker, Ray Stannard, 143, 144
Baldwin, Stanley, 194, 195
Barrington, E. *See* Beck, L. Adams
Bartlett, Mr., 318
Beck, Colonel, 207
Beck, L. Adams, 206–210
Belgian Congo, 246, 250
Bell, Mrs., 171–172, 173, 174
Bennett, Arnold, 194
Bennett, James Gordon, 220
Berenson, Bernard, 169
Bernhardt, Sarah, 327
Beveridge, Albert, 151, 163–164
Beverly, Massachusetts, Ellery Sedgwick's house at, 163, 218

Index

Bigelow, Dr. Sturgis, 208
Billings, Sherrard, 52, 53, 54, 55
Bixby, W. K., 163
Blaine, James G., 179
Bok, Edward W., 216, 290–291, 294; autobiography, 292
Borchgrevink, Carsten E., 108, 109–110, 111
Borchgrevink, Mrs. C. E., 110
Boston, 80, 166, 238; Boston Common, 78, 231; dining clubs, 167–168; eminent inhabitants, 168–175; Boston Arena, 231; police strike, 231
Boston Society for the Prevention of Cruelty to Children, 221
Bourbon, Françoise de. *See* Whiteley, Opal
Bourbon, Henry of, 263, 264, 265
Bourne, Randolph, 222–224
Boyden, Bert, 144
Bradford, Dr. Edward H., 327
Bradford, Mr., 97, 98
Bram, Thomas Mead Chambers, Mate, 312, 313, 315–319; story by Edmund Pearson, 319 *n.*
Brewer, Adele, 25
Brewer, Justice David J., 25
Bridges, Harry, 244
Briggs, Dean Le Barron Russell, 73, 330
British Weekly, 226, 227
Brogan, Billy, 10, 11, 33
Brooke, Rupert, 328–329
Brooks, Phillips, 31, 58, 78; quoted, 31
Brown, Alice, 176
Brown, Charley, 312, 316, 317
Browning, Mr. and Mrs. Robert, 171
Bryan, William Jennings, 246, 322–325
Buckle, H. T., 76
Buffum, David, 116–121; consequences of article, 121–123
Bulfinch, Charles, 167
Burne-Jones, Edward, 196

Butler, Charles E. (Ellery Sedgwick's uncle), 14, 17, 26
Butler, Ellis Parker, 124, 126
Butler, Sir Geoffrey, 291
Butler, Sigourney, 77
Butler, Susan Sedgwick (Ellery Sedgwick's aunt), 17, 26
Butler, Evarts, and Choate, 16
Butler, Evarts, and Southmayd, 14

CABOT, JUDGE FREDERICK, 238–239
Canadian Northern Railroad, 299
Canadian Pacific Railroad, 299
Canfield, Dorothy, an editor of *Leslie's Monthly*, 105; marriage, 106–107
Cather, Willa, 145
Caulfield, Jim, 126–132; and Ellery Sedgwick, 133–135
Century Magazine, 107
Chambers, Robert W., 151
Chapters of Erie (Charles Francis Adams), 22
Chesterton, Gilbert Keith, 253
Child, Francis James, 68, 69, 70, 305
Choate, George, 37
Choate, Joseph H., 16, 18, 34, 38, 179; St. Patrick's Day Speech, quoted, 35–37
Choate, Rufus, 171
Clark, James Beauchamp (Champ), Speaker, 185
Clarke, Mr., 40, 41
Clemenceau, Georges, 259
Cleveland, Grover, 178–179; visits Ellery Sedgwick's Harvard room, 77, 78
Coin's Financial School, 323
Collins, Patrick, 79
Comstock, Anthony, 149
Coney, Mrs., of Denver, 198, 199
Converse, Florence, 176
Coolidge, Calvin, 4
Cooper Union, Abraham Lincoln's address at, 21, 164

Index

Cosmopolitan, 107; prevented from publishing article on Martinique disaster, 112–115
Coudenhove, Count Hans, 246, 248–249; early history, 247, 250; death of, 251
Coudenhove-Kalergi, Count, 247
Crandon, Mr., 330, 331
Cross, Ada Cambridge, 203–206; quoted, 204
Crothers, Dr., 175
Cumnock, Arthur J., 149
Curzon, Lord, 259
Cutting, Bayard, 65

Dale, J. S. of. *See* Stimson, Frederic Jesup
Dame aux Camélias, La (Alexandre Dumas, *fils*), 327
Dana, Dr., 27
David Harum (Edward Noyes Westcott), 140
Davis, Richard Harding, 313
Dean, Mr., 40
Dickens, Charles, 173, 217
Dickinson, G. Lowes, 328
Dogs, Sedgwick, 28, 29, 30
Donnelly, Ignatius, 276, 282, 283
Dooley, Mr., 144
Doubleday, Frank, 292
Doubleday's, 149, 150
Doyle, A. Conan, 140
Dreiser, Theodore, 149, 150
Dumas, Alexandre, *fils*, 327
Duse, Eleonora, 327
Dwight, Colonel, 13, 14
Dwight, Abigail (Ellery Sedgwick's great-great-grandmother), 10
Dwight, Joseph, Brigadier General, 9
Dwight, Pamela (Ellery Sedgwick's great-grandmother), 10

Edmonds, Walter, 224–225
Education, mass, Ellery Sedgwick's opinions on, 76

Edwards, Jonathan, 11
Eliot, Charles William, 68, 71, 72, 75, 330–332
Elizabeth, Indian squaw, 6
Emporia Gazette, 298
Epictetus, 271, 273, 274; quoted, 272
Everybody's Magazine, 108

F., Colonel, 278–285
Fairyland Around Us, The (Opal Whiteley), 254, 260
Farrell, Nelly, maid, 28, 33
Field, Cyrus West, 24
Field, David Dudley, 21, 22
Field, Henry Martyn, 25
Field, Rachel, 25
Field, Stephen, involved in Terry Case, 22, 25; quoted, 23–24
Fields, Mrs. James T. (Annie), 173, 174
Fisher, Dorothy Canfield. *See* Canfield, Dorothy
Fisher, John R., 105, 106
Fiske, John, 59, 174–175, 276
Fitzpatrick, Teresa S., 191
Folk, Joseph W., 179
Folsom, Dr. Charles F., quoted, 83
Fortunes of Nigel, The (Sir Walter Scott), quoted, 43
Frank Leslie's Illustrated Weekly, 86
Frank Leslie's Popular Monthly. See Leslie's Monthly
Franklin, Benjamin, 270
French, Daniel Chester, 330 *n.*
Frick, H. C., 169, 170
Fugger Letters, 283

Gallop, Misses, 276, 282–285
Galsworthy, John, 194
Gardner, Miss, 169
Gardner, Amory, 59, 60
Gardner, Mrs. Jack (Isabella Stewart), 60, 61, 168–171, 249, 250, 301
Gardner, John L., 169
Gardner, William Amory, 52, 53
Gavitt, Chloe, 38

Index

Gavitt, Nellie, 38, 39
Gavitt, Pussie, 38
George V, King of England, 291, 292, 302
Gilroy, Thomas F., mayor of New York, 35
Godkin, Edwin Lawrence, 324
Good-bye, Mr. Chips (James Hilton), 226–228
Goodrich, Mrs. J. Z., 41, 42
Gordon, Dr. George A., 79
Gould, Alice Bache, 176
Grand Trunk Pacific Railroad, 307, 319
Grandgent, Professor Charles H., quoted, 71
Grant, Judge Robert, 175
Greshams' Law, 46
Grey, Sir Edward, 262, 327
Groton, 47, 179; Ellery Sedgwick a student at, 51–66; Ellery Sedgwick a master at, 48, 57; early days, 51, 52; Ellery Sedgwick a trustee of, 52, 57; founders, 52–56; visitors, 58–61; distinguished alumni, 62, 63; its emphasis on physical education, 63–65
Guiney, Louise Imogen, 176–177

H. D. P. *See* Monks, Lester
"H. M. and Company." *See* Houghton, Mifflin and Company
Hale, Edward Everett, 174
Haley, gardener, 45
Hall, Father (Bishop of Vermont), 58
Hall, James Norman, 220, 221, 222
Hanna, Mark, 167
Hapgood, Hutchins, 126
Hapgood, Norman, 126
Harriman, Averell, 320
Harrison, Juanita, 210–215; quoted, 212, 213
Harvard University, 67, 149, 157, 220, 224, 311, 327; Ellery Sedgwick at, 68–84; faculty members, 68–72; under Eliot, 72, 73, 330, 331; classmates, 73–75
Hearst, William Randolph, 136
Herbert Fuller, S.S., 311, 312, 314, 319
Higginson, Mrs. Henry, 170
Higginson, Thomas Wentworth, 174
Hill, Burbeck, 218
Hill, James J., 299
Hill, Sarah Althea, 22, 23
Hillman, Sidney, 244
Hilton, James, 226–228
Hofmayer, Mr., 39
Holmes, Oliver Wendell, 67, 172; quoted, 203
Holmes, Justice Oliver Wendell, Jr., 172, 177
Holworthy Hall, Harvard University, 77, 80
Hoppin, Fred, 111
Houghton, Mifflin and Company, 154, 157
House, Colonel Edward M., 287, 324
Howe, Mrs. George, 171
Howe, Mark, 299
Hugo, Victor, quoted, 54
Hunt, William Morris, 171, 305
Hurlbut and Johnson, 16
Hurlbut, Elisha P., 15

Ingersoll, Mrs., 11
Irwin, Will, 145

James, Henry, quoted, 3
James, William, 68, 78, 79, 189
Jefferson, Thomas, 245
Jenkins, MacGregor, 191, 296
Jewett, Sarah Orne, 173–174
Johns, Cloudesley, 271–275
Johnson, Samuel, 217; portrait owned by A. Edward Newton, 218
Journal of an Understanding Heart (Opal Whiteley), 255–256, 258, 261, 266

[338]

Index

Kay, Mr., 156
Keynes, Lord, 196
Kipling, Rudyard, 140, 196
Kittredge, George Lyman, 68, 285; and Francis James Child, 69–70
Knickerbocker Trust Company, failure of, 101–104
Koussevitzky, Serge, 9

Ladies' Home Journal, 294
Lane, George Martin, 70
Larrywang. *See* Lynch, Larry
Lawrence, Reverend Arthur, 26–27, 34; Sunday dinner stolen, 28–30
Lawrence, Billy, 27
Lawrence, Bishop William, 31
Leo XIII, Pope, 325–326
Leslie, Frank, 86
Leslie, Mrs. Frank, 89
Leslie's Monthly, 144; Ellery Sedgwick editor of, 86–137; proprietor, 87, 88, 91, 92, 96–97, 99, 136, 137; its financial condition, 90, 91–93; editorial quoted, 95; Ellery Sedgwick acquires stock in, 95; cashier's embezzlement, 99–100; article on Martinique disaster, 108–115; Buffum article, 116–123; editorial preface to Buffum article, quoted, 121; publishes "Pigs Is Pigs" (Ellis Parker Butler), 124; publishes "Maximilian Diamond" (Arthur Train), 125; change of name to *American Magazine*, 136; sale of magazine, 136–137
Lewis, Reverend Edward, 189–191
"Liberal," modern use of word, 244
Lidgerwood, Mr., 24
Lincoln, Abraham, 21, 158, 160, 163; anecdotes of, 161–162, 164–165; Lincoln legend, 162–163
Lincoln, Mrs. Abraham, 161–162, 163, 164
Lincoln, Joseph C., 151
Lincoln, Robert Todd, 159, 160, 163
Lliani, 118, 119

Lombroso, Cesare, 233
London, Jack, 272, 273
Lost Horizon (James Hilton), 226, 228
Lowell, A. Lawrence, 72, 175
Lowell, Amy, 175–176, 329
Lowell, James Russell, 178
Lucas, E. V., 218
Lynch, Larry, 9, 10

McAdoo, William G., 181
McClellan, General George B., 161
McClure, Samuel, 136, 311; character, 138–140, 141, 142, 143, 144; quoted, 140–141; original of Jim Pinkerton in *The Wrecker* by R. L. Stevenson, 140, 311; influence on employees, 143; Ellery Sedgwick's disagreement with, 146; in old age, 146, 147
McClure's Magazine, 107, 108, 136, 148; Ellery Sedgwick an editor, 137–146; working conditions at, 138
Mackenzie, Sir William, 299
McKinley, William, 323, 324
MacMonigle, Jimmy, 19
"Maine Law," 41
Manly, J. M., 285
Mann, Sir Donald, 299
Martinique, 108, 109, 110
Mary, Princess, of England, 292
Mary, Queen of England, 291, 292, 293, 294
Mary, Queen of Scots, Baconian play about her, 283
"Maximilian Diamond, The" (Arthur Train), 125
Memphis Appeal, 298
Mercier, Cardinal Désiré Joseph, 327, 328
Mifflin, Mr., 156, 157, 158, 165
Mill, John Stuart, quoted, 204
"Modern Voyage to Lilliput, A" (David Buffum), 118–121

[339]

Index

Monks, Mr. (Lester Monks's father), 318
Monks, Dr. George, 312, 313
Monks, Lester, adventures in the West, 306–310; letters quoted, 308, 09; adventures on the *Herbert Fuller*, 311–318; later career, 319–320
Monument Mountain, Stockbridge, 7, 9
Mooney, C. P. J. (editor of the Memphis *Commercial Appeal*), 298
Moresby, Lily. *See* Beck, L. Adams
Morgan, Pierpont, 51, 97
Moriarty, Patrick, 237–238, 239
Munsey's, 107, 108
Mutiny on the Bounty (Nordhoff and Hall), 187, 221

NASH, CAPTAIN, 312, 313, 314
Nash, Mrs., 313, 314
Neagle, guard, 23
New York Evening Post, 324
New York Herald, 220
New York Sun, quoted, 35–37
New York World, 143
Newcomes (William M. Thackeray), quoted, 153
Newton, A. Edward, 216, 220; appearance, 217; background, 218–219
Newton, Mrs. A. Edward, 218, 219
Nock, Albert J., 290
Nordhoff, Charles, 220–221, 222
Norton, Charles Eliot, 70, 71, 305

OAK KNOLL (home of A. Edward Newton), 218, 219
O'Connell, Cardinal William, 33, 327
Osborne, Thomas Mott, 232–233, 234, 236

P. E. N. CLUB, 192
Page, Walter Hines, 87, 154, 155, 178, 296
Palmer, George Herbert, 70

Peabody, Endicott, 52, 55–56, 57, 58, 59, 179
Peabody, Mrs. Endicott, 56, 57, 59
Pearson, Edmund, 319 *n*.
Pelée, Mount, Martinique, 108
Perry, Bliss, 155
Phillips, Mr. (partner of McClure), 139
Phillips, David Graham, 151, 152
Phillips, John, 144
"Pigs Is Pigs" (Ellis Parker Butler), 124
Pinkerton, Jim. *See* McClure, Samuel
Pisano, Nicolo, bust by Donatello, 300–302
Plato, quoted, 65
Platt, Tom, 144
Pliny, the Younger, 109
Poincaré, Jules Henri, 259
Poldi-Pezzoli Palace (Milan), 170
Pollock, Margaret, 12
Porter, Admiral David, 160
Portland Oregonian, 298
Portsmouth (New Hampshire) Prison, 232
Pratt, Mrs., 173
Pratt, Bela, 174
Precious Bane (Mary Webb), 195
Prescott, William H., 277, 278
Princess Ena, S.S., 307
Promised Land, The (Mary Antin), 270; quoted, 268, 269

QUARITCH, BERNARD, 218

RAPHAEL "THE RUSSIAN," 268
Rathbone, Frank, 39, 40
Rattlesnake Mountain, 7
Rayleigh, Lord, 259
Reedy, William Marion, 298
Reedy's Mirror, 298
Renan, Ernest, quoted, 206
Reni, Guido, 214
Revere, Paul, 167, 245
Reynolds, Sir Joshua, 218
Rhode Island, State Committee on Livestock of the State of, 120

[340]

Index

Rhodes, James Ford, 167
Riis, Jacob, 126
Risley, Eleanor, 200; quoted, 201–202
Riverside Press, 157
Roosevelt, Theodore, 58, 59, 145, 162, 269
Root, Elihu, 22
Roraima, S.S., 111, 112, 115
Rose, Hilda, 200
Royce, Josiah, 70, 326
Rublee, George, 52
Rupert, Elinore. *See* Stewart, Elinore Rupert
Russell, Bertrand, 196
Russell, "Billy," 79
Russell, Clark, 313

SACRED HEART, ORDER OF THE, 33
St. James's, Court of, 34, 159
Saint-Gaudens, Augustus, 78, 162
Sandringham, 291
Santayana, George, 73
Sargent, John Singer, 60, 61, 169
Saturday Club, 331
Schönbrunn, Court of, 247
Schurz, Carl, 163
Scott, Mr., of the *Portland Oregonian*, 298
Scott, Captain Ellery S., 111, 112
Scribner, Charles, 292
Scribner's, Messrs. Charles, Sons, 126
Scribner's Magazine, 107
Scudder, Horace, 154–155, 174
Sears, Joseph Hamblen, 148–149, 151
Sedgwick family, inheritance of characteristics, 4; homestead, 6, 7, 8, 19, 20, 93, 94; originally from Bedfordshire, England, 238
Sedgwick, Alexander (Ellery Sedgwick's brother), 20, 37
Sedgwick, Catherine (Ellery Sedgwick's great-aunt), quoted, 8, 11, 12
Sedgwick, Ellery, birth, 5; moves to Stockbridge, 6; eminent neighbors, 13–14, 15–20, 21–25, 34–38; relatives, 14, 32–33; fellow townspeople, 25–28, 38–42; his pet dogs, 28–30; at dame school, 38, 39; his opinion of coeducation, 46–47; his first boarding school, 48–51; student at Groton, 51–65; master at Groton, 48, 57; trustee of Groton, 52, 57; attends Harvard, 67–85; personal philosophy, 75; opinions on mass education, 76; meets President Cleveland, 77, 78; nursed by Jane Toppan, 80–84; editor of *Leslie's Monthly*, 86–137; advice to beginners in publishing business, 89–90; and financial problems of *Leslie's*, 91–93, 97–99; acquires stock in *Leslie's*, 95–96; marriage, 103; caught in failure of Knickerbocker Trust Company, 101–104; acquaintance with Dorothy Canfield, 105–107; covers Martinique disaster, 109–115; his article on midget horses, 116–123; friendship with burglar, 126–135; and sale of *Leslie's*, 136–137; editor for *McClure's*, 137–146; buys house on Park Avenue, 148; editor at D. Appleton, 148–153; buys *Atlantic*, 156; negotiates for Secretary Welles's diary, 158–165; early impressions of Boston, 166–168; on Mrs. Jack Gardner, 168–171; Boston friends, 172–177; admiration for Woodrow Wilson, 179–186; admiration for Al Smith, 186–187, 231–232; interest of material an editor's chief criterion, 187; publishes Rev. Edward Lewis, 189–191; meeting with Mary Webb, 192–195; and eminent women contributors to *Atlantic*, 198–210; Adams Beck (E. Barrington), 206–210; visits Japan, 208–210; story of Juanita Harrison, 210–215; friendship with A. Edward Newton, 216–220; summer home at Beverly,

Index

Massachusetts, 218; and famous men contributors to *Atlantic*, 220–228; on importance of having prejudices, 243, 246; on degeneration of language, 244–245; correspondence with Hans Coudenhove, 246–251; and story of Opal Whiteley, 254–266; on Mary Antin, 267–270; a hobo friend of, 271–275; encounters with Baconians, 276–285; on Albert J. Nock, 290; impressions of Edward Bok, 290–292, 293; meets Sir William Van Horne, 300–302; on taste as an ethical force, 302–304; story of Lester Monks, 306–320; reporter on the *Worcester Gazette*, 323; memorable faces in his experience, 325–332; friendship with President Eliot, 331–332

Sedgwick, Henrietta Ellery (Ellery Sedgwick's mother), 41
Sedgwick, Henry (Ellery Sedgwick's grandfather), 22
Sedgwick, Henry Dwight (Ellery Sedgwick's father), 41, 164, 165; his financial difficulties, 18–20, 93–94
Sedgwick, Jane (Ellery Sedgwick's aunt), 32, 33
Sedgwick, Mabel Cabot (Ellery Sedgwick's first wife), 103, 168, 180, 295, 329
Sedgwick, Marjorie Russell (Ellery Sedgwick's second wife), 5
Sedgwick, Nathalie (Ellery Sedgwick's cousin), 44, 45
Sedgwick, Robert (Ellery Sedgwick's grandfather), 22
Seward, William Henry, 158
Seymour, George, 40
Shakespeare, William, 278, 279, 285
Shaler, Nathaniel, 70
Shaughnessy, Sir Thomas, 299
Shaw, Robert Gould, statue of, by St.-Gaudens, 78

Sherbrooke, Viscount, quoted, 76
Sherwin, Tommy, 68
Sherwood, Rosina Emmet, 264
Siddall, Henry, 144
Sidney, Sir Philip, 56, 277
Sing Sing Prison, 229–230, 232, 236
Sister Carrie (Theodore Dreiser), 149, 150
Smith, Alfred E., 297; in Boston, 186–187; his sympathy for convicts, 231–232
Smith, Dean, 73
Socrates, quoted, 65
Southmayd, Charles F., appearance, 14–15; character, 16–17; robbed, 18; generosity to Ellery Sedgwick's father, 19–20
Spencer, Jonathan, 312, 313, 314
Stedman, E. C., 177
Steffens, Lincoln, 143, 144
Stella. See Toppan, Jane
Stevenson, R. L., 311
Stewart, Clyde, 198–199
Stewart, David, 168
Stewart, Elinore Rupert, 198–199, 200
Stewart, Isabella. See Gardner, Mrs. Jack
Strickney, Albert, 22
Stimson, Frederic Jesup, 174
Stockbridge, Massachusetts, 44, 67, 178; Sedgwick homestead, 6, 7–8, 19, 20, 93, 94; local names, 7; geography, 9; population, 9, 10, 12; denominationalism, 10–13; churches, 11, 26, 31, 32, 33; neighbors, 13–22, 24–29, 34–43
Stockbridge Bowl, 9, 34
Story of Opal (Opal Whiteley), preface to, quoted, 254–258
Swift, Jonathan, 80, 126

TAFT, WILLIAM HOWARD, 174
Tagore, Rabindranath, 326–327
Tanglewood, 9
Tarbell, Ida, 143, 144

Index

Tavern Club (Boston), 305
Tennyson, Alfred, Lord, quoted, 293–294
Terry, Judge David S., 22, 23, 24
Thackeray, William Makepeace, 173; quoted, 153
Thaw, Harry K., 73
Thayer, William Roscoe, 216
Three Gringos in Venezuela (Harding Davis), 313
Tocqueville, Alexis de, 230
Toppan, Jane, 80–84
Tragedy of Essex, Baconian play, 283
Train, Arthur, 125, 126
Tumulty, Joseph, 181, 183, 186
Tutt, Ephraim. *See* Train, Arthur
Tweed, William M. (Boss), 22
Tyrrell, Henry, 87, 88, 89

UNION LEAGUE CLUB, 164

VAN HORNE, SIR WILLIAM, 299, 300–302
Vanessa, nurse, 80, 81
Voyage to the Cape (Clark Russell), 313

WALD, LILLIAN, 126
Walker, John Brisben, 112–115
Ward, Mrs. Humphry, 138–139
Washington, Booker, 78
Washington, George, 162
Webb, Mary, 192–195
"Welcome to Alexandra, A" (Alfred, Lord Tennyson), quoted, 293–294
Welles, Edgar T., 158, 159, 160–161, 162, 165

Welles, Gideon, diary of, 158–160, 165
Wells, Fanny, 41
Wendell, Barrett, 167, 175, 322
West, Dr., 11
Westerburg, Justus Leopold. *See* Brown, Charley
Whistler, James McNeill, 169
White, Chief Justice Edward Douglass, 185, 186, 320
White, Mrs. Edward Douglass, 320
White, William Allen, 298, 299
Whiteley, Opal, 254, 259–260, 265–266; diary pieced together, 255–256, 261; puzzle of her birth, 257, 261–262, 263–264; diary published, 258
Whitlock, Brand, 179
Widener, Peter A. B., 170
Willard, Gus, 49
William, office boy, 88, 93
Williams, Deacon, 32
Williams, Ephraim, 10
Willkie, Wendell, 297
Wilson, Robert Cade, 89, 136
Wilson, Woodrow, 179, 297, 319, 324; his declaration of war, 180–186; quoted, 185–186
Wilson, Mrs. Woodrow, 183
Without Armour (James Hilton), 226
Wood, Leonard, 59
Woodberry, George, 174
Woodbridge, Professor F. J. E., 222
Wrecker, The (R. L. Stevenson), 140, 311

Yankee Lawyer (Arthur Train), 125, 126

The Happy Profession

WAS SET IN JANSON BY THE J. S. CUSHING COMPANY; PRINTED BY THE ROCKWELL AND CHURCHILL PRESS ON PAPER MADE BY THE S. D. WARREN COMPANY; BOUND IN LINEN BY THE RIVERSIDE BINDERY; AND DESIGNED BY OSCAR OGG AND ARTHUR WILLIAMS

SEPTEMBER MCMXLVI